KUWAIT AND THE SEA

By the same author

The Voyage of Al-Ghazeer
Kuwait, 1985

The Art of Dhow-building in Kuwait
Kuwait: Centre for Research & Studies on Kuwait, 2006
Arabian Publishing Ltd, London, 2002

Sons of Sindbad
by Alan Villiers
Introduction, with William Facey and Grace Pundyk
London: Arabian Publishing Ltd, 2006

Sons of Sindbad: The Photographs
by Alan Villiers
Introduction, with William Facey and Grace Pundyk,
London: National Maritime Museum, 2006
Arabian Publishing Ltd, 2006

KUWAIT AND THE SEA

A Brief Social and Economic History

Yacoub Yusuf Al-Hijji

Translated by
Fahad Ahmad 'Isa Bishara

Arabian Publishing

Kuwait and the Sea: A Brief Social and Economic History

© Yacoub Yusuf Al-Hijji, 2010

First published in 2010 by Arabian Publishing Ltd
4 Bloomsbury Place, London WC1A 2QA
Email: arabian.publishing@arabia.uk.com

Editor: William Facey

A catalogue card for this book is available from the British Library

ISBN: 978-0-9558894-4-8

Typesetting and digital artwork by Jamie Crocker, Artista–Design, UK
Printed and bound by ScandBook AB, Sweden

The walled city of Kuwait … has one of the most interesting waterfronts in the world. There are more than two miles of it, and the place is one great shipyard of Arab dhows.

Alan Villiers, *Sons of Sindbad*, 2006, p. 308

Ships, ships, ships, all along the sea. Sailors, quartermasters, carpenters, nakhodas, all along the shore road – what a place this Kuwait was. The ring of caulking irons, the throaty songs of sailors stepping the masts, the thump of Indian drums and the slapping of great hands as the undersides of the deep-watermen were paid with tallow and lime, the clank clank of ancient capstans warping in a pearler to the beach, the shouts of the sailors hauling out her yards to a newly floated boom, the ring of the marine blacksmith's irons as he beat out ironwork for the ships, the ripping of Persian saws through the logs of Malabar teak high on the cutting stage, the thud of drums and the burst of joyful song from a pearling sambuk coming in from the ghaus – these were the sounds of the waterfront all day and every day, with respite only for prayer.

Alan Villiers, *Sons of Sindbad*, 2006, pp. 349–50

Contents

List of Illustrations

PHOTOGRAPHS

Between pp. 48 and 49

1. Landsat view of Kuwait City, Kuwait Bay, Failaka Island, Bubiyan Island, and the mouth of the Shatt al-'Arab at the north-east corner, in 1997. Landsat data courtesy of NASA and USGS.

2. Aerial view of the western part of the old town of Kuwait in the 1940s. Photographer unknown; by courtesy of Kuwait Oil Company.

3. The dhow-building yard of the celebrated Kuwaiti shipwright Ahmad bin Salman, in the 1950s. Photograph by Badran.

4. One of the very last deep-sea *boum*s under construction in Kuwait, 1996. Photograph by the author.

5. Work proceeding on the hull planking of a *boum*, Kuwait, 1960s. Photographer unknown; by courtesy of the Ministry of Information, Kuwait.

6. Shipwrights constructing the hull interior of the hull of a large cargo *boum*, Kuwait, 1960s. Photographer unknown; by courtesy of the Ministry of Information, Kuwait.

Translator's Preface

I FIRST HAD THE PLEASURE of meeting Dr Yacoub Al-Hijji in December of 2006 and, having read just one of his publications, was immediately struck by his vast knowledge of the maritime history of Kuwait. Indeed, his deep love and respect for the dhows, shipbuilders and mariners of old Kuwait seemed unparalleled. As a student of the economic history of Kuwait, I was fascinated by the sheer amount of information accumulated by this one man over the years, and by his tremendous efforts in collecting and transcribing documents, recording interviews, and piecing together a past that has been reduced to little more than pictures and captions for members of my generation. Although our first meeting was brief, it was immeasurably informative and laid the groundwork for our later encounters.

Immediately upon returning to Kuwait from my first year of doctoral studies in the summer of 2007, I contacted him again, and he insisted on meeting up right away. The very next day, presenting me with the Arabic proofs of a book that he had just completed, he asked me to read it and let him have my opinion. I devoted the next few days to a careful reading of the work, my fascination growing with every page. At our next meeting, having passed on my more detailed observations, I told him that in general I found the book so useful that it had inspired me with the desire to translate it into English, enabling readers in both Kuwait and the West to have access to it. He jumped at the idea and, having settled various practical issues, I was able to start work.

The exigencies of translating a work from Arabic into English necessitate a certain freedom of adaptation. There is no question of anything so simple as a word-for-word translation, and one has to adopt the more readable approach of conveying the general sense. Thus I have to confess to the liberties I have taken in the process: ideas have been rearranged for reasons of clarity, repetitions acceptable in an Arabic work have been omitted even though their function in the original was to emphasize certain points, and certain poetic verses and song lyrics have been excised due to the complexities of conveying their meaning while preserving their structure. As a result of all this, the English version is shorter than the Arabic original and is perhaps a little less detailed. Nonetheless, I do firmly believe that this version is well tailored for an English-speaking readership and that it retains as much of the flavour and style of the original as possible. Any errors and shortcomings, of course, are my own.

I am indebted to Dr Yacoub Al-Hijji and Prof. Abdullah Al-Ghunaim for affording me the opportunity to translate this work and for all the assistance they have provided me with in my ongoing doctoral research. I am grateful too to the researchers and staff at the Centre for Research and Studies on Kuwait, from the librarian to the guards, for so tirelessly putting up with my daily visits and requests. It was both a pleasure and an inspiration to work amongst such fine scholars and devoted researchers.

Fahad Ahmad 'Isa Bishara
Duke University, USA, 2009

Introduction

M Y AIM IN THIS publication is to provide a compact and general
overview of the full range of maritime occupations engaged in by the
people of Kuwait, from the time of its establishment until oil was first
discovered and later exported – at which point the time-honoured bonds
forged by the Kuwaitis with the sea ceased to exist. While the overall scope
of the work is rather broad, the discussion and analysis will revolve chiefly
around the nature of these occupations during the early to mid-20th
century. The wide variety of maritime activities has meant that the narratives
and analyses are necessarily general; though the content of each chapter
might easily be fleshed out into an entire book, depth and detail have been
sacrificed for the sake of breadth and concision. The purpose of this
approach is to give both generalist and specialist alike a vivid idea of the
people of Kuwait's great exertions on behalf of themselves and their country,
of their dependence on sea and desert alike for their livelihood, of the skills
they managed to develop in this regard, and of the fortitude they displayed
in enduring the hardships of everyday life in a small country overshadowed
by three much larger neighbours.

The discussion does not confine itself to mere descriptions of these
activities and how they were carried out. Rather, it aims to convey a deeper
idea of their economic dimensions, including *inter alia* partnership and
profit-sharing arrangements, labour structures, geographical considerations,
and how they were all interrelated. This applies especially to the chapters on
pearling and long-distance trade – which together take up the majority of

the discussion – and to that on trade links with the Bedouin of north-east Arabia. With the notable exception of pearling, these activities have largely been ignored in existing Western literature on the Gulf, whose economic history before the appearance of oil has been viewed as unworthy of description and analysis. Examples of this phenomenon abound in works on the economic history of the Middle East and North Africa (for example in those by Charles Issawi), in which the Gulf is rarely mentioned.

This book is the fruit of many years' research, including numerous interviews with the *nakhodha*s (ship captains), merchants, sailors and ship-builders of Kuwait, surveys of secondary literature on the subject, travels around the coast of the western Indian Ocean, and of course forays into archival sources – particularly reports by British political officers in the region, and local logbooks and route guides. My hope is that this effort will provide the foundation for future research into the pre-oil history of Kuwait and the Gulf, and that students at all levels will find the book of some utility. If readers find the book as illuminating and fascinating to read as I have found it to write, then my work will have served its purpose.

Dr Yacoub Yusuf Al-Hijji
Kuwait, 2009

MAPS

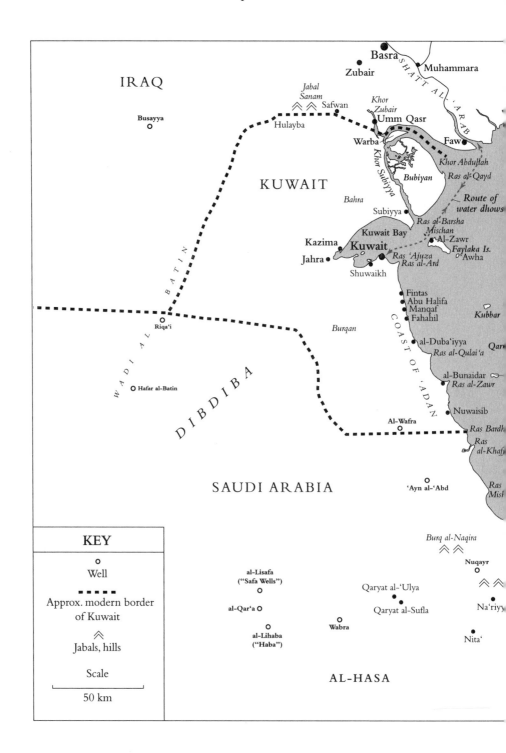

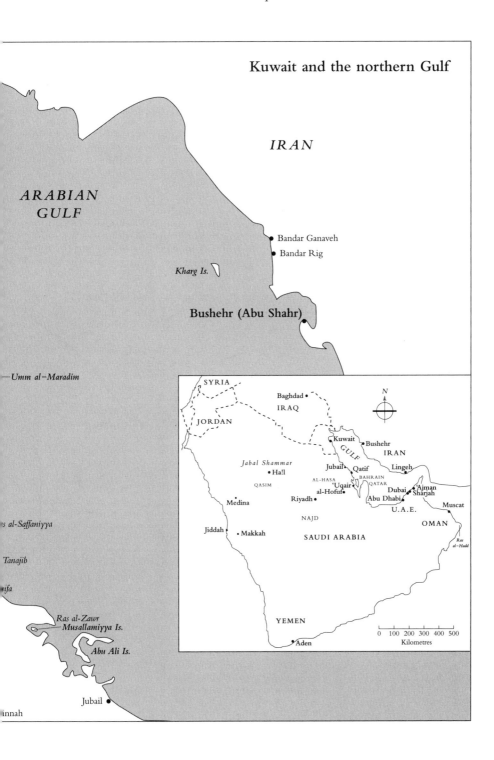

Kuwait and the northern Gulf

IRAN

ARABIAN
GULF

● Bandar Ganaveh

● Bandar Rig

Kharg Is.

Bushehr (Abu Shahr)

—*Umm al–Maradim*

s al-Saffaniyya

Tanajib

ifa

Ras al-Zawr
Musallamiyya Is.

Abu Ali Is.

Jubail ●

innah

SYRIA

Baghdad ●
IRAQ

JORDAN

N

● Kuwait   ● Bushehr

IRAN

Jabal Shammar   Lingeh ●
● Ha!l   Jubail ● Qatif
QASIM   'Uqair ● BAHRAIN
          AL-HASA   QATAR
          al-Hofuf ●   Dubai ● ● Ajman
● Medina   Riyadh ●   Abu Dhabi ● ● Sharjah
               U.A.E.   Muscat ●

NAJD   OMAN

Jiddah ● ● Makkah   *Ras*
          SAUDI ARABIA   *al-Hadd*

YEMEN

● Aden

0   100 200 300 400 500
Kilometres

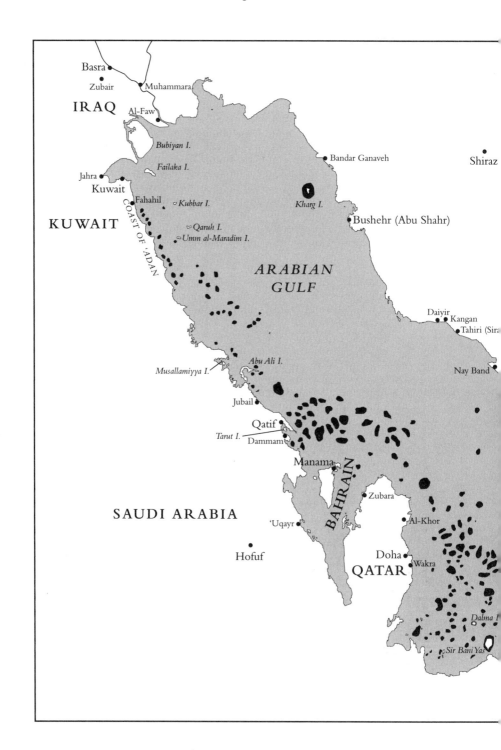

Pearl banks of the Gulf

Locations approximate only

Sources

- Information for the northern Gulf banks compiled by the author from interviews with pearling *nakhoda*s and UK Admiralty charts.
- Information on the lower Gulf banks is taken from the map compiled by Shaikh Mani' b. Rashid Al-Maktoum of Dubai in 1930 (published in *Records of the Persian Gulf Fisheries*, 1995).

Key

⬟ Pearl bank

◖ Island surrounded by pearl bank

Scale

0   50   100 km

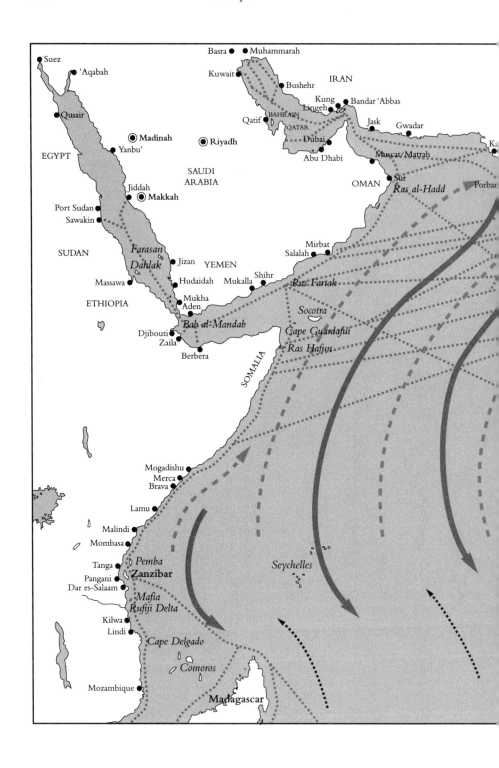

Dhow routes and winds of the western Indian Ocean

Based on Facey 1979: 90.

Key

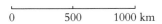

....	Dhow routes
▬ ▬ ▶	South-west monsoon winds (April–September)
➤	North-east monsoon winds (October–March)
▪▪▪▪▪▪▶	South-east trade winds

Scale

0   500   1000 km

1

Kuwait's Emergence as a Maritime Nation

THE INHABITANTS OF the town of Kuwait – or, as it was also known in the pre-modern era, al-Qurain – have had connections with the sea that are very ancient indeed, pre-dating the establishment of modern Kuwait by thousands of years. Sadly, because of the prevailing assumption that the history of Kuwait began with the arrival of the Al-Sabah and other families, the earlier part of Kuwait's history has hitherto been ill-documented and under-researched, with the result that thousands of years of Kuwaiti history have been ignored or even forgotten. Naturally any work on this era of Kuwait's distant past requires painstaking research and archaeological excavation, and all the patience they entail. Hasty attempts at piecing together a pre-modern history of Kuwait that ignore the need for evidence and scientific demonstration in support of conclusions are of little use, serving rather to retard our understanding of this era than sharpen it. Perhaps a good place for prospective researchers to begin would be with the archaeological investigations on Failaka Island (begun by the Danes in the 1950s), and those at al-Subiyya during 1998–2004 conducted by Drs Harriet Crawford and Robert Carter of the University of London, in which a vast number of artifacts relating to Kuwait's pre-modern history were found. It is from these findings and those of other ongoing archaeological expeditions that one can begin to shed light on the history of this area, as also of Kuwait Bay, which is usually thought of as little more than a tongue of water penetrating an arid land, devoid of life and civilization, before the establishment of modern Kuwait. While the account here does not pretend to fill any gaps in our understanding of Kuwait's pre–Al-Sabah history, it will refer broadly to this era insofar as it concerns the maritime activities of Kuwait's inhabitants.

It has frequently been observed that Kuwait Bay and its surrounding islands occupy a rather strategic location, lying as they do between Mesopotamia to the north and the fringe of the Arabian Peninsula to the south, and so forming a necessary zone of transition for travellers and goods coming from desert and sea alike. The Bay, which provides excellent shelter and natural facilities for the shipping of the northern Gulf, opens onto Failaka Island, an excellent transit point for ships sailing from the south to Mesopotamia and vice versa, a fact evidenced by the ancient ruins conspicuous on the island to this very day. At the western end of the Bay lay Kazma and Jahra, both of which – but especially the former – were stations for those travelling north and south by both desert and sea. Inward- and outward-bound ships found Kazma's harbour a sufficiently deep refuge from the rough *shamal* or northerly winds, while desert caravans found Kazma itself a welcome way-station on their journeys to Mesopotamia or southwards into the Arabian Peninsula. For both types of traveller, Kazma offered wells that tapped into the freshwater aquifer and collected rainwater, as well as a settled community of houses and a fortress.[1]

On the northern side of Kuwait Bay lies an area by the name of Umdaira and the island of Tabij, located near the wells of Umghaira. It is in the latter location that archaeological excavations during 2000 and 2001 uncovered signs of communal human life dating back at least 7,000 years, including the chance discovery of the mud-encrusted remains of a fishing boat most probably constructed of reeds and rope.[2] On the south side of Kuwait Bay lies the island of Qurain (known today as al-'Akkaz), on which digs have uncovered remains of a settlement pre-dating the Islamic era but also extending well into it. While absolute certainty cannot be claimed, it is highly likely that these communities did establish contact with one another by sea, if only for purposes of livelihood and security. It is pertinent to note

[1] See also Al-Isfahani, 1968.
[2] See Carter and Crawford, unpublished 2004.

in this regard that the raised sea level 5,000 years ago was particularly conducive to the establishment of maritime contact: the rather large Bubiyan Island that occupies the greater part of Kuwait's coastline today was not above sea level at that time, Failaka Island was much smaller, and Jahra was much closer to the coast than it is today (it currently lies around two miles inland).[3]

It is thus clear that any prospective researcher into Kuwait's establishment as a maritime nation would do well to investigate its origins long before its modern beginnings in the early 18th century under the rule of the Al-Sabah family. Furthermore, any archaeological dig setting its sights on these early origins must take into account the slight decline in sea level over the last 4,000 years and, in the light of this, focus the search farther inland than one would expect, as findings in Shu'aiba, Burgan, and the plateaux of Qurain near al-Wafra and Sulaibikhat have adequately demonstrated. Indeed, the importance of support for the continuation of such archaeological investigations cannot be overemphasized, for it is only through them that we can begin to clarify the blurred outlines of Kuwait's pre-modern history and appreciate the cultural contributions of its people.

The establishment of modern Kuwait

Despite all that we do know about the history of modern Kuwait since the 18th century, the exact date of its establishment is still something of a mystery even to the most expert scholars. Local historians record that al-Qurain (as Kuwait was known in its early days) was home to a small community of Arab fishermen and coastal traders whose maritime skills were developed only insofar as was necessary to meet their basic needs.[4] Failaka Island in particular deserves scrutiny, for what we know indicates that settlement there continued more or less uninterrupted, and that at least as far back as the 17th century AD it was home to Gulf people from such places as Bahrain, al-Hasa and southern Persia (the coast of which was

---

[3] Ibid.
[4] See Al-Rashaid, 1926, Ch. 1; and Al-Qina'i, 1988: 12–15.
[5] For Kuwaiti evidence for this, see Imam Malik's *Al-Mawatta'* (Malik, 2005), the republication of a manuscript written in the hand of Musa'id bin Ahmad on Failaka Island in AD 1682.

dotted with ports inhabited by Arab tribespeople), all of whom contributed to the development of the island's culture and technical skills.[5] Factors in the continuity of settlement on the island were its plentiful sources of fresh water enabling the development of cultivation, and the vital commercial contacts that were established with the people of al-Qurain.

In the same way, settled communities proliferated along the southern coast of Kuwait – the coast of 'Adan – and beyond. What it was that attracted settlers to this area is not clear, although one can speculate that the coast's proximity to the pearl banks of the northern Gulf must have played some role. To this one might add that during the 17th century the area came under the protection of the Bani Khalid, the tribal overlords of al-Hasa and its environs, from which it is possible to speculate that Bani Khalid guarantees of security to their protégés, if such they were, might have had something to do with the flourishing of settled life in the area. Certainly when the Syrian dignitary Murtada b. 'Ali al-'Alwan came this way in AD 1709, en route from Hasa Oasis, he found where Kuwait stands today "a sizeable town resembling al-Hasa" with a fort and towers, which was already, before the arrival of Al-Sabah, known as al-Kuwait as well as al-Qurain.[6]

So it can be said with some degree of certainty that these coastal communities, at some point long before 1700, would have developed maritime skills, and that their ability to build and sail simple boats of palm fronds lashed together has its origins far back in antiquity. And it is probable that by 1700 their skills had developed enough to enable them to build vessels from timber imported from India, in order to take part in pearl diving and short-distance trade with nearby communities, despite the difficulties of supporting such an industry with the necessary range of skills – a topic that will be discussed in greater detail in the next chapter.

It was into such a context that the Bani 'Utub – including the families of Al-Sabah, Al-Khalifa, Al-Jalahima and others – arrived in Kuwait from Zubara, on what is now the west coast of Qatar, and settled in al-Subiyya and al-Qurain.[7] Precisely what it was that attracted – or drove – them to this area is obscure. It is known, however, that they brought with them additional

[6] Haarmann in Slot, 2003: 37–40.
[7] Other writers insist that the 'Utub must have been scattered into a number of different ports before arriving in Kuwait. See Abu Hakima, 1988: 50; also Slot, 1998.

maritime skills undoubtedly learned during their sojourn in Zubara. While it is unclear whether they went first to al-Qurain then moved to Failaka Island and back, or settled in al-Qurain at once, the question is irrelevant to our story. The important facts are that there was virtually no opposition to their settling in the area, and that they eventually rose to pre-eminence among the communities there, maintaining their close ties with their protectors the Bani Khalid while at the same time carving out a relatively autonomous political space for themselves. The security derived from their Bani Khalid connection, combined with their relative independence, allowed the 'Utub to establish control over the carrying of trade through both the Gulf and the desert.[8] With their participation and protection, the economic activities of the area began to flourish: pearl diving, shipbuilding and commerce all developed under the rulership of one of the 'Utbi families, the Al-Sabah, who effectively established a system of justice and fair dealing in a secure environment, giving merchants the confidence to undertake commercial risks and enjoy the fruits of business.

The question of security is a vital one, for there existed tribal groups on the southern coast of Persia (going by the name of Banu Ka'b) who saw the commercial development of al-Qurain as a threat to their own economic prosperity, and also perhaps as a tempting target for raids and piracy. One local historian records how, in 1783, the 'Utub finally "placed their women and goods in one fleet of ships and set off in another to take on their enemies", a contest from which they emerged victorious, so establishing themselves as a force to be reckoned with in the Gulf.[9] Furthermore, it was roughly around this time – some record the year 1782 – that the Al-Khalifa, an 'Utbi clan that had previously left al-Qurain to return to Zubara in view of the abundance of pearl banks there, clashed with the Arabo-Persian Al-Madhkur tribe of Bahrain and, with the help of their al-Qurain brethren, were eventually able to win the day and claim the island for themselves.[10]

Having occupied such strategic locations and overcome the stiff competition of their rivals, the 'Utub established their maritime sway over the Gulf, emerging as rivals to Muscat in the regional carrying trade and, by the end of the 18th century, reaching and trading with the north-west

[8] Abu Hakima, 1988: 43.
[9] Al-Rashaid, 1926, Part 1: 3.
[10] Abu Hakima, 1988: 107–10.

coast of India. None of this could have been achieved had the 'Utub continued to sail in the small vessels recorded for earlier decades. Indeed, it is around this time that one sees the development of maritime technology among the 'Utub, including the building of *battils* and *baghlahs* – large cargo dhows – of around 400 tons.[11]

The commercial prosperity of the 'Utub of Kuwait soon came to rival even that of the port of Basra, then under Ottoman Turkish rule, where high customs duties – sometimes as high as 8.5 percent – drove a number of merchants to set themselves up in Kuwait/al-Qurain, which was close enough to Basra to allow for the overland carriage of goods between the two, and where customs duties were low or even non-existent.[12] Other motives persuading these merchants to transfer to Kuwait included the well-documented political unrest in Basra at the time, which undermined the stability of the commercial environment, and of course the sporadic outbreak of bubonic plague there, which drove even the British to move their trading factory to Kuwait (albeit temporarily) during 1775–79, and again in 1793–95.[13]

By the early years of the 19th century, so dominant had the Kuwaiti 'Utub and their fleet become that their ships were reaching Yemen and the Red Sea – including the ports of Mukha and Hudaida – and were bringing the renowned coffee of Yemen directly from its source rather than indirectly and at a marked-up price through the merchants of Muscat, who had once dominated the coffee trade. The 'Utbis were known for their trade in fine Arabian horses, brought in from central and northern Najd, which were in great demand in India, as well as in pearls, specie and dates – all of which will be discussed in more detail later. From India, the 'Utub would import varieties of timber from which to build their celebrated dhows, as well as foodstuffs, spices and other commodities.

British officials in the Gulf kept an eye on Kuwait throughout the 19th century, and some of their reports paint a graphic picture of the place during this time. In 1836, for example, Col. R. Taylor described it thus:

[11] The different ship types and their development will be discussed in greater detail in a later chapter.
[12] Manesty and Jones, 1986 (1790): 411; see also Fattah, 1997: 191–3.
[13] Abu Hakima, 1983: 15; Facey, 1992: 104–5 and 108; Facey & Grant, 1998: 10.

Grane or Koweit ... has an excellent harbour ... without, however, any other advantage. The country around is a salt and sandy desert, of the most barren and inhospitable description, without a tree or shrub visible as far as the eye can reach, except a few bushes which mark the wells, of which the water is particularly salt and bad.

Although wanting in almost every advantage, this town presents a singular instance of commercial prosperity. Its population consists of nearly 25,000 inhabitants, who possess 31 Buggalows [*baghlahs*] and Buteels [*battils*], from a hundred and fifty to three hundred tons burthen, which trade constantly with India; 50 smaller boats are employed in the coasting commerce of the Gulf, and about 350 boats are engaged in fishing on the pearl banks. It can produce 6,000 men capable of bearing arms.

The energy and courage of the people, who are closely united, and free from feuds and factions, render them respected and feared by all the other maritime tribes; and as, in fact, they are as prompt to resent insult or aggression towards themselves as they are cautious in refraining from injury and annoyance towards their peaceable neighbours, a piracy upon a Grane boat is of rare occurrence.

The Shaikh Subah, to whom the management of affairs has been made over by his father ... collects no taxes or customs, the port being entirely free; a small duty, levied upon the sales and purchases of the Bedouins who resort to the town, constitutes the only revenue realized by him, amounting to about 3,000 dollars annually.
...

The place on the land side is surrounded by a dilapidated mud wall, with round towers for bastions; in some parts the wall is levelled to the ground, and in others the sand has been allowed to drift nearly to its top. The seaward side has never been fortified, and in no part has anything like a ditch ever existed.[14]

---

[14] Kemball, 1845: 109. The information relates to 1836, as Kemball writes on p. 95 of these Memoranda that the information in them was "collected from living Native authorities, descriptive of the Coast of Arabia from the mouth of the River Euphrates to the ports of the Beniyas; by Colonel R. Taylor, Political Agent, Turkish Arabia. February, 1836."

British officials clearly regarded Kuwait as a small maritime utopia under benevolent shaikhly rule, and there is no reason to doubt their accounts. By mid-century we see a vigorous, united community whose trade had benefited from the maritime *Pax Britannica*. The pearling industry, in which the Kuwaiti fleet played a major part, had expanded greatly. The main exports were dates (from Iraq to India) and horses (from Najd to British India). Imports and exports included wheat, ghee, coffee, rice, sugar, wood for ship building and house building, spices, cotton cloth, dried fish, dried fruit and tobacco. By 1860 Kuwait's merchant fleet had became the largest in the Gulf, bigger even than Bahrain's, and in 1863 the British explorer William Palgrave was able to describe Kuwait as "the most active port on the Persian Gulf" – a remarkable achievement for a state with no natural resources of its own other than the skills and enterprise of its people. By the 1860s, with the arrival of steamships and the telegraph in the Gulf, the accelerating technological revolution in Europe was beginning to make itself felt in Kuwait. Col. Lewis Pelly, in Kuwait in January 1865, confirmed Palgrave's opinion:

> Kowait is one of the most thriving ports in the Persian Gulf. Its craft are large and numerous, trading with India and the Arabian Coasts. Its sailors are reputed the best in these regions. Its trade is considerable; importing rice from Shooshter, Busreh and the Malabar Coast; corn from the Persian Coast; dates from Busreh; and timber for ship-building from the West Coast of India. On the land side it barters with the Bedouins who, during the winter and spring, bring down "rowghan" [ghee], wool, and horses; exchanging these for coffee, rice, and other necessaries. ... No taxes or duties are levied. ... The Kowaitees have a considerable carrying trade, and are perhaps the best boat builders in the Gulf.[15]

In the last decades of the 19th century, perhaps by *ca.* 1885, Kuwaiti ships made their way to the Swahili coast of Africa, where they bought mangrove poles (known locally as *kandal* or *chandal*) and other commodities of lesser significance, following the general ban on the trade in slaves by the British and Omani authorities.[16] By the end of the 19th century, and with the

[15] Facey & Grant, 1998: 11–12; Pelly, 1978: 10.

accession of Shaikh Mubarak Al-Sabah (known among Kuwaitis as Mubarak the Great) to the helm of Kuwait, the principality's commerce had developed to hitherto unprecedented levels. Indeed, it was under the leadership and guidance of Shaikh Mubarak that Kuwait was able to preserve its autonomy during a time of intense regional upheaval and international competition for influence in the Gulf, and so to keep its commercial prosperity intact.[17] Mubarak not only provided the necessary legal and institutional protection for Kuwaiti traders and sailors in the Gulf and Indian Ocean, but was able further to facilitate commercial development by persuading the British India Steam Navigation Company (BISNC) – which by the early 20th century had come to dominate the region's trade – once again to make Kuwait one of its ships' weekly ports of call in the Gulf, so that Kuwait's merchants would be able to make use of its services.[18] To this list can be added Mubarak's support for the establishment of the telegraph in Kuwait (which was connected to the main station at Faw, at the mouth of the Shatt al-'Arab waterway) for use by Kuwaiti merchants, as well as the logistical and legal support he gave to Kuwaiti merchants wishing to establish agencies abroad in such ports as Bombay and Karachi.[19]

And so it was that Kuwait established itself as a commercial and maritime nation, making itself the centre of a network of routes by both desert and sea, and integrating its pearling vessels and cargo ships with the steamers of the BISNC into a prosperous whole. This state of affairs was first disrupted during the reign of Ahmad Al-Jabir Al-Sabah (r. 1921–50), whose difficulties with 'Abd al-'Aziz Ibn Sa'ud of Central Arabia resulted in a general desert trade embargo enacted by the latter. This was a harbinger of things to come for the maritime economy of Kuwait, which would soon be devastated by the collapse of the pearl market in the 1930s, and finally put to rest by the

[16] See also Sheriff, 1987.

[17] For a detailed account of Mubarak's reign and an assessment of his diplomatic achievements, see Slot, 2005.

[18] The BISNC service to Kuwait had first been instituted in 1862, but was suspended soon after by Shaikh Sabah II to assuage Ottoman anxieties. See Facey & Grant, 1998: 12.

[19] Among the first such merchants were Muhammad Salim Al-Sudairawi and 'Ali Humoud Al-Shayi' in Bombay, and Marzuq Muhammad Al-Marzuq in Karachi. See also Al-Ibrahim, 2003: 83–5.

discovery and export of oil and the massive transformation this brought to the livelihoods of Kuwait's people over the decades to follow.

2

Sina'at al-Sufun: Dhow Construction

BEFORE DISCUSSING the development of the dhow-building industry in Kuwait, it is necessary to define what a dhow is. The word "dhow", which has no equivalent in Arabic, is a term coined by Western seamen to denote any one of the wide range of local lateen-rigged sailing ships participating in the Indian Ocean trade system. Arab dhows, such as the larger long-distance trading *boums* and *baghlahs*, the mid-sized pearling *sanbuks* and *battils* and the others referred to below, were of various shapes and sizes reflecting their diverse uses. The specifications of these vessels and their building methods are the subject of this chapter. It should be borne in mind that, while "dhow" is employed as a generic term throughout this book, it does nonetheless cloud the differences, subtle or major, that distinguished these vessels one from another.

The establishment and growth of Kuwait's dhow-building industry

It is little wonder that a dhow-building industry should have arisen in a community as reliant on the sea for its livelihood as Kuwait, where the overwhelming majority of its people were employed as sailors, pearl divers, dhow captains and fishermen. In all likelihood it was their dependence on the sea for food that led the inhabitants of al-Qurain to recognize the need to develop boats – however basic – capable of extending their fishing range away from the shallow shores of the Gulf. Also, the close proximity of Failaka Island and the maritime know-how of the long-established community there must have helped to foster the development of similar skills on the mainland, for it would have been only natural for regular contact between the two communities to have led to the transmission of expertise. Communities on the mainland eventually developed the skills necessary to build medium-sized dhows, making possible increasingly far-flung contact and trade with littoral communities, and enabling them to participate in the age-old activity of pearl diving on the banks of the northern Gulf.

An important factor too would have been the arrival of the 'Utub in Kuwait in their own dhows, from which one can infer the presence on board of shipwrights (*qallafs*) to aid them on their voyage.[1] While it is difficult to be precise about the development of the dhow-building industry after the arrival of the 'Utub, one can surmise with some confidence that the 'Utbi *qallafs* must have pooled their skills with the existing master dhow builders (*ostads*) of Kuwait and thus accelerated the industry's evolution. One can further infer a boost in demand for vessels resulting from the participation of the 'Utub in the maritime sector. Furthermore, the stability and security brought by the rule of the Al-Sabah would have attracted progressively more *ostads* from Bahrain, Muscat and the ports of Persia to Kuwait, bringing further stimulus to the industry.[2] At least one local historian records that during the reign of Shaikh Abdullah I (1756–1814) a number of successful traders were attracted to the town, not least among them the father of the famous merchant Ahmad Ibn Rizq, whose financial investment brought about the building of dhows able to reach the ports of Yemen, the Red Sea and Western India – *baghlahs* and *battils* with an average carrying capacity of 300 tons.[3] Later, the skill and reputation of the Kuwaiti dhow builders was remarked upon by travellers: during his travels through the region in 1862–63, Palgrave noted that "among the seamen who ply the Persian Gulf, the mariners of Koweyt hold the first rank in daring, in skill and in solid trustworthiness of character".[4] As seen in Chapter 1, such

[1] See also Al-Rashaid, 1926, vol. 1: 15; Slot 1998: 110–11, in which he notes that the 'Utub arrived in al-Qurain by way of the Gulf; and Pelly, 1863–64: 72.
[2] Villiers, 2006a: 353.
[3] Al-Rashaid, 1926, vol. 1: 39   [4] Palgrave 1865, vol. 2: 386.

judgements were echoed by Col. Lewis Pelly during his trip from Kuwait to Riyadh in 1865.[5] With the accession of Shaikh Mubarak in 1896, the industry underwent even further development, attracting famous *ostad*s from Bahrain, Lingeh, Qishm Island and the like, and it was around this time that the *boum* came to the fore as the preferred long-distance trading dhow in the Gulf by virtue of its simple yet sturdy construction, seaworthiness and carrying capacity.

The reputation of Kuwaiti *ostad*s extended far beyond the Gulf, as one anecdote illustrates particularly well. During the Second World War, the Allied Powers needed local vessels to help transport their soldiers and equipment across the Shatt al-'Arab and, to achieve this end, requested Kuwaiti help, contracting the famous *ostad* Ahmad bin Salman and his assistant *qallaf*s to build them hundreds of barges (known as *dubah*s) in the years 1942–43. Upon the completion of this task and the subsequent Allied victory, Bin Salman was presented with a medal and the title of Khan Sahib in recognition of his contribution to the war effort – a testament to the expertise and reputation of Kuwait's dhow builders.

Nor did Kuwaiti *ostad*s confine themselves to building pearling and trading dhows in their home port alone. For a number of them went to the Persian coast to build dhows for merchants there, while others moved to Calicut on the west coast of India during the trading season to take advantage of the plentiful timber (specifically teak) at its source. Among the latter were the renowned *ostad*s Humud bin Hassan, Muhammad Al-Thuwaini, and Salih bin Rashid, builder of the famous 575-ton *Nur al-Barr wa 'l-Bahr* ("Light of the Land and Sea"), the largest *boum* ever built.[6]

Materials used in dhow building and their provenance

Perhaps the most striking aspect of the Kuwaiti dhow-building industry was its establishment and growth despite the total lack of timber in the region aside from the date palm, which was far from suitable for use in dhow construction. To overcome this basic obstacle, the merchants and *nakhoda*s of Kuwait looked abroad, importing a range of timbers from western India, as well materials such as iron for the fashioning of anchors

[5] Pelly, 1865a; Pelly, 1978 (reprint of Pelly, 1866): 10–11.
[6] Al-Hijji, 2001: 2.

and spikes (used in fastening the planks to the ribs), coal, cloth for sails, bales of cotton for use as caulking (filling the gaps between the hull planks), and other essential materials. The proceeds of shipping dates from Basra to India were often applied to the purchase of wood and other dhow-building materials. Rope, for example, was a common purchase, despite the fact that the fishermen of Kuwait could and often did make their own rope from palm-frond fibre. These materials, supplied to Kuwaiti dhows by branches of Kuwaiti merchant houses in the ports of western India, would be shipped home and kept in storage rooms at the dhow-maintenance yards scattered along the Kuwaiti coast. Nor must we forget the blacksmiths (*haddads*) of Kuwait, who played a crucial role in supporting the dhow-building industry by supplying the large iron nails used to clench the planking to the ribs, as well as anchors (*bawarah*), cooking equipment and other metal items. Prominent blacksmiths in pre-oil Kuwait included the Al-Haddad and Cherag families.

Timber

The first point to note is that in Kuwaiti maritime terminology, timber is referred to as *hatab* rather than by the standard Arabic term *khashab*. The latter was used as a generic term for dhows, particularly those of the long-distance trading variety. Next, it must be borne in mind that Kuwaiti merchants did not always purchase timber direct from India, where the various species of tree used in dhow building grew in abundance, but until the 1780s acquired it from the merchants of Muscat. During the 19th century, however, timber came to be imported direct by branches of Kuwaiti merchant houses established in western India. Notable among such merchant-house branches was the office of Yusuf Al-Saqr, the most prominent trader of timber between India and Kuwait, who directed his business from his office in Calicut, where he resided until the mid-1950s.

The most popular timber for dhow construction was teak (Ar. *saj*) which, due to its density and high resistance to heat and humidity, was the wood most suited for almost every part of the dhow. These qualities meant that teak was in heavy demand and commanded a high price, making it the costliest of the imported timbers. It was often sold in the form of large trunks as well as in bundles of planks or branches, the latter being used in constructing the dhow's interior hull.

In addition to teak, the various other types of timber included Indian Laurel (Ar. *janqili*) and benteak (Ar. *mintaij*), both of which were sold at prices corresponding to their quality. A special type of timber, poon (Ar. *fann*) was used for masts and yards because of its ability to carry weight combined with its flexibility under stress from the sail during heavy winds. Its importance to the dhow generated a high demand for poon trunks among *nakhoda*s during their trips to India, and the resulting high cost of a good mast and yard timbers might account for as much as one-fifteenth (6.5 percent) of the dhow's total costs.

What follows here is a short list of the main types of timber and the parts of the dhow they were used to build:[7]

Wood type	*Use in dhow building*
Indian Laurel (*janqili*) *Terminalia tomentosa*	Hull
Teak (*saj*) *Tectona grandis*	Keel; deck; ribs; hulls and keels of pearling dhows; and the rudder
Benteak (*mantij*) *Lagerstroemia lanceolata*	Keel and/or rudder in the absence of teak
Pali Wood (*faini*) *Palaquium ellipticum*	Topmost plank of the hull
Jack Wood (*fanas*) *Artocarpus heterophyllus*	Usually for ribs; sometimes for keels or hulls
Poon (*fann*) *Calophyllum inophyllum*	Mast and yard
Vaka (*baqah*) *Albizia molveanna*	Used in shaping the gunwale; also for the bulwark above the gunwale
Egyptian Thorn (*qarat*) *Acacia nilotica*	Sheaves for pulley blocks and as pins or shafts around which the sheaves rotate
Mango wood (*humbah*) *Mangifera indica*	Used only for fitting the dhow sweeps with square blades

[7] For more on this subject, see Al-Hijji, 2001: 37–42.

Types of dhow built in Kuwait

The evolving nature of the Kuwaitis' reliance on the sea meant that the types of vessel they built would have changed over time, in response to the needs of the people and the resources available to them.

Perhaps the simplest craft of all was the *warjiyyah* or *shashah* (as it is called in the lower Gulf), a small boat, almost a raft, of palm fronds lashed together with rope made out of palm fibre and stuffed with more fronds for buoyancy. While this is the most primitive and most probably the oldest of the sea-going craft of the Gulf, we shall focus on the larger, more sophisticated vessels — i.e. those with lateen-rigged sails to which the term "dhow" is applicable. Among these are the dhows used in the pearling industry — such as the *baqqarah, battil, sanbuk, jalbut, shu'i* and *boum* — as well as the medium-sized *tashalah*, which was used as a lighter and rock-carrier, and the much larger *baghlah* and *boum saffar* used in long-distance, ocean-going trade. Naturally, the design and size of each dhow was strongly influenced by the functions it was built to serve: the type of rudder, the keel and the openness or otherwise of the deck, all reflected these functions.[8]

The number of each type of dhow found in Kuwait at any particular time was never fixed, but naturally fluctuated in response to demand and other circumstances. What is clear is that until the decline of the pearling industry in the late 1930s (see Chapter 3), pearling dhows dominated the waters of the Gulf. During his time there in 1765, the explorer Carsten Niebuhr noted that there were roughly 800 dhows near the pearl banks, although he gave no numbers for long- or short-distance trading vessels.[9] The author Ahmad al-Bishr Al-Rumi recalled that in 1928 there were approximately 1,200 dhows used in pearling alone.[10] This figure should be set against that of 'Abd al-'Aziz Al-Rashaid, who noted that in the early 1920s there were roughly 2,000 dhows employed in various sectors and that around 800 of these were used in pearling.[11] In 1939, there were 106 trading dhows — a fleet that increased by 60 during the Second World War.[12] By the end of the 1940s, however, the pearling industry had completely collapsed and only a handful of pearling boats were still active. By the 1950s,

---

[8] For more on Kuwaiti dhow types, see Al-Hijji, 2001: 8–27.
[9] Niebuhr, 1792: 296.   [10] Al-Rumi, 1996: 21.   [11] Al-Rashaid, 1926, vol. 1: 68.
[12] From Villiers 1969, Introduction, and from various *Persian Gulf Trade Reports*.

many of these were sold or converted into motorized fishing and short-distance trading boats, reflecting the deterioration of Kuwait's trading links with the ports of the western Indian Ocean.

Building a dhow

As noted above, the master dhow builders were called *ostad*s and their assistants *qallaf*s; to this short list of actors can be added the client commissioning the vessel, whether a merchant or a *nakhoda*. The client would initiate the process by approaching the *ostad* with the request to build him a dhow of a particular type and size.[13] Thus commissioned and the cost agreed, the *ostad* would set about choosing 10–18 *qallaf*s. Construction would begin with the laying down of the keel (*bis*) of the dhow, and the selection of suitable timbers to form the stem- and stern-posts. Once those were in place, the lowest planks of teak (the garboard strakes) would be fixed along the keel between stem and stern. When this task was complete, the *ostad* would begin to form the hull of the ship using key ribs as templates against which to bend the hull planks. The rest of the ribs would then be fixed along the inside of the hull planking, after which the deck could be laid, leaving hatches giving access to the hold below deck for the storage of goods, and for the mast. Finally, he would prepare the masts and yards and notify the owner that his ship was seaworthy. All this might take just a couple of months (depending on the size and type of ship) after the laying down of the first plank. Work would begin at first light (usually around 7 a.m.) and continue until noon, at which point the *qallaf*s would have lunch at the expense of the buyer. They would return one hour later, working non-stop until the sunset prayer, when the cry of the *ostad*, "*Irfa'! Irfa'!*" ("Raise! Raise!"), signalled the end of the day's work. Following the prayer, both the *ostad* and the *qallaf*s would receive their daily wage, that of the former being twice that of the latter.

In building the dhow, the *ostad*s used only the simplest of tools, including the plumb-line (*bild*), the quadrant (*hindasah*), a cotton string (*khait*) used to

---

[13] The size and tonnage of the dhow is determined by the length of its base, measured by *ostad*s in arm's lengths (of roughly 1.5 feet). For detailed information on the techniques and materials of dhow construction, and the economics of it, see Al-Hijji, 2001: 29–97 and 142–5; and Villiers, 2006a: 367–74.

help draw straight lines, and a piece of chalk. *Ostad*s rarely, if ever, made use of blueprints, working by eye alone and preferring to make every ship as unique as possible. As for the *qallaf*s, they would use only such basic tools as a hammer, a saw, a bow-drill, a clamp, an adze for trimming and shaping planks and ribs, and a chisel, which was used for carving finer decoration. The launching of a newly completed dhow was an occasion for celebration, attracting a crowd of onlookers, as depicted in several early photographs. The *nakhoda*, who either owned the dhow himself or was hired by the owner to captain the dhow, would wait until the highest tide before ordering the vessel to be slowly hauled into the water and floated, after which he and the builders would partake in a feast held by the dhow owner in honour of the occasion and in anticipation of her first voyage. The task of hauling the dhow into the water would come at no extra cost to the owner, although he would necessarily bear the cost of such essential equipment as the sails and rope.

Transmission of dhow-building expertise

The art of dhow building was not one that could be learned by all, as it was passed down from generation to generation not by means of books or lessons taught in class, but through first-hand observation and hands-on experience from a young age. Indeed, scarcely any dhow builders – whether *ostad*s or *qallaf*s – ever attended regular school and were often unable either to read or write, as, from as young as six years, they spent most of their days in the company of their fathers and relatives in the shipyards.

Naturally real, hands-on work did not usually begin at such a tender age. As a general rule, youngsters were left to play in the shipyard and sometimes on the completed deck of a dhow, surrounded by the dhow builders and the timber, tools and materials with which they would familiarize themselves over the years. At times they would be asked to collect leftover pieces of wood to be used as fuel in the preparation of meals, and would be given planks of wood and tools ostensibly to play with, but in reality to familiarize themselves with, so that within a few years they would be able to assist the *qallaf*s by bringing them the tools and timbers they asked for, and by hammering nails into the planks for them. Eventually, the young man would become a *qallaf* in his own right, working directly under the supervision of an *ostad*. But not all *qallaf*s could become *ostad*s; only those who distinguished themselves in the eyes of their supervisors could hope to be asked to take on more specialized tasks, which required special training. The promising *qallaf* would eventually work his way up to the post of deputy *ostad* and, eventually, replace his superior. However, if he was unable to excel as a *qallaf*, he was likely to remain as such, up until his final days in the shipyard.

Although only around five percent of all *qallaf*s stood a chance of becoming *ostad*s, there were other ways in which a *qallaf* might excel. Normally this would entail specialization in a particular skill, such as the use of the adze (*jaddum*) in the fairing off of the dhow's hull to make its surface smooth, or the carving of designs into the wooden planks – both tasks demanding a degree of skill that only few *qallaf*s attained. Thus, there were various specialist positions between that of *qallaf* and *ostad* that a shipwright could aim for in order to gain distinction and perhaps an added bonus for his work.[14] A shipwright whose work set him apart from the rest could expect to find himself in great demand by other *ostad*s – not only in Kuwait but also in other Gulf ports, all of them competing to build the best dhows and to boast the best team of shipwrights. Indeed, a particularly well-crafted dhow would have its fame and beauty extolled in all the ports around the western Indian Ocean, and its builders could expect to have their names perpetuated in the memories of other dhow builders, merchants, *nakhoda*s and sailors alike. Of such renown were the *Dhow*, the *Bin Rashdan*, the *Muhallab* and *Taysir*, to name but a few.

The economics of dhow building in Kuwait

Linked to the process of building a dhow were a number of ancillary trades separate from the construction itself. These included the supply and manufacture of appropriate materials and equipment for the vessel in addition to the purchase and shipping of timber from India to Kuwait. While it would be useful to explore all such linked activities and their impact on the economics of dhow building in Kuwait, to do so would entail a more detailed discussion than is possible in a concise overview such as this. So we shall focus our attention on the two main activities involved: the purchase

---

[14] Personal interviews with various *ostad*s.

and shipment of timber, and the construction of the dhow itself.[15]

The price of timber and its shipment to Kuwait

As noted earlier, timber was often sold in the form of trunks, which were sawn into planks later. These were measured in volumetric units called *gandi*s (in India, *kandi*), each *gandi* being approximately 13 cubic feet, although teak would sometimes be sold by the cubic foot in units called *kweek*s. One *kweek* or cubic foot of teak typically cost between Rs 13 and 16. Curved branches to form the ribs of the dhow were called *shalman*, and they were gathered into bundles known as *kurijah*s. Because *shalman*s came in a variety of sizes, they fell into different categories, each known as a *gari*, a reference to the carts they were carried on. Thus there was the *gari* 20, a load of 20 *shalman*s in a cart; likewise the *gari* 15, and, for very large curved branches or crooks, the *gari* 5.

First, however, the timber would be brought from the interior in the form of large trunks and distributed to the sellers in the ports according to their orders. Once an order had been placed by a buyer, the timber would be sawn into the requisite lengths, bundled up tightly, and transported by an Indian mariner to the buyer's dhow. Once there, the timber would be lifted in by the sailors and stowed in the hold under the supervision of the first mate (*mujaddimi*), who would ensure that it was stacked in such a way as to maintain the balance of the vessel and avoid listing in rough weather.

The price of timber naturally fluctuated according to its type, supply, demand and quality. What follows is a rough breakdown of the prices of the different types of timber purchased in western India:

Wood type	*Price in Indian Rupees (Rs)*
Teak	Between Rs 13 and 16 per foot in India; Rs 24–30 upon reaching Kuwait
Pali Wood	Between Rs 80 and 90 per *gandi*
Indian Laurel	Between Rs 50 and 65 per *gandi*
Poon	Between Rs 111 and 147 per 5 *gandi*s
Mango Wood planks	Approx. Rs 7 per plank

[15] For a good exposition of the economics of a deep-sea dhow, see Villiers, 2006a: 367–74.

To these prices should be added the cost of transporting the timber from the source to the seller (in 1959, Rs 40 for two *kandis* worth Rs 130); moving the timber from the seller to the ship (in 1948, Rs 26 for a quantity worth Rs 1,186); an Indian government sales tax of 1.5 percent; and the commission of the timber merchant or broker, which was usually about 2 percent.[16]

Of course, the price of the timber and the additional transaction costs was not the final price, as a merchant had also to factor in the cost of freightage (*noul*), the main source of income for the mariners. While there were standard prices corresponding to the size and weight of the timber, they often fluctuated slightly according to whatever deal had been struck between the merchant and the dhow owner – who was sometimes the *nakhoda* himself – regarding the distance to be freighted and the amount to be paid; usually one-third or one-half of the amount paid for the timber itself was agreed. In the early 1950s, for example, freightage for one *gandi* of poles was between Rs 25 and 32.[17] Of the total freightage collected by the *nakhoda*, one half would go to the vessel's owner and the other half was to be distributed among the mariners in a fashion to be discussed in greater detail in the chapter on long-distance trade. It is also of note here that, generally speaking, merchants did not insure cargo carried on Kuwaiti boats by Kuwaiti crews, although they did begin to do so in the 1940s and 1950s when transporting their cargo on steamers and Indian ships.

Dhow building and its costs

As described above, the shipwrights were paid wages on a daily basis and the wage of an *ostad* was double that of a *qallaf*. Wages naturally fluctuated according to the supply of available shipwrights, the reputation of the *ostad* and other factors. In his survey of the Gulf in 1904, J. G. Lorimer noted that there were around 25 dhows built in Kuwait every year and that there were roughly 300 shipwrights (of varying ranks), each of whom earned between a quarter of a Maria Theresa Dollar (roughly half a Rupee) and one Maria Theresa Dollar (roughly Rs 2) per day.[18] The cost of labour varied according to the type and size of dhow; a pearling dhow, for example, cost

[16] For more information, see Al-Hijji, 2000 (Arabic): 345–9; Al-Hijji, 2001: 142–3.
[17] Ibid.: 349. [18] Lorimer, 1908–15/1986, vol. 5: 2319.

less than a trading dhow because of its smaller size. Such economic factors as supply and demand also played a role. During the two World Wars, for instance, trading dhows were in high demand due to the recall of steamers for the war effort, but were highly priced because of the difficulty of obtaining the necessary timber to build them. These factors have escalated in more recent times, as the ban imposed by the Indian government in about 1990 on the export of dhow-building timber, and the near-extinction of skilled shipwrights, have served to boost the price of dhows dramatically.

To give an idea of the changing nature of dhow building and its effect on the prices of dhows, we can compare the prices of dhows in three separate years: 1937, 1986 and 1997. In 1937, it was possible for a prospective dhow owner to travel to Calicut himself to secure the necessary timber at a favourable price (both for the timber itself and its shipment to Kuwait), for it was almost guaranteed that he would find timber in ready supply and at a price lower than would be the case in Kuwait. For example, a medium-sized trading dhow (i.e. of 225 tons with a keel of 64 feet in length) of the *boum* variety was sold for Rs 14,880. The *boum Bayan*, built in 1937 and described by traveller and sailor Alan Villiers, had a carrying capacity of around 200 tons and cost roughly Rs 12,500.[19] The construction of a similar dhow 50 years later would cost a bare minimum of 81,000 Kuwaiti Dinars (KD1 = Rs 13) but could cost as much as KD 250,000.[20] To give another hypothetical example: a pearling *sanbuk* would have cost the prospective buyer about Rs 6,000 in 1937, but fifty years later would have cost roughly KD 17,000.[21] In 1997, however, the *boum Muhallab II* – which was constructed by order of the late Amir Jabir Al-Ahmad Al-Sabah and was roughly the same size as *Bayan* – cost KD 300,000. To put this in perspective, the *sanbuk* constructed that same year by the *ostad* 'Ali Jasim Al-Sabaghah for the Kuwait Foundation for the Advancement of Sciences, cost just KD 12,000.

Dhow building in Kuwait today

Even after the Government of India banned the export of timber in about

---

[19] Villiers, 1969: 397; Villiers, 2006a: 367–9.
[20] This obviously depended on the price of the timber itself, which to this day is subject to fluctuations. Interview with the *ostad* 'Ali 'Abd al-Rasul.
[21] Al-Hijji, 2001: 143

1990 and after the involvement of Gulf people in the Indian Ocean trade system had ceased, the *ostad*s of Kuwait continued their work, building yachts as well as fishing and short-distance trading boats adapted for engines. Indeed, this noble industry would not grind to a complete halt until the dawn of the new millennium, which brought with it the proliferation of fibre-glass boats that were cheaper and less maintenance-intensive. This new maritime era demanded technical and mechanical expertise that the *ostad*s – few of whom in any case still survived – simply did not possess, and their sons, seeing no future in an industry eclipsed by the modern age, chose not to follow in their fathers' footsteps as generations before them had done. As the demand for dhows waned after the Second World War and the start of the oil era, merchants, owners and *nakhoda*s sold their vessels to the merchants of the Persian coast, particularly those of the port of Kung. Among the dhows sold in Kung in 1949, history has preserved the names of the following:

- The *Muthanna* of 'Abd al-Latif Muhammad Thunayyan Al-Ghanim, built by the *ostad* 'Ali 'Abd al-Rasul and sold for Rs 45,000
- The *Bayan* of 'Abd al-'Aziz Al-'Ali Al-Mutawwa', built by the *ostad* Musa Sabti and sold for Rs 42,000
- The *Khaldi* of Khalid Al-Hamad and his brothers, built by the *ostad* Husain Al-Ghadban and sold for Rs 50,000
- The *Suhail* of Muhammad Da'ud Al-Marzuq and his brothers, built by the *ostad* Musa Sabti and sold for Rs 21,000
- The *Ziyad* of 'Abd al-Muhsin Nasir Al-Khurafi, sold for Rs 40,000[22]

What follows is a list of the number of dhows built annually in Kuwait between 1919 and 1948 and the total price (if known) that they fetched:[23]

Year	No. of dhows built	Total price (Rs)
1919/20	26	332,500
1920/21	12	193,005
1921/22	36	96,300

[22] Interview with the *nakhoda* 'Isa Al-'Uthman, 1985.
[23] Al-Hijji 2001, pp. 143–5

1922/23	14	38,100
1923/24	23	120,000
1924/25	24	116,250
1925/26	46	247,995
1926/27	33	20,700
1927/28	40	67,005
1928/29	48	134,205
1929/30	21	39,405
1930/31	15	31,200
1931/32	27	607,500
1932/33	4	425,000
1934/35	12	1,210,500
1935/36	40	1,513,500
1936/37	23	1,158,750
1937/38	49	1,051,500
1938/39	11	180,000 – 450,000
1939/40	19	150,000 – 450,000
1942	24 dhows, 180 barges	Unknown
1943	7	35,000
1946	10	Unknown
1948	3	Unknown

3

Al-Ghaws: The Pearl-diving Season

O F ALL OF THE MARITIME activities of Kuwait's people, none was as important or had such a profound effect on their lives as pearl diving, by which is meant the gathering of oysters from the underwater pearl banks of the Gulf. These are to be found chiefly in the shallower waters off the Arabian coast, but were also exploited to some extent on the Persian side too, for example around Kharg and Qish Islands.[1] But pearling was not limited to diving for oysters; any account of pearling in general must include the knowledge and experience involved in locating the banks, the skilled navigation and manoeuvring of the pearling dhows, the sale of pearls both in the Gulf and abroad, the economic bustle that the diving season brought with it, and the social impact of its customs and traditions. The pearling season was unrivalled in its impact, clearing the town of Kuwait of all its able-bodied men for four months at a time, from June to September, leaving behind only the women, children, the elderly and the infirm.

Despite pearling being a centuries-old pillar of the traditional Gulf economy, there was nothing certain about it. Imponderables abounded: the quantity and quality of the catch, the price that it would fetch at market, and the ability of the divers to repay the money advanced to them at the

---

[1] Qish Island, today part of Iran, was well known in medieval times by its Arabic name, Qays.

beginning of the season by the *nakhoda* (usually borrowed in turn from a pearl merchant or *tawwash*). Money, health and safety were all staked on the pursuit of temporary employment and a precarious income. Indeed, the only certainties from one season to the next were that the divers were going to dive, and that they were going to dig themselves deeper into debt – and, by the early 1940s, even those could no longer be counted on. In the heyday of pearling, however, the Kuwaiti fleet could be reckoned among the largest and most productive in the region, second only to that of Bahrain, which is situated close to a cluster of pearl banks known as the "southern banks" by the Kuwaitis and the "northern banks" by the Bahrainis.

A brief history of pearling

During their excavations at Subiyya in 2001–02, Drs Carter and Crawford of the University of London discovered the area's early inhabitants to have been already actively engaged with the sea around 7,000 years ago, fishing and diving for pearls just like the people of Kuwait in more recent times. Their conclusions were based on the find of a pierced pearl – perhaps the oldest yet to come to light – and the remains of a fishing boat.[2] While it cannot be stated with absolute certainty, on the basis of a single find, that the inhabitants of Subiyya were regular participants in this ancient activity, it is certain that pearling took its place as a feature of Gulf economic life from the 3rd millennium BC on. It is recorded by Greco-Roman writers in the late centuries BC, and seems to have grown in importance through the early Islamic centuries, pearl diving in the Gulf being described in recognizable detail by the Arab geographer al-Mas'udi in the 9th century AD.[3] By the 14th and 15th centuries AD, pearls are known to have formed an important part of the exports of Hormuz and Julfar (modern Ras al-Khaimah). And, by the time of the arrival of the 'Utub in eastern Arabia in the early 18th century, pearling had become a cornerstone of economic life. This became all the more so after the invasion and occupation of Bahrain, later that century, by the 'Utub – led by the Al-Khalifa who, a little time before, had left Kuwait to return to Zubara on the north-west coast of the Qatar peninsula. The occupation of the island brought with it access to the rich pearl banks of the area, and the kinship and camaraderie between

[2] Carter & Crawford, 2002.   [3] Donkin, 1998: 44–50, 80–9, 107–9.

the Bahrainis and Kuwaitis – who still refer to each other as cousins – created a safe environment for sailing and pearl diving along the southern littoral of the Gulf extending between the two shaikhdoms.

It was under such circumstances that the Kuwaiti fleet grew and pearling flourished, to the point where it accounted for at least one-third of the town's annual income.[4] Its development both stimulated and was in turn supported by a growing labour force, not only within Kuwait itself but also from the adjacent Arabian interior, from where Bedouin families would emerge to set up camp outside Kuwait during the summer months and to send out their men (who made up roughly 30 percent of the diving force) in Kuwaiti ships to earn some income. Men from the southern Yemeni coast of Mahra too came to Kuwait to serve as sailors on board the vessels of the *tawwash*es, as did occasional divers from Najd (in central Arabia), Basra, Zubair and the ports of southern Persia.[5]

Preparing for the diving season

The main pearl-diving season occupied the hot summer months, during which Gulf waters were warm enough for the divers to work continuously. In the autumn, the water begins to cool, making diving too risky. The main season, known as *al-ghaws al-kabir*, or "the big dive", began in June on a specific date set by the ruler, who likewise ordained a particular closing date in September. While weather prospects dictated the precise beginning and end of the season, it was the ruler's role to enforce an official date, which was binding on everyone on pain of a fine or other punishment. The set dates did not, however, prevent some crews and *nakhoda*s from trying their luck a few weeks before the season's official opening, in what was called *al-ghaws al-khanjiyyah*, usually in the month of April, although a *nakhoda* would not set out without some indication of clement weather conditions and the prospect of a worthwhile catch. All such dhows, however, would return in time to prepare for the start of the main season.[6]

Upon deciding to take part in the pearling season, a *nakhoda* would set

---

[4] This was recalled by the merchant Muhammad Thunayyan Al-Ghanim on the television series, *Safhat min Tarikh al-Kuwait* ("Pages from the History of Kuwait"), Kuwait Television, 1966.
[5] See also Al-Dhuwaihi, 2001.

out to choose a first mate (*mujaddimi*) to be in charge of the crew and to help him prepare the dhow for the trip. The first task of the *mujaddimi* was to assemble the crew of divers and haulers (*saibs*). The haulers' job was to lower the divers into the water and pull them back up, emptying their catch into a common pile and so making it impossible for anyone to tell whose were the pearl-bearing oysters. The crew would also include young boys (called *radif* and *tabbab*) to carry out such duties as cleaning and attending to the *nakhoda*'s requests, as well as a cook and the *nahham*, the on-board singer/chanter. Once assembled, the crewmen would gather in the boatyard to help repair the dhow and prepare it for the season.

On completion of repairs, preparation of the sails, and stocking up with sacks of rice, lentils, ghee, sugar, coffee and dates, the *nakhoda* would set a time and place to meet up with his crew and advance them their seasonal loans (known as the *salaf*), enabling them to provide for their families while they were away. The amount advanced varied from season to season depending on market prices, but was always set by the ruler. Under this arrangement, the sum advanced to a diver was invariably a little higher than that advanced to a hauler, and was recorded in the *nakhoda*'s account book in the presence of the *mujaddimi*.

Once the business of advancing loans was done, the *nakhoda* would set a departure date, before which each crewman had to prepare his personal belongings to take on the trip – usually clothing, simple bedding and sometimes a little tobacco. These he would place in a bag on board. Some divers opted to spend some money on equipment to facilitate the diving and gathering process, such as baskets for oysters, stones to weigh them down, and light cotton trousers known as *shamshul* or *sirwal*.[7] At dawn on the day of departure, the *nakhoda* would appear on the shore near his dhow, showing the sailors that it was time to board, hoist and unfurl the sail, and set off

---

[6] If the pearling season coincided with the month of Ramadan, the dive would be split into two intervals: one that took place just before the holy month and ended with its commencement, the other beginning after the 'Id al-Fitr celebration had concluded. Aside from the physical strain entailed by pearl diving, the reasoning behind this was that mariners feared that the entry of water into their system through their mouths and ear canals would nullify their fast.

[7] A basket usually cost around half a Rupee, while stones could cost as much as three-quarters of a Rupee. Interview with the pearling *nakhoda*, Rashid Abu Gammaz, 2004.

with the fleet to the pearl banks. This was done to much fanfare and sorrowful farewells under the *amir al-ghaws*, or admiral of the pearling fleet. Once they reached the pearl banks, they would drop anchor and set about the long and arduous process of collecting oysters from the seabed.

Generally speaking, no special factor determined which bank would be selected first. A particular bank might be chosen on the basis of the captain's luck there during the previous season. Proximity to the home port and coastal watering places might also be taken into into consideration. However, if a particular bank had revealed itself during the pre–main season diving (*al-ghaws al-khanjiyyah*) to be a plentiful source of oysters, it would most probably be targeted again during the main season.

The diving procedure

The dhow's position over a bank was usually orchestrated with other dhows, so that it could be systematically picked over by the divers. All pearling dhows were equipped with oars or sweeps, which had a dual purpose: first, for rowing the vessel over short distances on the banks; and, second, for use by the divers in the water to hang onto while the dhow was stationary.

The diving process began with the lowering of ropes over the gunwales into the water, with the responsibility for each rope and the safety of the diver using it being that of the hauler assigned to it. The ropes were tied to the sweeps, which helped to keep the ropes evenly spaced and prevent them from becoming entangled. The divers themselves were separated into two teams, each detailed to do ten dives while the other rested so as to ensure a continuous and orderly diving process. Each diver would hold on to a main rope (the *'idah*), and would slip his foot through a loop in a second rope (the *zaibal*) tied to a lead weight; this second rope was also held by the hauler. The *'idah* was also sometimes attached to the basket (the *dayyin*) in which oysters were placed. Once ready to submerge himself, the diver would clamp his nose shut using a peg called a *futam*, grasp the main rope, and signal to the puller that he was ready to be lowered into the water. Upon reaching the seabed, the diver would detach his foot from the weighted rope, which the hauler would pull up to the surface. Then, hanging the basket around his neck and grasping the *'idah* between his toes, the diver would set about collecting oysters.

Having gathered as many shells as he could while holding his breath – usually for a minute to a minute and a half – the diver would take the basket from round his neck, grasp it by the rim, and then tug at the main rope to signal to the hauler that he was ready to be pulled to the surface. His ascent would be rapid, with one hand gripping his basket and the other covering his eyes to shade them from the dazzling sunlight. Having surfaced, his hauler would empty his basket's contents onto the deck. Then the diver would repeat the process nine more times before resting – at which point the second team would take over. The two teams alternated back and forth even during the midday prayer, with one group praying while the other carried out its ten dives. There was no respite until the evening prayer, after which the cool evening air and failing light made their work impossible. Next day their toil would resume all over again right after the dawn prayer, with a session of opening the oysters collected the previous day. Hopes of finding a prize pearl ran high, and they would turn all the pearls they found over to the *nakhoda*.

Despite a tendency in recent times to romanticize it, diving was far from being in the slightest degree enjoyable, and placed an overwhelming and intolerable physical strain on the diver. So chilled did he become in the depths that he had to warm himself by the cooking fire between bouts of diving, even in the heat of a blazing Gulf summer day. Divers had to cope too with hearing and breathing problems caused by the pressure differential between seabed and surface, and with the trauma caused by their rapid ascent and descent. These pressure changes also affected their diet, which was necessarily simple – usually no more than a small cup of coffee and a few dates – because of the intense nausea brought on by diving after even a modest intake of food. The only meal of any size was dinner, which consisted most often of rice and ghee and perhaps a little fish if any were to be had. Life on board was no better for the haulers, who were allowed to eat no more than the divers and were prey to the scorching sun, from which only an awning provided any protection. Nor did sleep bring respite or comfort, for divers and haulers alike were crammed together on deck like sardines and were unable even to turn over without disturbing their neighbours.

While the summer months were the most suitable for diving, the weather was not always favourable, as high winds and dust storms could force the boats to seek shelter in a neighbouring bay until conditions improved. In such spots the crews would look to replenish their supply of water and other essentials, although they would also be able to purchase these from water-carrying dhows and others whose sole purpose was to purvey provisions to the pearlers.

Such was the pattern of life on the pearling banks for four consecutive, gruelling months, ending only on the day of the *quffal*, on which the pearling dhow of the *amir al-ghaws* would fire a cannon to signal the end of the diving season. All vessels were obliged to stop work immediately, raise their sails and return to Kuwait, the fleet appearing over the horizon like a flock of seabirds. Once home they would sing and drum their way into the harbour. Any dhow captain attempting to return early or late without good reason – even a plentiful catch was no excuse – would be subjected to interrogation in the presence of the ruler, who would either impose a penalty or, in the case of an early return (which was usually done to fetch a better market price in advance of the other boats), command the *nakhoda* to return with his crew to the pearl banks. This rather rare infringement was treated severely, as a deterrent, so that the other crews did not have grounds for complaining that they were being unfairly deprived of the returns from a full season's catch, and so that there would be no ill will between them and the *nakhoda*s, whose reputation for fairness was of paramount importance.

The close of the season (the *guffal*)

Much though Gulf pearling has been written about, there has been little specifically on the *guffal* and its attendant celebrations, which surpassed all others in scale. Just as the atmosphere of joyous anticipation on shore defies description, as families awaited the return of fathers, sons and brothers, so too is it hardly possible to convey the excitement on board the homecoming vessel, with its sails unfurled and flag raised aloft. Even the visual images that survive of life on board and ashore fail to conjure up the electricity in the air during the *guffal*, which brought to an end months of arduous toil, carried out under the additional burdens of debt and absence from family and friends. While the *guffal* was chiefly a celebration of return, it was also a collective acknowledgement of the pivotal position occupied by pearl diving in the economy of the Gulf, bringing as it did employment to the mariners and capital to the merchants, enabling them to finance the import of the foodstuffs, clothing and other goods traded in Kuwait's renowned market (*souq*).

The first act of the *guffal* was the homeward race, which begin the moment the cannon was fired. Each boat would sail in as fast as it could, and moor in the basin closest to the home of the owner or the *nakhoda*. Once inshore, the *nakhoda* would disembark first, followed by his crew, some of whom would be greeted straight away by their families, while others stayed to help lower the masts and yards and prop the hull up on its crutches. For some there was grief instead of joy, as news of the death of a loved one was reported and his meagre belongings handed over.

While the mariners spent the first few days after the *guffal* resting at home with their families, for the *nakhoda* there was still work to do. The very next day he had to meet with the *tawwash* who had advanced him money, to show him the season's catch (*igmash* or *itbabah*), which he was obliged to sell him in its entirety, or at least give him first pick. However, in the few cases where a *nakhoda* had borrowed from merchants who did not deal in pearls, he was under no obligation to sell the catch to his creditors; he could sell it instead to whichever merchant offered what he considered the best price.[8] Most often, though, loans were advanced by pearl merchants.

Once left with the net profit (the exact division of profits will be described in greater detail below), the *nakhoda* would subtract the amount loaned to each mariner before the trip from whatever share of the profit each man was entitled to. In the end, a mariner might have earned enough to live on for the next few months, but often this was not so. More usually, he found himself still in debt to the *nakhoda* and thus compelled to borrow even more to provide for his family during the coming winter months, during which he would most probably be away on a long-distance trading voyage. And, the following pearling season, he would be obligated by his debt to serve on the boat of the *nakhoda* who was his creditor. Indeed, he would not be entitled to serve on a new dhow without presenting a letter

---

[8] In some cases, *tawwash*es would approach the *nakhoda*s by dhow while they were out near the banks. In this scenario, a *nakhoda* that needed money to purchase provisions would be compelled to sell part of his catch to the *tawwash* without knowing exactly how much the pearls might fetch later on shore.

(known as a *barwa*) from his *nakhoda* stating either that he was clear of debt, or, if not, how much was owed and would have to be paid to the latter for the mariner's employee status to be transferred. Alternatively, one *nakhoda* might allow a mariner to work for another if the mariner agreed to pay the first one one-third of his net earnings (called *thulth al-makadda*) until his debt was repaid, the first *nakhoda* giving him a letter formally attesting to the agreement. This, however, was an arrangement that came rather late in the game, as the standard practice was for the *nakhoda* to take all of the mariner's earnings, so as to cover his own debts. Such arrangements were open to much abuse and manipulation by merchants and *nakhoda*s alike, and it was only in 1939 that a bureau was established providing sailors with their own personal account books in which their debts were registered and could be verified, so protecting the rights of all participants in the pearling industry.

Financial duress might induce some dhows to return to the banks in October, roughly one month after the season's close, to try their luck again in what was known as the *ghaws al-raddah*, or "return dive". However, because by then conditions were unfavourable, most dhows would stay for only a few weeks, sometimes returning yet again for a short time in November. On such trips, impelled as they were by a shortage of money, divers would often not be advanced any money beforehand and provisions on board would be minimal.

The pearling *nakhoda*

The success of the dive was heavily dependent on the *nakhoda*, who was at once captain of the crew, responsible for order on board, a native pilot skilled at locating pearl banks, and an experienced accountant. He could do duty as an imam, leading his sailors in prayer, and, should medical treatment be needed, act as doctor. As a merchant, he could buy and sell. He was arbitrator in disputes among the crew, and would also act as lawyer in defence of his sailors' rights in case of trouble in foreign ports.

Upon reaching the intended pearl bank, the *nakhoda* would give the order for the anchor to be dropped so that diving could commence. The anchor would not be weighed when the vessel's location needed to be only slightly adjusted over the bank; the anchor rope would merely be lengthened or shortened to adjust the vessel's position, skilfully utilizing the currents in order to gain the divers more access to oysters. It was only when all the oysters on the bank had been collected that the *nakhoda* would order the anchor to be weighed and the boat to be sailed or rowed – to the rhythm of the *nahham*'s chanting – to a new location. Unless the *nakhoda* gave orders for a return to the coast, it was rare for the mainsail to be lifted, most preferring instead to row or use a small sail to manoeuvre between the numerous banks – a job that the divers, in view of their already heavy workload, were spared. It was only the sweet voice of the *nahham* (who never toiled with the divers) that made the arduous task of rowing more bearable, by boosting morale and giving the oarsmen the rhythm they needed to co-ordinate their efforts. It was for this reason that the *nakhoda* often took pains to hire the very best *nahham* that he could find in Kuwait, and might even look farther afield for one.

The farther a dhow voyaged for pearls – many smaller dhows stayed close to Kuwait – the more experienced its *nakhoda* needed to be.[9] Many a *nakhoda* acquired a name for navigational and pilotage skills and firm leadership, and their reputations live on to this day. Among such outstanding names are Rashid bin Ahmad Al-Rumi, the captain of the *As'ayyid* (a famous *battil*), who was reputed to know every single pearl bank on the southern shore of the Gulf, and Abdullah bin Nasir Bu Risli, captain of the *Naif* (a *boum*, and the largest pearling dhow in Kuwait and perhaps in the entire Gulf), who commanded a crew of at least one hundred of the best pearling mariners in the country.

Other diving arrangements

Besides the standard dive described above, and the Ceylon dive, which will be described below, there were three smaller diving arrangements in which fewer dhows and crew members participated. These were the *ghaws al-khammas*, the *ghaws al-'azzal*, and the *ghaws al-munawwar*.

The *ghaws al-khammas* involved just a handful of divers and haulers, who would typically band together to rent a small dhow from its owner for one-

---

[9] Indeed, this was also true for the crew as a whole; smaller dhows that stayed closer to home would often not even need haulers in view of the shallowness of the waters they plied. In such a scenario, the diver would often be able to reach the seabed and launch himself upwards using his feet, without any other assistance.

fifth or one-tenth of the value of the catch. They would then borrow a small amount of money or pool their meagre resources in order to prepare the boat for the trip, after which they would set out with the rest of the fleet to try their luck on nearby banks. Under this arrangement, the mariners would end up with more and larger shares of the net profit – three for the divers and two for the haulers – than was the case under the standard arrangement described below.

In the *ghaws al-'azzal*, a diver would sail with a pearling dhow during a regular season but bring along his own hauler and would not borrow money from the *nakhoda*. Instead of emptying the contents of his basket into the common pile he would keep his catch for himself, opening the oysters and selling on his own account whatever pearls he might find. His sole obligation to the *nakhoda* or dhow owner was to hand over one-tenth of his net profit and his share of the food and water expenses. The remainder of the profit he would divide between himself and his hauler on a 3:2 basis.

Finally, the *ghaws al-munawwar* was a dive which took place close to the coast, in shallow water such that the diver would not need a weight or stone to help him descend, but would be able to do so by himself with relative ease. By this method, the diver would wait until the water was sufficiently still and clear for him to be able to see if there were any oysters beneath, and then dive. Sometimes he might pour fish oil (*sil*) onto the surface of the water and use a box with a clear glass bottom to help him locate oysters. This method – that is, the use of the box – was the preferred one in Yemen and was also practised on the Farasan Islands, just to the north of the Yemeni Red Sea coast. Following the sale of the catch, the net profit would be distributed equally between the divers, who would often not need to spend the night on the boat, thus minimizing their expenses.

The pearl banks

Pearling *nakhoda*s knew all the pearl banks (*hair*, pl. *hairat*) by name, as well as their depths, and whether they were sandy, muddy or covered in sea-grass. Accessible banks ranged from 5 to 13 fathoms (*ba'*) deep, or 30 to 80 feet; any greater depth caused the diver difficulties, so that any catch he might make was not worth his while.[10] The vast majority of Gulf banks were, and are, located close to the southern littoral, extending westwards

from Sharjah to the east coast of Qatar and thence from the north of the
Qatar peninsula all the way to Kuwait. The relative shallowness of these
waters not only made the banks accessible to divers, but also gave rise to sea
temperatures and other conditions that were conducive to the development
of pearl-bearing oysters. This is not to say that there were no pearl banks on
the Persian coast: the waters surrounding Kharg and Qish Islands and the
stretch between the ports of Lingeh and Tahiriyyah contained pearl banks,
but they were neither as numerous nor as clustered as those along the
Arabian coast, which were rich enough to attract Persian pearling boats. In
addition to engendering oysters in abundance, the environmental conditions
of the southern (i.e. Arabian) coast of the Gulf were thought to encourage
the growth of the highest-quality pearls – the banks in the vicinity of
Bahrain being held in especially high regard in this respect.[11]

Although the Bahrainis enjoyed a comparative advantage in the pearl
trade because of the abundance of banks nearby and the quality of their
pearls, it must be stressed that no group was held to be exclusively entitled
to the banks that happened to lie close to its home territory. The pearl
banks were all regarded as common property, and as long as the divers
continued to use the traditional method of diving described above – scuba
gear and other accessories being strictly prohibited – then all was deemed
fair under customary law. Though the banks were given such general names
as "the Kuwaiti banks", "the Bahraini banks", etc., this was only an
indication of general location and implied no claim to property rights or
privileged access.

Why some banks produced oysters in abundance and others did not
remained a mystery, nor did anyone have any inkling why a particular bank
that had produced plenty of pearl-bearing oysters (known as a *tibrah*) one
season, might produce none the next. Not even the most knowledgeable
and experienced *nakhoda*s, who could identify a pearl bank by name after
just one glimpse, were able to answer these questions, nor did they try to.
And this was by no means out of ignorance on their part, for some seasoned
*nakhoda*s were able to identify which bank a pearl came from just by seeing
and touching it.[12]

[10] Some pearl merchants, however, held the unsubstantiated belief that the deeper the
water, the better the pearls, and so they recommended pushing divers to the limits of
their endurance.
[11] Villiers, 2006a: 325–6.   [12] Villiers, 2006a: 326; Lorimer, 1908–15/1986: 2220.

The Ceylon dive

The pearl banks of the Gulf were not the only ones tried by Kuwaiti divers. Some even used to sail to Massawa in the Red Sea to try their luck, but this was unusual due to the prevalence of shoals and reefs there and the consequent dangers to navigation.[13] More commonly, after the end of the main pearling season, those who eschewed the lesser dives and employment on the long-distance trading dhows might try and earn some money diving off the island of Ceylon (modern-day Sri Lanka), where the warmth of the water even during the winter months made diving possible all year round. During this dive, which usually began in January or February, the local people would hire out boats and cottages for the season to the Kuwaitis and other Gulf mariners. The dive took place in the Gulf of Mannar – the stretch of sea between the southern tip of India and the northern part of the island – and was regulated by the Ceylon Pearl Fisheries Company, which supervised all diving activity in the area. On the first day of the dive, the boats would congregate near the pearl bank assigned to them by the company – usually around 20 miles from the coast – and wait for the signal to begin at first light, after which they would dive until midday, to depths ranging from 8 to 11 fathoms.

The number of Kuwaitis participating in the Ceylon dive peaked at around 3,000 in 1905, but declined soon afterwards to 400 in 1907, collapsing to none by the 1909/10 season when the company dispensed with foreign divers. While their employment by the company was restricted in later years because of the First World War, some 285 Kuwaiti divers are known to have taken part in January and May of 1925. Kuwaitis, however, could find this dive to be of dubious profitability. Abdullah Rashid Al-'Alaiwah, for example, recalled that in 1928 he was paid around 119 British Pounds (approximately Rs 1,400) for a season's work; but he had to pay for his steamer trip from Kuwait to Bombay, and then pay again for the train fare from Bombay to Ceylon, to take part in a dive no more than 40 days long; and, once there, he also had to pay for housing and boat rental.[14] A take

[13] In an interview, the *nakhoda* Rashid Abu Gammaz recalled how some pearl merchants, among them Yusuf Al-Bakr, used to encourage him to try the banks of the Red Sea.
[14] Interview on the television series "*Safhat min Tarikh al-Kuwait*" ("Pages from the History of Kuwait"), Kuwait Television, 1966.

of Rs 1,400 was regarded as average, but takings could fluctuate wildly: in some seasons the divers grossed as little as Rs 500, and in others as much as Rs 2,000.[15] A further discouragement to participation in the Ceylon dive was provided by Shaikh Mubarak (r. 1896–1915), to whom pearl merchants and *nakhoda*s alike complained that upon their return Kuwaiti divers were simply too exhausted to take part in the main diving season.[16]

The diving process in Ceylon differed hardly at all from that in the Gulf, either in the number of crewmen needed for a single operation or in the techniques of the dive itself. The only differences were that the local divers in Ceylon – that is, Indians and Sri Lankans – never used a nose clip, preferring instead to use their hands, and that divers were not allowed to eat for the entire duration of the day's work. This was no great hardship, as the dive lasted only until midday, at which point the company supervisor would give the signal that the day's diving was done. The most marked difference lay in the division of the catch and in the method of paying the divers. First, the divers would keep one-third of their oysters and hand over the remainder to the company, which would auction the pearls and pay the divers a flat rate for their labour. The divers were free to do whatever they pleased with their own oysters: some might choose to sell them unopened, while others preferred to try their luck by searching for pearls, especially if they had heard that the banks from which the oysters originated were renowned as pearl-bearing.

Pearls and their sale

The trade in pearls developed and flourished over the course of hundreds of years, regulated by customary law and operating outside the purview of formal government control. The government merely levied a tax to the tune of one diver's share on each boat. Until the 1930s, the only government interference in the pearling industry took the form of the appointment of a deputy from among the pearl merchants known as the *ra'is salifat al-ghaws* ("head of the pearling court") whose function was to resolve disputes between merchants, *nakhoda*s and mariners. The celebrated *tawwash*,

---

[15] Al-Shamlan, 1975, vol. 2: 86.
[16] See the reports by the British Political Agent in Kuwait, *Persian Gulf Administration Reports*, vol. 6 (Reports of the Political Agency, Kuwait, 1906/07): 109.

Salim bin Ali Abu Gammaz, for instance, was appointed *ra'is salifat al-ghaws* during the reign of Shaikh Ahmad al-Jabir Al-Sabah (r. 1921–50). If a dispute went to court, the opinion of such an individual would carry greater weight than that of an ordinary merchant because of his long experience in the pearl trade, his grasp of its lore, customs and principles, and his perceived honesty and scrupulousness.

As already described, upon his return from a pearling trip, the *nakhoda* was obliged to sell his catch to a pearl merchant (*tawwash*), usually his creditor, at a price agreed between themselves and usually at a rate of 10 to 20 percent below market price, before he was allowed to sell the remainder to anyone else. Having purchased pearls from the *nakhoda* in this way, the *tawwash* would travel to distant pearl markets to offer his stock to bigger pearl merchants. Just as was the case with the *nakhoda*, the *tawwash* in turn had often borrowed money from such merchants, to help finance his business and advance his loans in Kuwait, and would thus be obliged to sell to his own creditor, although this was not always the case. Of these pearl markets, the most popular in the Gulf were those at Bahrain and Lingeh (on the Persian coast), as well as Dubai and, in the more distant past, Basra. *Tawwash*es, however, were not limited to markets within the Gulf and often went to Bombay (and, before that, Surat), where some of the wealthiest jewellers in the world were concentrated until the decline of the market for pearls in the mid-20th century.[17] Bombay attracted buyers and sellers from all over the world, among them the likes of the Kuwaiti pearl merchants Jasim Muhammad Al-Ibrahim, 'Abd al-Rahman Al-Ibrahim, 'Abd al-Latif Muhammad Al-'Abd al-Razzaq (a famous broker), and Muhammad 'Ali Rida Zainal, a Hijazi notable who played an important role in protecting the rights of the Arab merchants in Bombay. These merchants, who resided in Bombay, acted as middlemen, buying pearls from Gulf *tawwash*es and selling them on to the throng of foreign buyers drawn to the port during the season. Among these buyers some famous European names stand out, such as Victor Rosenthal, a wealthy French Jewish merchant who spoke

---

[17] In an interview on the television series *Safhat min Tarikh al-Kuwait* ("Pages from the History of Kuwait"), Yusuf bin 'Isa Al-Qina'i recalled a letter from Shaikh 'Abd al-Latif Al-'Abd al-Razzaq in which the latter recorded how the pearl merchants of Kuwait used to go to the pearl markets of Surat and Baghdad before those of Bahrain and Bombay rose to prominence.

Arabic and had stores in Paris, Bombay, Bahrain and London, and Albert
Habib, another French Jew with stores in Bombay, Bahrain and Paris, who
often bought stock from Hilal Al-Mutairi.[18] It was via these channels that
the pearls of the Gulf would make their way to the display cases of society
jewellers in Paris and New York.

The price that pearls fetched in the market varied and depended in the
first instance on their size, weight, colour and sparkle. A large and perfectly
spherical white pearl (known as a *danah* or *hasba*), weighing at least one
mithqal (see Appendix D), could fetch a relatively high price in a favourable
market provided the merchant's judgment was sound. To be sure, there were
standard objective methods by which pearls were classified according to the
criteria above, and all who participated in the trade were well versed in
them. The pearls would first be sorted according to size by means of a
cascade of three sieves, called *tasah*s, whose bases were perforated by standard
holes in descending order of size. The pearls would be rolled about in the
topmost sieve until they separated, the largest (called the *ras* or "head"
pearls) being retained there, while the smallest (the *dhayl* or "tail" pearls) fell
through to the lowest sieve; those caught in the middle sieve were called the
batn or "middle" pearls. The very smallest pearls (some called *sihteet* and
others *bukah*), which fell through the holes of the lowest sieve, were not
much sought after and fetched a very low price.[19]

As a general rule, the pearls held by the topmost sieve would fetch a price
roughly equal to twice that of the middle pan, while those of the lowest
sieve would fetch a price equal to only one-eighth of those of the former.[20]
A *danah*, however, would be sold separately from the others: it would
normally be weighed in *mithqal*s, after which that weight would be squared
and then multiplied by 330 to give its weight in *chau*, the standard term for
units of weight of pearls in the markets of Bahrain, India and the Gulf.[21] The
weight in *chau* would then be multiplied by the standard price for a *chau* of
pearls in that market – and this naturally fluctuated according to market

[18] Al-Shamlan, 2000:166.
[19] Al-Shamlan, 2000: 80–2.
[20] Lorimer, 1986: 2220.
[21] Though the *mithqal* as a general unit of weight varied from market to market, when
it came to pearls the Kuwaiti *mithqal* was the same as the Gulf *mithqal*, which in turn
was the same as the Bombay *mithqal*. The differences in the *mithqal* in other contexts
were common knowledge among pearl merchants and merchants in general.

conditions – to ascertain the pearl's market price, which would then be adjusted to account for aesthetic qualities such as colour, smoothness, lustre and sparkle.[22]

A detailed study of these systems leads one to a true appreciation of the mathematical and commercial acumen of the merchants, whose simple outward appearance belied their ability to manipulate and adjust these equivalences so as to weather economic fluctuations, which might involve losses of thousands of rupees one season and compensating gains the next. Those trading from both Kuwait and India kept various resources at hand, exploiting whatever was available in the way of dhows, steamers, couriers, agents, brokers and other intermediaries to afford them the flexibility they needed to minimize transaction costs and to find ways around impediments to the smooth flow of commerce.

Above all, these merchants had a detailed and compendious knowledge of every different category of pearl and its characteristics, including size, colour, lustre and sparkle. The different categories of sizes have already been discussed; what appears below is a short list of the broad categories of pearls and their general characteristics:

Name	Characteristics
jyoon (= "G one")	Fully round and with no blemishes
shireen	Fully round with a few blemishes
daraj	Round, but smaller than the above two
qōlōh	Shiny and clear, but not perfectly round
badla	Same as the above, but with more blemishes
nā'im	Small, but fully round
fus	Embedded in the oyster in which it was found

As for colour, with rare exceptions, the most sought-after pearl was the pure white variety, after which came yellow-white, then yellow, and then sky blue.[23] The standard categories included:

---

[22] For *tawwash* manuals detailing these practices, see also Al-Manna'i 1886.
[23] See also Al-Ghunaim, 1998: 199; Al-Zayyani, 1998: 187

Local name for colour	Characteristics
mishir	White with a pink tint; the rarest of the colours
nabāti	White with a yellow tint
zujāji	Sparkling white with a clear glossy exterior
samāwi	Sky blue
niqbās	Blue-grey
khadra	Greenish in tint
shagra	Pale yellow
aswad	Black; can be worth a small fortune if fully round

Some exceptional pearls fetched such enormous prices on the market that they quite literally made history. Notable among these was the *nakhoda* 'Ali Dawb's *danah* which, at 300 *chau*, was the largest ever found in Kuwait, and which in 1935 was sold for Rs 20,000 (it was in fact worth much more) to Shaikh Ahmad Al-Jabir, Kuwait's ruler, who in turn gave it to HM King George V of Great Britain as a state gift. Then there was the one found by the *nakhoda* Abdullah bin Yaqut, which weighed 170 *chau* and was sold for Rs 110,000 to a *tawwash*, who in turn sold it in India for Rs 170,000 in 1918. Also memorable was the pearl of the *nakhoda* Hashim Al-Rifa'i, sold to the famous *tawwash* Hilal Al-Mutairi for Rs 45,000 and then resold by him in Dawra (near Kuwait) for Rs 100,000. These, however, were the exceptions; the vast majority of pearls fetched a good deal of money, but rarely fortunes like these.

The economics of pearl diving

Until its decline in the late 1930s, pearl diving was a cornerstone of economic activity in the Gulf. Its economic implications were not limited to the activities directly linked to it, but had a trickle-down effect on various other sectors too, so that in all it accounted for nearly one-third of the country's national product.[24] Pearl diving was a source of income not only for mariners and dhow-owners, but also to the dhow-builders, whose work

[24] Interview with the Kuwaiti merchant Muhammad Al-Thunayyan Al-Ghanim, on the television series *Safhat min Tarikh al-Kuwait* ("Pages from the History of Kuwait"), Kuwait Television, 1966.

– and that of all who were linked to that sector, such as blacksmiths – was stimulated by the demands of an active pearling sector. Furthermore, the sale of pearls by the Kuwaiti *tawwash*es brought them income that allowed for further activity and spending, as did the onward sale of those same pearls by the merchants in India and Bahrain. The pearling season also brought income to the state, which levied a tax of one diver's share on each boat. Indeed, the economic impact of pearling was not limited to Kuwait Town alone but also extended into the desert, as members of nearby Bedouin tribes were frequent participants in the dive and spent their share of the profits in Kuwait's market on goods that they would either consume or resell in the markets of the interior. Taking all of this into consideration, it is little wonder that Kuwait's rulers went out of their way to ensure the stability of the market. Mubarak Al-Sabah, for example, once travelled personally to Bahrain to appeal to the renowned pearl merchant Hilal Al-Mutairi and others to return to Kuwait, after a crisis in their relations with the ruler over the continued use of their labour force as soldiers in his campaigns against the Muntafiq tribe of southern Iraq.[25] As alluded to above, the dive for pearls was structured on a hierarchy of debt and obligation that penetrated deep into Kuwaiti society. Indeed, the entire industry was sustained by a system of monetary advances, from the merchants in the markets of India and Bahrain all the way down to the mariners. In a society in which taking interest on loans was strictly forbidden under religious law, other means were found by which the merchant could reap a benefit. It has already been noted how *nakhoda*s, who were generally cash-strapped, had to borrow from local merchants – and sometimes also the ruler – to enable them to prepare for the season by advancing loans to their mariners, buying provisions for the trip and so forth, and how they were then obligated to sell their catch to their creditor before they could offer it to anyone else, and usually at a price that was lower than that of the market by 10 to 20 percent. However, if their creditor was not a pearl merchant and had no interest in purchasing the catch, before the season began he would resort to the method known as "double sale", which works as follows.

A *nakhoda* needing to borrow 100 rupees in cash would come to the merchant, who would agree to give him that sum, on condition that the

[25] Al-Rashaid, 1926, vol. 2: 111; Slot, 2005: 334–9.

nakhoda paid him back R 120 at the end of the season. In order to do this in a way that did not involve actually making a loan bearing interest, the merchant would "sell" the *nakhoda* some sacks of rice on credit for R 120, to be paid at the end of the season. The merchant would then immediately "buy" the sacks of rice back for R 100 in cash, which he would give to the *nakhoda*. Thus the *nakhoda* received R 100, and the sacks of rice never changed hands. He is now under an obligation to pay the merchant R 120 at the end of the season. The merchant thereby secures a gain without actually taking any interest. This ploy of the "double sale", in which no goods actually changed hands, was used by Muslim borrowers to circumvent the ban on interest.

The *nakhoda*, however, was not always compelled to borrow money, as sometimes he would have sufficient capital of his own to fund a pearling venture; this, however, was the exception rather than the rule, with most *nakhoda*s straddling the area between profit and debt. Should a *nakhoda* be unable to pay back the amount he had borrowed from the merchant – and he always took measures, detailed below, to ensure that he could – he could be compelled to sell his dhow, if it belonged to him, or even his house.

As we saw, this debt hierarchy extended all the way down from the *nakhoda*s to the mariners, who would often be advanced small loans at the beginning of the season – in the 1930s, Rs 20 to 30 – and would thus be tied to that *nakhoda*, working for him until their debts were cleared. While this would ideally be achieved within a single season, a catch that failed to bring in sufficient money meant that the mariners' debts would accumulate, as they would be compelled to borrow from the *nakhoda* to provide for their families during the off-season, during which they would either dive elsewhere or work as sailors on the long-distance trading dhows. In order to do this, however, the mariner would have to present the *barwa* or letter of attestation to his new *nakhoda* so that the responsibility for seeing that the mariner's debts were paid would pass to the latter, who would then debit the mariner's account accordingly. It should be noted here that *nakhoda*s too sidestepped taking interest on their loans to the mariners by marking up the price of the provisions they supplied to them during the voyage, thereby securing their financial gain at the expense of their crew. While most mariners were in perpetual debt, there was no bar to one becoming a merchant himself; Hilal Al-Mutairi, for example, started off as a diver and, with luck and financial acumen, rose to become one of the largest pearl merchants in the entire Gulf. Again, a skilled diver was in heavy demand by *nakhoda*s and could command a bonus on top of his share of the profit. This was why the Bedouins of the interior preferred to work as divers rather than haulers, who were paid less, had less opportunity to distinguish themselves, and had to carry out the rowing and sail-raising.

While this hierarchy of debt and obligation may seem unjust, it should be emphasized that participants in the system did so voluntarily and with a clear idea of the financial implications of it all.[26] True, they were driven to accepting such harsh labour conditions by the lack of employment opportunities in other sectors and by the general poverty of the region. Furthermore, debt was regarded as normal and, while the mariners were often aware of their exploitation by those further up the hierarchy, few ever went so far as to contest the system. Only in a few cases did *nakhoda*s resort to harsh measures by forcing mariners out of their homes and onto the dhows, and in doing so they earned notoriety.[27] Mostly, *nakhoda*s were known for their fair treatment of crewmen. And to prevent injustices the government increasingly intervened, for example by appointing a deputy to resolve conflicts between *nakhoda*s and their men, by enacting certain laws regarding debt, notably the Pearling Law of May 1940, and by making compulsory such devices as the mariner's personal account book.

The sheer amount of luck involved in pearling and the hardship it brought led some merchants to choose not to participate in it despite its profit potential, and to prefer instead to "leave it to its people". This negative image of hardship and precariousness, however, did not alter the fact that pearling was one of the few sectors that could be relied upon to bring

[26] See Appendix A: The Pearling Law of 1940, for the codification of the debt system towards the end of the pearling era. One informant, an ex-diver, defended the system by remarking that people today are as much indebted, through their mortgages and credit cards, as the divers used to be; why, then, single out pearling for special criticism?

[27] The Pearling Law enacted in 1940 (see Appendix A, article 19) did not provide for a diver's debt to be nullified with his death; the debt continued be passed on to his living relatives, as had been the practice beforehand. Article 19 of the Law merely allows the diver and his descendants to repay his debts by any means possible, and not necessarily by diving as had been the case prior to the Law. See Appendices A and B. For a vivid description of the workings of the debt pyramid in Kuwait up to 1939, see Villiers, 2006a: 322–3, 327–30.

money into the generally cash-poor Gulf. In 1911–12, for example, the average share on board a pearling boat amounted to between Rs 1,500 and 2,000. In his survey of the region, Lorimer recorded that in 1904–05 Shaikh Mubarak could expect to receive an annual income of 60,000 Maria Theresa Dollars (roughly Rs 150,000) from the pearling sector alone. In general at the height of pearl trade, the Kuwaiti ruler could expect to receive an annual revenue of between Rs 90,000 and Rs 180,000 from pearling. In 1924–25, the total value of the export of Kuwait's pearls was Rs 2,829,990, as against the total value of exports by sea of Rs 8,199,765. There were, however, years in which pearls fetched an exceptionally low price in the Kuwaiti market: in 1933, for example, the total domestic value of the catch was a mere Rs 450,000.[28]

Turning to the division of profits for the season, the procedure went as follows. The *nakhoda* would take the catch to the *tawwash* and, having agreed on a price, the two of them would subtract the amount owed to the latter (or to any other merchant) from the gross profit. If the two parties were unable to come to an agreement on the price of the pearls, they would refer the issue to an arbitrator known as the *muthammin* – the names of Ibn Duwaisan and Ibn Rashid stand out in the record – to determine the value of the catch. After the catch had been sold and the loans cleared, one-fifth of the money would be given to the owner of the boat, who was sometimes the *tawwash* himself or occasionally even the *nakhoda*, but who could also be an independent party.[29] Following this deduction, the net profit would be divided by the total number of shares on board to determine the value of each share; the total number of shares being reached by adding up the entitlement of every crew member. The shares were then distributed between the mariners in the following standard proportions: three shares to the *nakhoda*; three shares to the diver; three shares in government tax; two shares to the hauler; one share each to the cook and singer (*nahham*); one share to the first mate (*mujaddimi*) or head of the mariners, as well as a bonus in the form of a sack of rice, sugar, dates, etc.; and one share to the apprentice (*radif*).

[28] Lorimer 1908–15/1986, vol. 8 (Geographical): 1076; *Persian Gulf Trade Reports*, vol. 1 (1924–25): 3; vol. 2 (1932–33): 3.
[29] The boat-owner one-fifth was always paid out of the gross profits of the season, before other loans were repaid. See Al-Qitami 1976: 213 (appendix added by one of 'Isa Al-Qitami's sons).

This profit-sharing process is perhaps best illustrated by a hypothetical scenario. Let us say that on a pearling boat there were one *nakhoda*, 25 divers, 29 haulers (who also acted as rowers and sailors), two apprentices, one cook, one singer, and the first mate. On the basis set out above, this adds up to a total of 141 shares. The government also takes three shares (a diver's entitlement), bringing the total to 144 shares. Let us then assume that the season's pearls were sold for Rs 80,000. One-fifth (i.e. Rs 16,000) would go to the boat owner, leaving the *nakhoda* with Rs 64,000 from which he would have to subtract the costs of the provisions – typically 1,000 Rs in the early 1930s – which would leave him with Rs 63,000. This net profit would then be divided by the total number of shares, 144 in this example, meaning that a share would equal Rs 437.5. This amount would then be multiplied by the number of shares due to each person. The profit-sharing process would be completed once the divers' advances and other loans had been deducted from the money due to them, thus repaying the *nakhoda* (and ultimately his creditor).

Prices fetched by pearls

The prices fetched by pearls in the markets of Bahrain, Bombay and other places fluctuated widely from year to year, especially during the World Wars and the inter-war years, which saw not only the worldwide economic depression of the early 1930s that reverberated through Kuwait's pearl markets, but also the disruption and uncertainty caused by the introduction of Japanese cultured pearls. But it is difficult to ascertain exactly to what degree prices fluctuated, as the only sources we have to rely upon are reports by British officials in the Gulf. The dearth of local merchants' documentary records means that one can only speculate about approximate prices fetched by pearls in the markets of Kuwait and Bahrain. In Bombay, where in 1915 the Government of India exacted a tax of 7.5 percent on pearls sold, the picture is slightly clearer. However, even here the waters are muddied by the various debts and obligations involved in the pearl business, as it is impossible to ascertain whether the recorded prices were the real market prices or only the sums of money that actually changed hands.

A few Kuwaiti merchants did however record the total annual prices fetched by pearls. Yusuf bin 'Isa Al-Qina'i, for example, noted that in the year 1330 AH/AD 1912, the total value of the catch was roughly Rs 6 million. Another historian, Al-Nabhani, commented that pearls usually fetched Rs 8 to 10 million, although he gives no dates for his estimate. Finally, the *nakhoda* Rashid Salim Abu Gammaz recalled that in the early 1930s they fetched only Rs 3 to 5 million.[30] To give the reader a rough idea of the prices, the following tables list some transactions noted by different British political agents in the area as well as average prices in India.

Some Noteworthy Transactions[31]

Year   Pearl prices (in Indian Rupees)

1915   One *danah* was sold in Kuwait for Rs 12,000 and resold for Rs 110,000; another was sold in Kuwait for Rs 19,000 but was resold for Rs 50,000.

1918   One *danah* was sold in Kuwait for Rs 110,000 and resold (also in Kuwait) for Rs 150,000, although its real value was Rs 220,000.

1923   The total export value of pearls registered by the Kuwait Political Agent was equivalent to £6,667, or Rs 100,000.

1933   The *tawwash* Musa'id Al-Badr sold a pearl for Rs 20,000 that fetched a price of Rs 40,000 in India.

1935   A *danah* was sold to Shaikh Ahmad Al-Jabir Al-Sabah for Rs 20,000 but in actuality was worth far more than that.

1936   The largest *danah* found this year was said to be worth Rs 90,000 and was sent to India to be sold there.

Pearl Prices in India, 1945–49 (in Indian Rupees)[32]

Year	Jyoon	Shireen	Nā'im	Qōlōh	Badlah
1945	200	100	60–65	50	15–20
1946	500	150–250	60–70	30–50	10–15
1947	80–120	–	35–40	15–25	5–8
1948	150–200	–	60–65	35–40	8–12
1949	150–200	–	60–85	35–40	8–12

[30] See Al-Qina'i, 1988: 71; Al-Nabhani ,1949, vol. 8: 181; Abu Gammaz's information was gleaned during an interview in 2004.

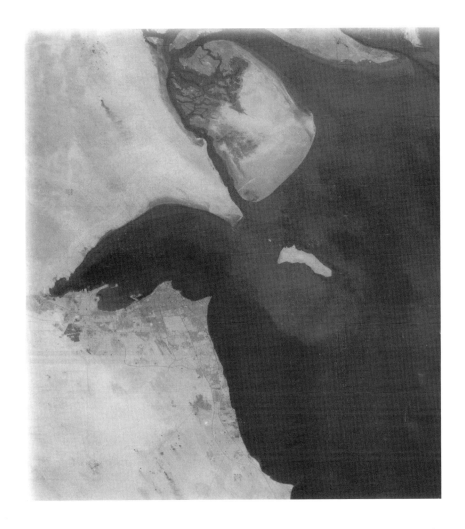

1. Landsat view of Kuwait City, Kuwait Bay, Failaka Island, Bubiyan Island, and the mouth of the Shatt al-ʻArab at the north-east corner, in 1997.

2. The western part of the old town of Kuwait in the 1940s, before but on the brink of modern development.

3. *Above* The dhow-building yard of the celebrated Kuwaiti shipwright Ahmad bin Salman, in the 1950s.

4. *Above* One of the very last deep-sea *boum*s under construction in Kuwait, 1996.

5. *Opposite, top* Work proceeds on the hull planking of possibly the same *boum*, just above the high tide mark, Kuwait, 1960s. In front of it is drawn up a small fishing craft, a *balam fudiri*. In the dhow basin beyond lie two more *boum*s, which will be floated by the incoming tide.

6. *Opposite below* Shipwrights construct the hull interior of the hull of a large cargo *boum*, Kuwait, 1960s.

7. The Kuwaiti dhow builder Muhammad bin Abdullah in the 1960s.

8. *Above* Kuwaiti pearl divers, hanging on to the *bulbus*, a rope tied to the sweep, prepare for their next descent to the seabed, 1950s.

9. *Below* A pearl diver, grasping the rim of his basket to which his *ʿidah* is attached, gasps for air as he breaks surface after being hauled up from the seabed, 1960s.

10. *Left* A pearl diver with his nose clip and oyster basket, 1960s.

11. *Below* Two *barwa*s, letters formally recording a diver's debts to a previous *nakhoda*.

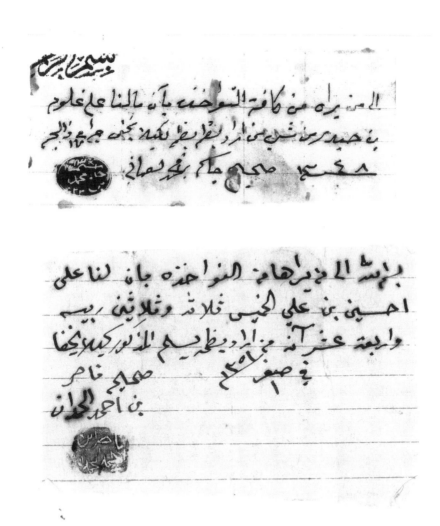

12. *Above* Two of Kuwait's biggest pearl merchants, Shamlan bin Ali Al-Saif (left) and Hilal bin Fajhan Al-Mutairi (centre), in the 1930s. To the right sits a youthful Shaikh Abdullah Al-Salim Al-Sabah, later to be Amir of Kuwait, 1950–65.

13. *Below* A pearl merchant's equipment included weights, a small balance, graduated sieves, small shovels, small chests or cash boxes, and red cloths to hold the pearls. These were photographed in the 1960s.

14. *Above* Kuwait's long-distance dhow trade was dependent on the dates of the Shatt al-'Arab plantations, which supplied the bulk commodity for export all over the western Indian Ocean. The date packages also served as effective ballast for the dhows on their outward voyage. These are Iranian date packages, in 2000.

15. *Below* Yusuf Al-Saqr's guesthouse at Calicut was a famous meeting-place for Kuwaiti merchants and *nakhoda*s. Seen here in 1983, it has since been demolished.

16. *Right* Husain Al-'Asusi, a Kuwaiti deep-sea *nakhoda*, like other deep-sea *nakhodas* was adept at the use of a sextant, the use of which he here demonstrates at his house in 1989.

17. *Far right* Thunayyan Al-Ghanim, seen here in the 1930s, was a well-known Kuwaiti timber and date merchant.

18. *Below* The Kuwaiti merchant and broker Yusuf Al-Saqr, photographed here at Calicut in the 1940s with British officials, was a notable figure on India's Malabar coast.

The compass diagram shows the 32 compass points in English on the outer rings (reading clockwise from the top): N, N by E, NNE, NE by N, NE, NE by E, ENE, E by N, E, E by S, ESE, SE by E, SE, SE by S, SSE, S by E, S, S by W, SSW, SW by S, SW, SWbyW, WSW, W by S, W, W by N, WNW, NWbyW, NW, NW by N, NNW, N by W.

The inner rings contain the Arabic star names (matla' / maghib):

مطلع العيوق · مطلع السماك · مطلع الواقع · مطلع الثريا · مطلع الطائر · مطلع الجوزاء · مطلع النير · مطلع الاكليل · مطلع القلب · مطلع العقرب · مطلع الحارثين · مطلع النعائم · مطلع الذابح · مطلع الناقة · مطلع الحصين · مطلع الفرقدين

مغيب العيوق · مغيب الواقع · مغيب السماك · مغيب الثريا · مغيب الطائر · مغيب الجوزاء · مغيب النير · مغيب الاكليل · مغيب العقرب

19. *Above* Arab navigators in the Gulf and Arabian Sea used a system of 32 compass points based on the rising (*matla'*) and setting (*maghib*) of certain stars, as shown here.

20. *Opposite, top* On the East Africa run, once date cargoes had been disembarked by Kuwaiti dhows at Aden and Berbera, a popular commodity for further shipment down to the Swahili ports was salt. This old postcard shows a salt production site at Aden.

21. *Opposite, below* At Aden, the office of the Kuwaiti merchant and broker Khalid Al–Hamad, seen here in 2000, was situated in the town of Crater, and was a vital point of contact for Kuwaiti *nakhoda*s and Yemeni traders.

Aden - Salt Works

22. Once in East Africa, Kuwaiti *nakhodas* would call in at the offices of various brokers to sell their cargoes. This building in the port of Mombasa, seen here in 2000 was the office of an Arab broker in the 1940s.

The end of pearling in the Gulf

A confluence of factors contributed to the decline and eventual extinction of the Gulf pearling sector. In the first case, the market for pearls had changed completely: gone were the maharajahs and the Persian and Chinese emperors that had once formed a regular core market for Gulf pearls. Moreover, the tastes of European women were changing, and the hard times brought about by the World Wars and the Great Depression meant that those who once wore pearls as an ostentatious display of wealth no longer felt inclined to do so. To these factors, of course, must be added the introduction of Japanese cultured pearls, which to the untrained eye looked indistinguishable from, but were far less expensive than, their Gulf counterparts.

This is not to say that there was no market at all for pearls. Demand persisted for cheaper pearls of the non-cultured variety as well as for mother-of-pearl, chiefly from Indian women who continued to use them in jewelry for special occasions – just as is the case today, albeit in much smaller numbers than before. Despite the changes that were having their impact well before the natural pearl market's eventual demise in the late 1930s, however, the pearl-diving process continued just as before, with divers taking loans that they knew they would be unable to repay, and continuing to dive for lack of better economic options.[33] The pearl-diving sector was dealt its final, crushing blow by the introduction of oil into the economy of Kuwait and the employment opportunities provided by it for the male inhabitants, who no longer found it necessary to participate in pearling in order to make a living.

Thus it was that one of the pillars of the Kuwait's pre-oil economy collapsed. While the pearling industry is remembered and celebrated to this

[31] *Persian Gulf Administration Reports, 1873–1957*: for 1915, vol. 7: 71. Ibid. for 1918, vol. 7: 62. Ibid. for 1933, vol. 9: 62. *Persian Gulf Trade Reports, 1905–1940*: for 1923, vol. 1: 18. Ibid. for 1936, vol. 9: 35. Al-Shamlan, 2000: 84.

[32] *Persian Gulf Administration Reports, 1873–1957*, vol. 8.[33] It should be noted here that at least two participants in the pearling sector, the merchant Mishari Al-Rawdan and the *nakhoda* Rashid Abu Gammaz, noted that in 1948 the Indian government banned the import of Gulf pearls because of the capital flight that it caused, although this happened well after the market had entered on its sharp decline. Both were interviewed on the television series *Safhat min Tarikh al-Kuwait* ("Pages from the History of Kuwait"), Kuwait Television, 1966.

[34] Villiers, 2006a: 347.

day by the descendants of those who toiled with such fortitude to wrest their meagre livelihoods from it, not one of its practitioners – save perhaps the merchants – was sad to see it go, for the dive for pearls was customarily likened by its exponents to a season in hell. As Alan Villiers confirmed after his experiences on the pearl banks in 1939, "… judged by any standard I know, compared with any form of maritime hardship I have experienced, or seen, or read about, pearling in the Persian Gulf can be terrible indeed. I came away from Kuwait favourably impressed by most aspects of its life, enthusiastic about its ships, and an admirer of its seamen. But the infernal *ghaus* [*sic*], the hellish diving, is another matter."[34] But these men had little other option, and it was only the death of the pearl market and the bankruptcy of many of the pearl merchants that impelled most Kuwaiti mariners quite literally to jump ship to the long-distance trade sector, which continued unabated for a number of decades and to which the discussion will now turn.

4

Al-Safar: The Long-distance Dhow Trade

OCCUPYING THE PLACE of honour in the maritime history of Kuwait, long-distance trade by dhow, or *al-safar* in Kuwaiti parlance, denotes the seasonal voyages undertaken by Kuwaiti dhows to the numerous ports of the western Indian Ocean – i.e. western India, southern Arabia and East Africa – to transport goods either on behalf of Kuwaiti merchants and their agents or, occasionally, of the *nakhoda*s or captains themselves. While there were similarities between the pearling sector and the long-distance dhow trade, particularly in their labour hierarchies and profit-sharing schemes, the two also differed in significant respects. Debt in long-distance trade was not common, as it was in pearling, as a long-distance voyage provided a sailor with opportunities to make some money on his own account, however little it might be. Nor was a sailor was ever obligated to return to a particular dhow to sail again the following season. Furthermore, much less uncertainty attached to a trading dhow's seasonal profits than to those of a pearling dhow, and mariners were generally far more amenable to the idea of working on the former than on the latter.

Although work on board a trading dhow was arduous and even more time-consuming than on a pearling dhow – trading dhows were gone for nine months of the year – the adventure of sailing to distant ports and interacting with people of different cultures made work on these vessels a much more enticing prospect to the prospective sailor. Even the food on trading dhows was better, more varied and more plentiful than that of their pearling counterparts, whose meals were meagre and barely nutritious. As an added bonus, sailors were allowed to carry out a little petty trading on their own account and often did so, bringing in goods from the ports of India and East Africa and selling them at a substantial profit in the markets of the Gulf – an option that was simply not available to pearl divers.

A brief overview of Kuwait's involvement in long-distance trade

Kuwaiti trading dhows catered to the needs of their homeport for goods from abroad, but in doing so also served the needs of their destination ports in Iraq, Yemen, India and East Africa. Of course, some decades were required for the technical development of vessels capable of reaching these ports. One local historian records that Kuwaiti dhows reached the western coast of India by around 1780, although this did not become the norm until the beginning of the 19th century, and that they did not reach East Africa until the mid-19th century.[1] In his report of 1863, Colonel Pelly, the British Resident in the Gulf, observed that the total value of dates exported from Iraq to India on Kuwaiti dhows was around Rs 60,000 and that these dhows also carried Rs 180,000 worth of Arabian horses to India that year. From India, he noted, they brought back rice, textiles, coffee, timber and spices worth approximately Rs 200,000, on board the 30 or so dhows that employed around 4,000 mariners in total.[2] By 1927 the number of long-distance trading dhows had grown to 88, and then to 106 just 12 years later.[3]

Long-distance trade was conducted on *baghlahs* and *booms* with cargo capacities ranging from 150 to 500 tons and with crews of between 20 and 70 mariners (on average, 10 mariners per 75 tons). Typically, the *nakhoda* of such a vessel would be contracted by a merchant to pick up goods (usually dates) from the Shatt al-'Arab waterway just south of Basra, and deliver them to his agent or a broker in one of the many ports of the western Indian Ocean at an agreed rate, or freightage (*noul*). The principal would not necessarily be a merchant, but could sometimes be a ship-owner, the *nakhoda* himself, or both in partnership. When the goods reached their

[1] Abu Hakima, 1983: 96.   [2] Pelly, 1863: 73, 118.
[3] *Records of Kuwait, 1896–1961*, vol. 4: 210.

destination, the *nakhoda* and his crew would seek other cargoes – the nature of the goods depending on the location of the vessel – to transport back to Kuwait or one of the other Arabian ports along their homeward route. Sometimes, however, dhows voyaging to India would put whatever spare time they had to good use by transporting goods along the Malabar coast (the western coast of India) for extra money, or might even make the direct ocean-going voyage from Mangalore to the Swahili coast of East Africa, having taken on tiles (*kabrail*) for shipment. From there they would carry mangrove poles (*chandal*) back home.

The westward voyage (i.e. that to southern Arabia and East Africa) was more of a two-stage process than the India voyage. On this trip, the dhows would transport the cargo – again, usually dates – to the ports of South Yemen, such as Mukalla or Aden, where the *nakhoda* would receive the freightage payment for transport of the goods. He would then put part of this capital towards the purchase of other goods (usually salt) for sale in the ports of East Africa, to make enough money to purchase mangrove poles. Their light weight, durability, resistance to termites and low cost created a brisk demand for these poles for use as roofing material in Gulf houses. Whatever net profit the poles fetched in the markets of the Gulf would be split among the sailors and the ship-owner in standard shares. The only money to which the commissioning merchant had any right was the profit made from the sale of his own goods, usually dates. In addition to the freightage earned from transporting goods, the ship-owner and sailors also earned money from fares charged for taking passengers from port to port.

It is important to note that the government rarely interfered with the long-distance trade sector, preferring instead to leave it to the *nakhoda*s and merchants. Thus, it would not compensate a ship-owner for a damaged ship or a merchant for lost goods, nor would it impose any insurance requirements on either party; indeed, it was the merchants who often fulfilled this role, helping fellow merchants in their time of need. While credit advanced by the merchant to the captain and crew had to be paid back irrespective of what happened (as in pearling), if a ship's *cargo* were lost, the *nakhoda* could not be held liable.[4]

---

[4] This notion is embodied in the Long-distance Trade Law of 1940, Article 25 (see Appendix C); and is implied in Villiers, 2006a: 350, where he says, in case of shipwreck and loss of cargo: "But the merchants argued that they they lost the dates, and that was enough."

However the government did impose a duty of 4 percent on goods imported into Kuwait, and Mubarak Al-Sabah and his son Jabir introduced a levy of another 4 percent on goods re-exported from there. One important role that the government did play was in protecting the rights of its merchants and mariners abroad, often corresponding directly with other governments or with the British Resident in the Gulf should any legal troubles arise. The government also appointed a deputy (*ra'is al-salifah*) – usually someone of considerable influence and experience – to adjudicate in disputes over commercial and maritime matters; for example, the *nakhoda* and merchant Muhammad Shahin Al-Ghanim acted as deputy under Shaikh Ahmad Al-Jabir Al-Sabah, as did his father before him.

*Nakhoda*s of long-distance trading dhows

The long-distance *nakhoda* was responsible for ensuring the safety of the dhow and those on board, maintaining order amongst the crew, and keeping accurate accounts of the voyage's income and expenditure. In this respect he was not just a ship's captain, but also an accountant responsible for the income of his crew and some of the business affairs of the merchant. Assisting the *nakhoda* in maintaining discipline was the first mate (*mujaddimi*, just as on the pearling dhows), who assigned the crewmen their various roles and acted as main liaison between them and their *nakhoda*. The greatest responsibility on board was vested in these two individuals, but each and every sailor too was responsible for his own safety as well as that of the dhow and its passengers. The role of the *nakhoda* was well expressed by Villiers in 1939:

> An Arab nakhoda had a great many worries which are spared the ordinary shipmaster. Not only does he sail the ship, and navigate and pilot her, but he controls all her spending, all her people, all her papers. He buys and sells the cargo without benefit of agents; he finds the passengers and suffers them too, and rules them; settles their disputes and gets rid of them, which is not always easy. He is a business man, astute and capable, a judge of timber, of sugar and rice and ghee and frankincense and dried fish, an appraiser of dhows small and large, a master shipwright, a master sailmaker, a master

maker of ropes. He knows the best places to sell things as diverse as a cargo of Malabar logs or Rufiji mangrove poles, of sesame and coconuts and Berbera goats, cotton-goods, and salt. He knows a good agent from a bad, even in Sur; a solvent Arab from an insolvent. Sometimes he errs. He has much on his mind, conducting that great ship over the face of the eastern waters, tending her people and her trade, and bringing her back safe to her home at the head of the Persian Gulf.[5]

The typical budding *nakhoda* came from a family of *nakhoda*s, from whom, having acquired the basic skills in reading, writing and arithmetic necessary for the task, he would learn the art of navigation. Those not hailing from such families or without such hands-on tutelage rarely became *nakhoda*s, though there was no bar to a sailor becoming a helmsman (*sukkuni*) after some years' experience – a job requiring only a basic knowledge of the waters, winds and other practicalities related to navigation. A good helmsman stood a chance of being noticed by the *nakhoda* and serving on successive voyages with him, and could thus hope one day to become a *nakhoda* in his own right, though this was rare. It was more common for a *nakhoda* eventually to become a merchant, though this could only be achieved either when he had saved enough money to buy a ship of his own and finance a voyage, or when a merchant invited him to pool their resources in a commercial venture. Under the latter arrangement, the *nakhoda* would be at once the dhow's captain, its part-owner, and both principal and agent in the commercial venture, receiving the shares of each and earning a potentially substantial sum of money.

Preparing for a voyage

The start of the trading season, with the onset of the north-east monsoon winds in October, followed neatly on the end of the pearling season in September. As the trading season drew closer and the dhow crews began to prepare for their voyages, there would be an unprecedented amount of activity in the town of Kuwait. Before any of this could happen, however, the ship-owning merchants (*tajir*, pl. *tujjar*) had to find *nakhoda*s to captain

[5] Villiers, 2006a: 150.

their vessels. Once taken on, the *nakhoda* would start the search for a first mate, upon whose obedience he could rely, to maintain order among the crew. If the *nakhoda* happened also to be the owner of the vessel, the only requirement would be for an appropriate first mate. It was the first mate who set about putting together his crew.[6]

A ship's size was calculated in terms of its carrying capacity. The unit of measurement used was the *mann*, by which packages (*gallahs*) of dates were measured, at the rate of two packages per *mann*, each *mann* weighing about 76 kilograms. Crew strength would of course depend on the size of the vessel: a dhow with a cargo capacity of 3,000 *mann*/6,000 packages of dates – or 225 tons, with each 1,000 *mann* equalling approximately 75 tons – would require a crew of 30 sailors, i.e. 10 sailors per 1,000 *mann*.

The crewmen would be taken on for a variety of reasons, some being chosen for their willingness to come along or because of kinship with another crew-member, while others' reputation as exceptionally brave or skilled sailors ensured a ready recruitment by the first mate. Invariably, however, a crew would comprise able seamen, a shipwright (*qallaf*) to see to whatever small repairs might be necessary at sea, a cook (*tabbakh*) to prepare at least three meals a day for the hungry crew, and an assistant to the first mate (*al-mujaddimi al-saghir*). Dhows often carried a *mu'allim* (pilot or navigator) as well, if the *nakhoda* was not a navigator himself.

Having recruited a full crew, the first mate would set a date for equipping the dhow for its voyage, and on the day the crew would assemble at the dhow basin. First they would remove the mats protecting it during the summer off-season, and then set about washing it down and cleaning it. Meanwhile the *qallaf* would set about any small repairs necessary, taking particular care to replace the caulking between the hull planking with new oil-soaked raw cotton so as to prevent water penetration. The sailors would then remove the crutches on which the vessel was propped and, resting it on its bilge, winch it slowly into the water while readying other crutches to hold it up at low tide – a very complicated and laborious process, as can be imagined. The helm was then attached to the various ropes and pulleys controlling the rudder, just as had been done for centuries, there being no need for levers or intricate mechanisms. When the helm was ready, and during low tide, the sailors, using their bare hands, would coat the hull with

---

[6] *Nakhoda*s not owning their vessels were known as *ja'di nakhoda*s.

a mixture of animal fat and powdered lime called *shunah* (Swahili, *chunum*) to ward off damage from corals and ship worm (teredo molluscs). Once the dhow was fully prepared, the mariners would hold a celebration known as the *sangini*, involving singing, music and dance – an occasion always attracting a crowd of onlookers on shore. The following day would be taken up with transferring provisions such as rice, dates, flour and lentils from shore to hold, where they would be stored below the poop deck in what was known as the *dabusah*. At the same time the crew would bring on board their clothing and other personal belongings, usually in wooden chests, using the ship's lifeboat or longboat if the tide were high.

Using the first mate as an intermediary, the *nakhoda* would then set a date for a meeting with his crew, at which he would announce the departure date and advance them their loans for the season – between Rs 50 and 65 in the 1940s – which the sailors would use to provide for their families during their absence. While most crewmen were advanced similar amounts of money, the first mate could prevail on the *nakhoda* to advance a larger sum to a particular man if his work or reputation distinguished him from his peers. On the day of the voyage, the mariners would gather around the longboat and await the *nakhoda*, who on arrival would give the signal to begin rowing to the dhow, which was usually by now anchored off the coast of what is now Shuwaikh, and which had only its smaller mast erected as there was no heavy cargo just yet to act as ballast. The mariners would row to the sound of the *zuhairiyyah*, sung by the *nahham* whose chanting – as in a pearling dhow – served not only to raise the men's morale but also gave them a rhythm to unify their efforts.[7] Once at the dhow, the *nakhoda* would climb on deck and, with the sailors all on board, order the anchor to be weighed and the sails unfurled as his vessel embarked on the first leg of its voyage.

The Shatt al-'Arab

Kuwait possessed almost no agricultural resources of its own, except around Jahra, and its people were heavily reliant on produce from estates on the Shatt al-'Arab in Iraq, the waterway combining the Tigris and Euphrates rivers that flowed south of Basra to the head of the Gulf. For it was in this

[7] See Chapter 10 for more details.

area, on the banks of the Shatt, that the famous Basra dates were grown. More will be said about these dates as a cash crop in the section on Kuwait's export merchandise in the next chapter, but for the moment it is worth noting that several Shatt al-'Arab estates, since the middle of the 19th century, had come into the possession of the Al-Sabah shaikhs and various merchant families. By the 1930s, Iraq had become the world's largest date producer, accounting for about 80 percent of world production, harvested at the end of each summer from at least 15 million palm trees. Dates were both a cash crop and an important staple food for the entire Kuwaiti population. And not only were they the main export of Kuwait's long-distance trade, but the heavy clods of dates compressed in palm-frond baskets provided vital stabilizing ballast in the holds of the ships on their outward voyages. Other agricultural produce included grains, lucerne (alfalfa) for fodder, the dried fronds and cut trunks of date trees for mats, building materials and firewood, and cows and goats for their meat and milk products. In addition to the omnipresent dates, a cornucopia of fruits and vegetables was harvested from June to November: cucumbers, melons, grapes, figs, peaches, pumpkins and lemons.[8]

Thus as dates replaced horses as the chief export during the later 19th century, the Shatt al-'Arab came to form not just a vital part of Kuwait's ability to feed itself, but also an essential component of the Kuwait trading system: it provided the amirate's bulk export for distribution over the western Indian Ocean, so enabling it to acquire the imports that it needed.

So, irrespective of its eventual destination, a long-distance Kuwaiti trading dhow always called first at the Shatt al-'Arab. The dhows would sail out of Kuwait Bay, leaving the west coast of Failaka Island to starboard, by way of the *mafras* – the narrow channel between Failaka and Mischan Island – if the wind and size of the vessel permitted. If the dhow was too large – i.e. any larger than 4,000 *mann* or 300 tons – it would have to skirt the islands of Failaka and 'Awha, leaving them to port, and then turn northwards to the Shatt. Entering the Shatt under sail was a tricky business depending on wind direction, currents, the tide, and the sand bars accumulated at its mouth; a *nakhoda* not fully prepared for these conditions would need to hire a steamboat to tow him, thus incurring an extra expense.

At the Shatt's entrance stood the Faw customs station, where every dhow

---

[8] See Toth, *From Maritime Amirate to Oil State*, unpublished MS.

was required to register with the Iraqi authorities – be they Ottoman, British or Arab – in order to be allowed to carry dates out of the area. Should the ship-owner also be a merchant, he would often arrive in the Shatt before the *nakhoda* to arrange with a merchant there to prepare a cargo of dates for transportation. While it was not always the case, it sometimes just so happened that the date merchant in Basra was a Kuwaiti himself, which eased the task of reaching an agreement. However, if the *nakhoda* was the ship-owner, he himself would have to see to it that his dhow left fully loaded, either by purchasing a cargo of dates to sell on his own account or, if finances did not permit, by finding a local merchant willing to pay freightage for a cargo to be sent to the markets of India or South Arabia. The freightage rate, which was calculated by the number of *mann*s of dates to be shipped, was never constant and fluctuated from season to season in response to market conditions. Furthermore, the dhow was never loaded at once, but would take on consignments of dates from the plantations incrementally over the course of weeks or even a month. These consignments would be ferried to the vessel by smaller boats, or lighters, as dhows drew too much water to moor directly by the plantations on the riverbank. The packages would be lifted aboard by the crew who, under the supervision of the first mate, would begin the process of packing them in the hold so as not to upset the balance of the vessel. Before loading, however, the mariners would take care to lay planks on the floor of the hold and cover them with mats, so that the dates would not be exposed to any water in the bilges. The disc-shaped packages were then packed so tightly that they became cuboid under compression.

Unless the merchant owned a date plantation himself, dates were usually sold in advance by the lot by the agent of the owner (usually but not always a member of Al-Sabah) to the merchant, having hired local peasants (*fallahin*) to harvest them from the palms and package them. This process, however, could not take place until a local Iraqi government official had assessed the number of dates (specified in *mann*s) in a particular plot and had been paid a tax proportionate to the amount; only once that had been done could the plantation owner mark off a plot and sell its produce to prospective buyers, of whom there was no shortage. Whether or not the *nakhoda* was also the buyer, he often sent along his crew to help transport the dates so as to speed things up and not leave his men idle for too long. The evenings, however, were for leisure. The *nakhoda*s would visit each other's vessels, and so would the sailors, gathering on deck to feast and entertain each other and the *fallahin* with music, singing and dancing. This was just part of the joy of being in the Shatt; mariners also looked forward to treating themselves to the fresh local produce, water, milk, butter and bread, and the fine autumn weather.

Sailing out of the Gulf

Once fully laden, outward-bound dhows would get their papers stamped at the Faw customs station and then gather at the mouth of the Shatt, where they would await a favourable wind to carry them along the Persian coast and through the Strait of Hormuz en route to India or Yemen.[9] Once under way, the *nakhoda* would commence his daily entries in a log known as a *rozenameh* (from Persian: literally, day book or diary, thus logbook), in which he would record noteworthy events, the route taken, weather and water conditions, and other important information for review at the end of the voyage.[10] At this point too the first mate would set about allotting the mariners their various tasks, detailing their night watches, for example, and even assigning them to particular ropes for the hoisting and lowering of the yards and sails. The mariners, for their part, were expected to be awake and on duty at dawn, to bail out any water in the hold, and generally to be at the ready for the *nakhoda*'s or first mate's orders.

In the Gulf the dhows, as far as possible sailing in convoy, would pass the Persian island of Kharg and the port of Bushehr (Abu Shahr; Bushire), and then head south until they reached the *mataf*, a sandy bar at the Persian port of Daiyir. Thence they sailed past the islands of Shu'aib, Qish (Qais) and Furur en route to the Strait of Hormuz, which they would have to negotiate very carefully as far as the island of Salamah – by which point they knew they had safely navigated the straits and were in the Gulf of Oman. All was plain sailing if the winds were favourable; if they were not (i.e. if they were

---

[9] Some *nakhoda*s would wait until 20 November to leave, as the ten days preceding that date was the time during which the squally *ahaimir* wind blew, indicating that the seas were going to be stormy and dangerous to navigate.

[10] For more on this, see the seventeen *rozenamah*s published by the Center for Research and Studies on Kuwait.

blowing from the south and against the dhows) the process would take far longer and the dhows might be forced to run for shelter in one of the many Gulf ports. On reaching the port of Matrah, by Muscat, the dhows would go their separate ways, with some heading westwards to Yemen and East Africa, and others sailing east towards the west coast of India.[11]

The eastward voyage to India

As indicated above, a Kuwaiti voyage to India had first to wait upon two events: the ripening of the dates in the Shatt al-'Arab, and the first breezes of the north-east monsoon (known as the *azyab* winds) during October. These winds intensify as the weeks pass, and blow steadily over the Arabian Sea and western Indian Ocean until April. The dates begin to ripen a couple of months before the north-east breezes begin. This allowed the *nakhoda*s to plan their voyages so as to arrive in the Shatt al-'Arab in early September, just as the date harvest was getting into its stride, giving them ample time to load their vessels and catch the seasonal winds for the voyage to western India.

While most *nakhoda*s would aim to set out around 24 September, some left a month before that, as a result of which they were known as *harfi* ("start-of-the-season") *nakhoda*s.[12] The risk in such a voyage was that they might leave the Gulf during the period when the dangerous *ahaimir* winds can blow and thus expose their dhow to possible damage and unfavourable currents. The rationale behind such a voyage, however, was purely economic: the first cargoes of dates to reach India would command the best prices on the market, and would be exempt from the customs duties imposed by the Government of India on incoming dates. More important still, a *nakhoda* setting out for India would be able to fit in three round trips to Karachi – at the time a part of India and a major market for dates – into a single season, whereas the others would only be able to make two. This last point is significant: it was rare for a *nakhoda harfi* ever to sail to ports south of Karachi or Bombay precisely because doing so would jeopardize the completion of

---

[11] The separation of the voyages into two is somewhat artificial and is only for convenience of discussion. Some dhows making the India voyage would then make the deep-sea passage to East Africa, as will be described in a later section.

[12] In the 1920s and 1930s, three *nakhoda*s in particular were renowned for their early voyages: Ahmad Al-Gasar, 'Isa Al-Nashmi and Salih Al-Muhaini.

three such voyages. The nature of the *nakhoda harfi*'s voyage conferred a
further advantage still: he would not have to navigate the open sea like the
dhows returning from Malabar, but could coast his entire voyage, first
westwards along the Makran coast to the mouth of the Gulf, and then all
the way up the Persian littoral to the Shatt al-'Arab or Kuwait.

Dhows sailing to western India would first have to cross the Gulf of
Oman from Matrah to the Makran coast, which is now shared between
Iran and Pakistan. Before reaching Karachi a dhow would sail past a number
of minor ports, stopping only if forced for provisions or for refuge from
rough weather. Dhows only called in even at Karachi if the merchant for
whom they were carrying the dates had instructed them to deliver them to
that port (which was also called Kas Bandar) or, if the *nakhoda* himself had
purchased the dates and he thought it prudent to do so. If he was unable to
sell all of his dates in Karachi – or unwilling to do so at the market price
there – he would sail on to one of the other major ports, such as Porbandar
or Veraval, and all the way on to Bombay, at which point he would be
compelled to sell what was left of his date cargo. In these ports, the *nakhodas*
would either deliver the dates to a merchant's agent, or deliver or sell them
to a local date merchant or commission agent, such as Yusuf Maklai in
Veraval and 'Abd al-Shakur in Bombay. As can be seen from their published
logbooks, some *nakhodas* only rarely voyaged south of Bombay (e.g. to
Calicut and the surrounding ports) for the specific purpose of selling dates.

It should be borne in mind that the establishment of branches and
agencies of Kuwaiti merchant houses occurred only when Kuwaiti dhows
were able to reach India themselves, as all trade with India prior to that was
done first through Omani intermediaries and then by way of the merchants
of Bahrain, whose island was home to a sizeable community of Indian
traders. This is not to say that there were no Kuwaiti merchants at all in
India in former times – among others, the Al-Bassam family was active in
the tea trade and the Al-Ibrahim family in the pearl trade – but that their
presence was on a rather limited basis. It was with the accession of Shaikh
Mubarak Al-Sabah after 1896 that Kuwaiti merchants were given the
encouragement and protection that enabled their presence in India to
develop as rapidly as it did in the early 20th century. Indeed, it was Shaikh
Mubarak himself who requested the merchant Salim Al-Sudairawi to set
up shop in Bombay, and by his request too that Marzuq Muhammad Al-

Marzuq set up his agency in Karachi in 1909 with the aim of establishing direct relations with its merchants.

It was also through such agencies that Kuwaiti merchants were able to import the necessary foodstuffs into Kuwait for local consumption and re-export them to the markets of the Gulf and the Bedouin of the interior. When a Kuwaiti merchant needed certain goods from India, he would send a telegram or letter to one of the many agents and brokers (*dallals*) in a particular port and place his order, which would be sent to him by way of dhow or steamship – whichever was more feasible and cost-effective. These agencies also facilitated the sale of pearls by Kuwaiti *tawwashes*; as noted in the previous chapter, the Kuwaiti merchants residing in India would buy the pearls themselves and sell them on to Indian and European jewellers. These merchants in India would also offer hospitality to Kuwaiti merchants and *nakhodas* on trading visits, accommodating them in their guest quarters and seeing to their needs during their stay.

As trade with India flourished, more and more Kuwaiti merchants set up agencies there, and eventually a Kuwaiti merchant could be found in every major port, including Bombay, Karachi, Goa, Veraval and Porbandar. Indeed, it was these merchant houses that kept Kuwait's economy intact during the two World Wars and after the decline of the market for pearls, which ravaged the economies of other Gulf ports. Such agencies were not confined to India, but were established in other ports too across the western Indian Ocean, especially in the Gulf, Oman and Yemen, selling goods to the merchants of Kuwait in return for a small commission (usually no more than 2 percent) and buying their goods from them for sale into their local markets.[13]

The proceeds from the sale of dates went either to the *nakhoda*, if he had purchased them himself, or to the account of the merchant – either with an agent of his at that port or with a broker to whom a number of merchants entrusted their affairs. When the last of the dates was sold and the proceeds or freightage collected, the *nakhoda* would often look around for

---

[13] In an interview in 2000 with the merchant Salih 'Ali Humoud Al-Shayi', he recalled the names of the following merchant houses: in Bombay, Salim Al-Sudairawi and his son Muhammad, Humoud Al-Shayi' and his sons 'Ali and Muhammad, Muhammad 'Ali Al-Bassam, Husain bin 'Isa and his brothers, 'Abd al-Razzaq Al-'Adwani, Salih and Ibrahim Abdullah Al-Fadl, Hamad Al-Qadi, Khalid Al-Fawzan, 'Abd al-'Aziz Al-'Arfaj, Musa'id Al-Badr, and Khalid Al-Khamis. In Karachi, there

goods to transport southwards to Calicut. If there were none, he would arrange to load his vessel with natural salt from the Tranja Coast of Bombay for shipment to Calicut, where it was in demand as fertilizer for the coconut trees. The crew, for their part, would set about cleaning the dhow and making whatever repairs were necessary for the voyage to Calicut, which had no breakers to protect it from the wind and waves and was thus sometimes dangerous to anchor off. Any risk, however, was offset by the fact that Calicut was the main source of teak which, as discussed in Chapter 2, was in high demand in the dhow-building ports of the Gulf and was often ordered by merchants there. Securing a cargo of teak, however, was something of a rigmarole, and *nakhoda*s would try to put the wait to good use by seeking cargoes for shipment to neighbouring ports.

The best time for a dhow to be in the port of Calicut was in December–January, giving it plenty of time to locate and load cargo. If it did not reach Calicut until March, it would soon be time to return home. A *nakhoda* trading on his own behalf would purchase and load whatever quantities of timber, rope and tamarind he could afford to take back to Kuwait for sale there. However, if he was not trading on his own behalf, he would seek cargo to transport for another merchant or agent to Kuwait or another Gulf port, in return for the freightage. Available to assist him in this search were various agents and brokers in Calicut ready to locate a cargo for him in return for an agreed commission. Among them were the famous timber merchant, Yusuf Al-Saqr, the Indian broker Kanji Ahmad, and the Barami brothers. Once a price or a freightage fee (whichever was applicable) had been agreed between *nakhoda* and broker or agent, the cargo would be delivered to the dhow by Indian labourers and taken on board by the crew, who would stow it in the hold under the ever-watchful eye of the first mate. He would ensure as usual that the cargo was evenly stowed and packed securely so that it would not shift during stormy weather and upset the trim of the vessel.

was the Marzuq family, 'Abd al-Rahman Shahin Al-Ghanim, Muhammad Abdullah Al-Sa'd, and Humud Al-Jasir. In Calicut, there were Yusuf Al-Saqr, whose relative 'Abd al-'Aziz Hamad Al-Saqr was based in Porbander. In Goa, there was 'Abd al-'Aziz Al-Jallal and Marzuq Boodai. In Aden, there were Khalid 'Abd al-Latif Al-Hamad and his brothers, as well as Jasim Shahin Al-Ghanim. In Bahrain, there were Badr Al-Sayir and Khalid Al-Sa'dun; while in Dubai there was Murshid Al-'Usaimi. It is interesting to note that the Bombay offices of Husain bin 'Isa and Muhammad Humoud Al-Shayi' still survive, although very little business is any longer done there.

None of this should be taken to imply that life in Calicut and other ports was all work and no play. After a hard day's work the sailors would clean themselves up, don fresh clothes and, via longboat, visit the port's markets, where they would promenade, take in the sights and have a meal before returning to the dhow to sleep. The *nakhoda* himself seldom slept on board ship, spending his nights instead in the guest quarters of a merchant's or broker's home, or even in a hotel – in Calicut, the Beach Hotel was the most popular amongst *nakhoda*s. While they often had a good time in the ports of India, the fun would last only as long as there was no work to do. As soon as the dhow was laden with cargo and the weather in their favour, our mariners would waste no time in setting out on their homeward voyage.[14]

The return from India

The return voyage from India to Kuwait, known as the *ta'lah*, marked the end of the trading season and usually took place between the end of February and the beginning of April. Those leaving Calicut before February would do so in order to give themselves time to make a second return voyage from Kuwait to India, usually no farther than Bombay. After 15 May the seas were too stormy and dangerous to navigate safely. Those unable to make it out of India by then would have to wait until the next season. The vessel would be left moored at Calicut while its *nakhoda* and crew either returned home by steamer, or else stayed in India till the following sailing season, in which case they were known as *barrasu* or *tawahu*.

The homeward route differed slightly from the outward-bound one. From Calicut, the *nakhoda* would sail northwards to Mangalore so as to avoid the many small islands on the way, after which he would set his course north-westwards into the Arabian Sea, making for Ras al-Hadd on the eastern tip of Oman. Those making only a single voyage to India might continue northwards from Mangalore to Goa, where they would restock with food and the famous fresh water of that port before heading into the open sea for Ras al-Hadd and then Kuwait. The crossing of the Arabian Sea, called the *'abrah*, typically took as its starting point the island of Netrani, from which the *nakhoda* would plot his course on his chart in the hope of

---

[14] Dhows in the port of Calicut would often travel to the nearby Beypore Creek, where they would make any repairs needed before taking on cargo.

a following wind and a smooth passage for what was anticipated to be a two-week voyage. It was now that a *nakhoda*'s ability to navigate using his instruments and a map came into play, as those who were unable to do so would not undertake such a voyage unless accompanied by another *nakhoda* with the requisite knowledge and skill – in which case the unskilled *nakhoda* would be called a *sinyar*, or "follower". In keeping with the custom of the sea, if for some reason a dhow encountered another under the command of a *nakhoda* incapable of navigating the open sea, then it was obliged to escort it all the way to the Omani coast (or the coast of Makran, if this occurred during the first leg of the voyage). There was seldom a case of an unskilled *nakhoda* surviving the trip unaided across that body of water.

Once successfully across the Arabian Sea and close to Oman, the *nakhoda* would order an exceptionally sharp-eyed sailor to the top of the tallest mast to look for any sign of land. The sighting of grebes (*kreek*) was especially welcome, as they were a sure sign of land being close at hand. At the first glimpse of the Omani coast he would shout excitedly to his fellows, at the top of his voice, and thank God for their safe arrival, while the cook set about preparing the sweet known as *shinyali* (made up of dates, butter or ghee, and flour) in celebration. Sailing past Ras al-Hadd or Masirah Island, the sailors would sing and drum their way into Matrah Bay, raising their Kuwaiti flag at the sight of the dhows at anchor there and at the familiar faces of other Gulf seamen. Having dropped anchor in that bustling port, the *nakhoda* would set out in search of one of the agents in Matrah, such as Muhammad Al-Khanji, to inform the owner of the dhow (should he not be the *nakhoda* himself) via telegraph of the safe arrival of dhow and crew. The stay at Matrah would never exceed two or three days and would rarely involve the sale of goods, as that honour was reserved for the much more vibrant markets of Bahrain and Kuwait.[15] That said, the Kuwaiti crews would rarely leave without purchasing containers of Muscat's famous *halwa* sweetmeat as gifts for their families and friends back home.

Upon leaving Muscat on the northward voyage, the *nakhoda* would be on the alert for any sight of Umm Al-Fayarin, an islet signalling the proximity of the Strait of Hormuz. After passing safely through the Strait, the dhow would coast along past the ports of southern Persia to Kharg Island, and

---

[15] The *nakhoda* 'Abd al-Wahhab Al-'Uthman, for example, often stopped in Bahrain to sell his cargo of wood before returning to Kuwait. Interview in 1995.

from there cross over to the islands of 'Awha and Failaka and so enter Kuwait Bay. One should not assume from this brisk summary that sailing from the Strait to Kuwait was easy: the *shamal* or northerly winds were contrary during this season, and for roughly forty days they could make the voyage extremely slow and difficult. These winds not only impeded the dhows, but could also whip up heavy seas and carry dust, so reducing visibility, all of which could force vessels to run for shelter in a nearby Persian port until conditions eased. On reaching Kuwait Bay, the mariners might be greeted by their families coming out in their boats even before they anchored at Shuwaikh, where there would be an outburst of celebration involving the slaughter of a lamb (if one was available) and the holding of a feast, complete with servings of Omani *halwa*.

The return home, if late in the season, marked the end of the year's voyages. Should a dhow have made its return to Kuwait by mid-January, however, it would stay for only a week or so before preparing for a second voyage – usually back to India, though only as far as Bombay, Calicut being too far to allow for a timely return.[16] For this trip, called the *mutrash al-thani*, the *nakhoda* would advance his crew a second sum of money, not paying them their earnings – or the ship-owner his share – from the first voyage until the entire season concluded and their account for the whole season could be calculated. The second trip to India was usually shorter than the first and often easier on the *nakhoda*, for on this short voyage he did not have to cross the Arabian Sea but could coast along in sight of Makran from one of the north-western ports of India, such as Karachi or Porbandar. Furthermore, the cargoes brought back were different, chiefly comprising sacks of rice or coal and textiles, rather than timber, though crooks of certain species of wood used for crafting specific parts of a dhow were brought from the coastal town of Daman just north of Bombay. Most of these goods, however, would be purchased from Kuwaiti merchants resident in India, many of whom, as we have seen, had offices or branches in the major ports there and sold a wide variety of goods.[17]

The final return home of the trading season coincided neatly with the beginning of the pearling season, with only about a week of rest before a

---

[16] There were, however, a few *nakhoda*s who were famous for being able to complete two voyages to Calicut in a single season, among them Yusuf Jasim Al-Mubarak, the *nakhoda* of the *boum Tariq* belonging to the merchant 'Abd al-'Aziz Al-Saqr.

man was forced to dive if he owed a pearling *nakhoda* a debt he was unable to repay from the proceeds of his trading voyage. Before going off on the dive, however, the crew made sure to unload all the cargo from their dhow – especially the timber, which was tied together in bundles and rowed or taken by lighters to the shore. Once the cargo had been discharged, the mast was lowered and taken to shore, followed by the dhow itself, which would be hauled in at low tide, propped on crutches so that it could stand on its own, and covered or skirted with hand-made palm-leaf matting from Basra or coconut matting from India to protect it from the scorching summer sun. The hull planking was then coated with fish oil to keep it from drying out, and a guard was paid a monthly wage to watch over the vessel and adjust the stilts as necessary during high and low tide.

Not every dhow, however, sailed home from India, nor did all dhows sail to Calicut having discharged their cargoes of dates. There were a few (though never many) dhows that shipped timber and rope from Calicut to Aden, where they joined the vessels sailing direct to that port from the Gulf – a voyage that will be described below. Other *nakhoda*s opted to sail from Bombay (or wherever they had sold the last of their dates) to Mangalore, where they would look for a cargo of tiles to transport across the Indian Ocean to East Africa. Those unable to find a cargo to transport on someone else's behalf sometimes chose to purchase a cargo on behalf of a Kuwaiti merchant or even on their own account. In either case, the tiles would be taken on board, where the local Indian workers stowed them carefully in straw to prevent breakage at sea, a process taking an efficient *nakhoda* roughly two weeks. Of course, only the most experienced of *nakhoda*s risked this voyage, as success depended on navigational expertise. Those reaching the East African coast in good time would sell their tiles in the port of Kilindini at Mombasa, and then sail southwards to Zanzibar, where they joined the vessels which had sailed direct from the Gulf – a voyage to which the discussion will now turn.[18]

---

[17] Fortunately, price lists have survived from such stores, including that of the Al-Marzuq brothers in Karachi and Hamad bin 'Isa in Bombay, to name but two, and indicate that they carried a very wide range of goods, from textiles to shoes.
[18] For an excellent example of this type of journey, see Al-Hijji, 2003: 437, for the 1947 voyage (number 20) in the *rozenameh* of *nakhoda* 'Isa Bishara.

The westward voyage to Yemen for East Africa

The westward voyage from Kuwait to Yemen and East Africa (the latter known as the *Sawahil*, or "coasts"), differed in a number of ways from its Indian counterpart, the most obvious difference being its length. While dhows sailing to India could expect to make two trips per season, those going to East Africa had time for just a single voyage of nine to ten months' duration. Also, a dhow on this voyage tended to call in at more ports along the route than their Indian counterparts, and had to pay much closer attention to the rhythm of the monsoon winds. Finally, Africa-bound cargoes tended to be more varied than those bound for India.

Dhows for Africa set off in exactly the same way those for India, loading dates in the Shatt al-'Arab before sailing down the Gulf, through the Strait of Hormuz and into the Gulf of Oman. After staying in Matrah for a day or two, however, the East Africa dhows would coast south-west along southern Arabia until they reached the Yemeni ports of Shihr or Mukalla where, if the price was favourable, the *nakhoda* would attempt to sell his cargo of dates to a local merchant. If the price was too low, or if his instructions were otherwise, he would sail on to the port of Aden (specifically, into Mu'alla Bay), where he would have to sell whatever dates he had, unless news about the market for dates in Berbera, on the Somali coast, made it seem worth his while to make the round trip there.

Yemen and the Red Sea

Upon returning to Aden from Berbera on the Somali coast or from the south Arabian ports, a *nakhoda* might be asked by a local merchant – Kuwaiti or otherwise – to transport cargo, including dates, wheat, corn, rice, sugar and textiles, to one of the ports of the Red Sea, including Mukha, Hudaida,

[19] In *Sons of Sindbad*, Alan Villiers noted that in 1938 the Kuwaiti *nakhoda* Ma'yuf Al-Badr transported a cargo of dates on behalf of the Kuwaiti merchants Khalid Al-Hamad and his brothers to the port of Jizan on the Red Sea, returning home with a cargo of soap (Villiers, 2006a: 320). On another voyage, during the Second World War, he took a cargo of corn from Aden to Jiddah, returning home with a cargo of cement from the port of Massawa in Eritrea (information from author's interview with Jasim Al-Khashti one of Ma'yuf's crew). Villiers himself voyaged in a *zarouk* from Aden to Jizan in 1938 (Villiers 2006a: 13–17).

Jizan or even Djibouti, for a high rate of freightage.[19] In this event, he would need the assistance of a knowledgeable local pilot to negotiate the numerous shoals, reefs and islands dotting the Red Sea coasts and making its waters treacherous. The pilot would spend the entire voyage perched on a board fixed to the highest mast, from which he would bellow orders to the helmsman and which he would seldom leave, even having his lunch sent up there. At night, poor visibility meant that the dhow would have to anchor at one of the numerous roadsteads, whether on an island or the mainland, and the pilot would climb down, resuming his post at first light. When the dhow reached its destination, the cargo would be discharged and, having received his dues, the *nakhoda* would give orders for the ship to return to Aden. In view of the time required to sail to East Africa, most *nakhoda*s returning from the Red Sea preferred to head back to Kuwait, purchasing only empty cans at Aden. These they would fill en route with fish oil, used for coating dhow hulls to protect them from sun damage, bought from the smaller ports dotted along the South Arabian coast on the homeward voyage, such as Qishn and Sayhut on the Mahra coast of Yemen, where fish oil was produced.

There were, of course, smaller dhows that only sailed from Kuwait to Yemen and back, only rarely venturing into the Red Sea. These would transport dates from the Shatt al-'Arab and exchange them with Kuwaiti merchants in Yemen for containers of fish oil, which they would ship back to Kuwait on their behalf, receiving freightage only after its sale there – of both the oil itself and the containers it came in. While such operations were on a much smaller scale than those involving timber and other goods, they were just as lucrative: the *nakhoda* Muhammad Shahin Al-Ghanim rapidly acquired a reputation and fortune in this trade.[20] *Nakhoda*s on this voyage also brought back labour: Yemenis from the Mahra coast would pay a fare of about Rs 5 in the 1930s to be taken to Kuwait and Bahrain, where they would work as pearl divers and mariners on pearling dhows during the summer months. The dhows that only sailed from Kuwait to Yemen and back, however, comprised only a small percentage of those making the westward voyage; for most Kuwaiti dhows, Yemen was but a necessary stop on the way to East Africa.

[20] Other famous *nakhoda*s in this trade include Ibrahim Al-Nasrallah, Ahmad 'Isa Al-Asfour, and 'Abd al-'Aziz Al-Harb: Al-Hijji, 2005: 110–12, 321–2, 485–6.
[21] See Villiers, 2006: 69.

The onward voyage to East Africa

Having sold the last of their dates in Yemen or Somalia, *nakhoda*s on the East Africa run would anchor at Aden for a few days to prepare for the voyage down the Swahili coast, buying provisions and making whatever repairs were necessary. In Aden too cargoes were purchased that were in demand in East Africa, notably sea salt and such goods as rice, textiles, pots and other utensils. Once the goods were stowed in the hold, the dhow would sail back eastwards along the southern coast of Yemen to collect passengers (sometimes in the hundreds) to take to the East African ports, the fares from this being added to the freightage and split between the mariners and ship-owner. While male passengers and children travelled and slept on deck, female passengers had to be segregated in the cabin under the poop in view of the religious restrictions placed on contact between men and women.[21]

Loaded with goods and passengers, and having sailed eastwards, the dhow would try to get to windward along the South Arabian shore as far as Ras Sharma, to east of Shihr. It would then fall off south-westwards before the wind and run directly for Ras Asir (Cape Guardafui) on the Horn of Africa, using the north-easterly *azyab* wind and the favourable current. The first Somali ports of call would be Haifun, if any business was to be done there, and then Mogadishu, if passengers were to be delivered there. If the *nakhoda* had no business in either port, he would coast onwards to Kenya, perhaps calling in at Lamu and Malindi, until he reached the famous port of Mombasa. As the waters here teemed with fish, the sailors would catch whatever they could and salt it (the salt fish was known as *tiraih*) to preserve it for later consumption.

When approaching the old port of Mombasa – the new port of Kilindini having long been reserved for steamships – the *nakhoda* always made sure to steer well clear of the coast and tried to enter the harbour in the morning, for fear of fouling one of the many reefs littering its entrance. Having safely negotiated the reefs and anchored in the harbour, the dhow would be boarded by the immigration officer and port doctor, to check the identity papers of passengers and crew, and to vet them for any contagious diseases before allowing them to disembark. Once cleared, the *nakhoda* would go to whichever broker he normally dealt with in Mombasa for help in selling the goods brought in from Aden, while his crew explored the city and set about repairing the dhow in anticipation of the trip to Zanzibar and the Rufiji Delta.[22] After the goods had been sold, the dhow, lightened of its cargo and therefore high out of the water, would have its smaller sail hoisted and would set out at night, planning to reach Zanzibar in the morning to avoid running aground on the sandy shoals guarding its entrance and making navigation extremely difficult at night.

Upon reaching Zanzibar harbour, the *nakhoda* would disembark and set off to meet the various brokers whose acquaintance he had made over the years, in order to ascertain the current price of mangrove poles (*chandal*) in the area.[23] As already mentioned, these poles were in high demand in the Gulf as rafters, in view of their lightness and strength, low cost, and resistance to sun, heat and termites. Should it be the *nakhoda*'s first time in Zanzibar, he would also look about for a local pilot to guide him to the Rufiji Delta, the southern and primary source of the stouter grade of mangrove poles, where they were cut and loaded direct onto the dhows. The pilot was also required to act as intermediary with the Swahili-speaking natives. When the pilot's fee had been agreed, the crew would assemble for the voyage south to the Delta, stopping at the island of Kwale to submit the dhow's papers to the authorities there, for collection on its return and payment of the appropriate tax on its cargo of poles. The dhow might also be overhauled on the beach at Kwale, and the *nakhoda* would also sometimes leave whatever sails were not needed for the trip on the island for safekeeping until he returned.

At the Rufiji Delta, the *nakhoda* and his guide would look for a local *shimamizi*, the head of a Swahili pole-cutting crew, to agree on a quantity of poles and the fee to be paid for the labour. Of course, the poles themselves had to be paid for, and to do this the *nakhoda* would have to report to the delta authorities – who usually represented whichever company had the rights to the poles in the delta – to place his order and be assigned an area from which the *shimamizi* could cut poles. The process of cutting and transporting the poles was in itself a dangerous and laborious task, carried out as often as not under the watchful eye of a company

---

[22] A well-known broker in Mombasa was Sayyid Muhammad Abdullah Al-Shatry, an Arab from the Yemen.

[23] Such brokers in Zanzibar were the Arabs Abdullah Ba-Haroun and Bin Gurnah.

representative, who would count the poles, note their quality and mark them before allowing the sailors to transport them via longboat to their dhow. Loading the dhow could take as much as an entire month, during which the pole-cutters and sailors all slept and ate together at the mariners' expense on board, where they were subjected to unremitting attack by mosquitoes and other insects. And at all times the men had to be on the alert for snakes, crocodiles and hippopotami.

*Nakhoda*s nonetheless managed to circumvent the official control over the sale of mangrove poles, and would acquire up to half their poles in secret and at a much lower price direct from the Swahili cutters. Though this was technically illegal, it was not regarded as theft, as the company agents were well aware that if the dhows were forced to comply with every petty regulation, they would stop coming to the Delta and business would dry up.[24]

With loading complete, the *nakhoda* and two or three of his crew would set off on a two-day trek to Dima, a town at the edge of the Delta where the company responsible for the sale of poles had an office. Here the *nakhoda* would pay whatever he owed for the poles out of the freightage accumulated thus far. It is important to stress that the purchase and sale of poles was never on behalf of any merchant, but was a business venture undertaken by agreement between the *nakhoda* and his sailors on their own behalf: they would sell the poles at the Gulf ports and split the proceeds just as they would the freightage, according to a system to be detailed below.[25] Once the money had been handed over at Dima and the *nakhoda* had returned with a paper from the company, the crew would sail back to Kwale Island to pay the tax and retrieve the dhow's papers and sails before returning to Zanzibar, where they would rest up for however many weeks were left before the first breezes of the south-westerly monsoon (the *suhaili* winds) arose to give them a fair passage to Oman and home. If he had time while waiting for the south-westerlies, the *nakhoda* might tout for a cargo of corn to ship from Zanzibar to Dar-es-Salaam, Lindi or some other neighbouring port for a nominal freightage fee.

---

[24] Villiers, 2006a: 216–19.
[25] It was very rare for a Kuwaiti merchant to send a *nakhoda* to purchase mangrove poles on his behalf, for most preferred to simply buy them from the *nakhoda*s when they arrived in Kuwait.

Some dhows arrived in East Africa from Yemen too late to visit the Rufiji Delta for mangrove poles, and would have to do so from Lamu, slightly to the north of Mombasa. While stacks of Lamu poles were made readily available on the beaches for latecomers, they were generally rather thin and of a poorer quality than those from the Rufiji, which commanded better prices. That said, there was always a market for Lamu poles because of their cheapness, although a crew could not expect to earn nearly as much from them as from Rufiji poles.

When the south-west monsoon winds began to blow in mid-April, the dhows would set off from Zanzibar and Lamu, staying inshore so as to make good use not just of the winds but also of the coastal currents. Thus they would sail north non-stop up the coast of East Africa and then southern Arabia to Muscat and Matrah, where their course rejoined that of the Kuwaiti dhows returning from India. After a few days' rest in Matrah, off they would set once more, to the markets of Bahrain and Kuwait, selling their poles wherever they thought the best price could be got. Whatever was left unsold in Bahrain the crew would take on to Kuwait for sale to local merchants, before splitting the profits between themselves.

Long-distance trade during the two World Wars

While Kuwaitis merchants and *nakhoda*s carried on their business with the ports of the western Indian Ocean for scores of years as the dominant Gulf dhow traders, it should be borne in mind that British steamships – in particular those of the British India Steam Navigation Company – had been introduced into the Gulf in 1862 and had come to dominate the transport of most goods in the region since the late 19th century.[26] This came to a halt during the two World Wars, when all British steamships were recalled to play their part in the war effort. The recall left an enormous gap in the carrying trade of the Indian Ocean and especially of the Gulf, which had come to depend on the regular calls by steamships laden with commodities from India that figured in the everyday diet of the region. While this caused hardship everywhere, conditions were especially bad in places with no sailing fleet available to take the steamships' place.

Naturally Gulf dhows and especially those of Kuwait stepped in to fill this

---

[26] Facey and Grant 1998: 12.

gap, shipping staple goods from India to the Gulf ports in disregard of the quotas imposed by the government of British India on goods exported from there. This boost to the Kuwaiti dhow business also stimulated activity in the amirate's boatyards, which were building more *boums* than ever before to meet the demand of Kuwaiti merchants. The First World War also witnessed the building of *boums* of unprecedented size to accommodate the large orders of goods. Such *boums* included the 400-ton *Fatih al-Karim* (also known as "The Dhow" or *al-Daw*), which was built in 1914 for the merchant Hamad Abdullah Al-Saqr; the 550-ton *Muhammadi*, built for the Ma'rafi family in 1916; the 575-ton *Nur al-Barr wa 'l-Bahr* ("Light of the Land and Sea"), built for the Bahraini merchant 'Abd al-Rahman Al-Zayyani in 1918; and a number of famous *boums* of lesser size, including the *Taysir* of 'Abd al-'Aziz Al-'Uthman, and the *Mansour* of the *nakhoda*-cum-merchant Ahmad Al-Khurafi. While dhow-building and trade activity declined a little during the inter-war period and was not nearly as profitable during the world-wide economic depression of the 1930s, it picked up again with the outbreak of the Second World War, during which Kuwaiti *nakhoda*s transported food and other goods to the ports of southern Arabia and the Gulf – particularly to the Persian coast and Qish Island, where the shortage of food hit the population much harder than anywhere else.[27]

Freightage rates during the two World Wars were especially profitable for Kuwaiti *boums*, which found good business shipping goods for the merchants of Basra, where steamers had called regularly before the war, linking with large markets such as Baghdad. One *nakhoda*, for example, earned freightage of Rs 40,000 for a single cargo of textiles that he brought from Bombay to Basra during the Second World War; and another earned approximately Rs 28,000 taking dates from Basra to the ports of India.[28] The high rates paid to *nakhoda*s continued during the period just after the Second World War when the Kuwaiti fleet expanded to around 166 dhows, and freightages of up to Rs 55,000 for one return trip to India were to be had. Indeed, a *nakhoda* could count on a profitable voyage even in the 1950s:

---

[27] During an interview in 2007, the Kuwaiti *nakhoda* 'Isa Bishara recalled bringing food to a starving population on Qish Island, and how a number of Kuwaiti mariners brought families from there back with them to Kuwait, where conditions were better.
[28] Interview with the *nakhoda* Husain Al-'As'usi of the *boum Muhallab*, 1987.

in 1952, for example, one dhow earned Rs 21,093 for transporting a cargo of dates to India, grossing Rs 50,460 following the return trip.[29]

The gradual decline of Kuwaiti long-distance trade

While Kuwait's long-distance trade sector was able to survive various shocks and carry the Kuwaiti economy through the decline of the pearl trade, the challenge of the nascent oil industry proved too great for it. While the profits to be made from dhow voyages to India and East Africa climbed steadily even after the discovery of oil and during the early years of its exportation from 1946, voyages made by Kuwaiti dhows show a year-on-year decrease. This was due mainly to the new work opportunities in the oil sector that were eagerly snapped up by Kuwait's seafarers, and which thus deprived the *nakhoda*s of their crews. As one *nakhoda* recalled: "We [the *nakhoda*s] never abandoned long-distance trade for lack of profit ... the freightage was good and the profits were great. We only stopped trading because the sailors stopped coming with us."[30]

The post-war years were also ones of independence from British rule in India and the partition of India and Pakistan. These and other political disturbances in India created an unstable business environment for Kuwaiti merchants there. At the same time, Kuwait's domestic economy was developing rapidly, holding out to the Kuwaiti merchants of India the prospect of making much more money at home without having to reside abroad. By the early 1950s, most Kuwaiti merchants had all but shut up shop in India and moved back to Kuwait, leaving behind their homes and offices – some of which still survive, just, to this day. While trade with India continued, the nature of the trade changed radically, leaving no room for Kuwaiti intermediaries as had been the case in the past.

Changes in economic conditions also undermined the staple commodities of the old trading system. For example, the dates of the Shatt al-'Arab completely lost their economic importance after the discovery of oil. Employment opportunities offered by the oil companies meant that fewer people than before were willing to work in the date palm groves. Without the necessary care and management, the Shatt plantations were no

---

[29] Interview with the *nakhoda* 'Isa Al-'Uthman, 1985.
[30] Interview with 'Abd al-Wahhab Al-'Uthman, 1995.

longer impermeable by the saline water of the Gulf and, as a result too of the gradual silting of the mouth of the waterway, the palms no longer produced as plentiful a crop. No dates are exported from the Shatt today; the palm groves have fallen into dereliction, and the ravages of military conflict have reduced their numbers to a fraction of what they once were.

The decline in the production and export of dates, the decreasing availability of Indian timber discussed in Chapter 2, and the growing business opportunities in Kuwait, all served to strangle Kuwait's long-distance maritime trade sector. With its loss came the concomitant demise of maritime skills and traditions. While many Kuwaitis today still enjoy the sea and own vessels of various sizes, it is rare indeed to find anyone with a knowledge of sailing and navigation, as most people prefer motorized craft. The curtain came down on Kuwait's age of sail with the fading of its long-distance trade in the late 1950s, relegating this bedrock of its traditional economy to the annals of history.

5

The Economics of the
Long-distance Dhow Trade

JUST AS WAS THE CASE with pearling, the long-distance trade sector was characterized by various types of costs, income, debts and profit-sharing arrangements between the various parties, all of which contributed to its distinctive structure and development. What follows is a brief description of the economics of this sector.

Costs of dhow ownership

While the dhow-building business has already been covered in some detail in Chapter 2, it will be useful to recapitulate the information directly relevant to the economics of long-distance trading, as it is in many ways impossible to separate the dhow from the voyage.

By the 20th century, most trading dhows were of the *boum* variety (with a pointed bow and stern), which had emerged as the distinctive Kuwait vessel type in the later 19th century. There survived a handful of *baghlah*s (with pointed bow and decorated transom stern and poop, very much in the Portuguese galleon style), just three of them still being in use in the late 1930s.[1] Most, whether *boum* or *baghlah*, were medium-sized dhows with storage capacities of between 2,000 *mann* (i.e. 150 tons or 4,000 packages of dates) and 5,000 *mann* (i.e. 375 tons or 10,000 packages), although there were a few exceptionally large vessels. The average *boum* would cost anywhere between Rs 16,000 and 18,000 to build, a sum that did not include the two masts and six sails, which could come to an extra Rs 2,000. These prices would be higher if the buyer bought the necessary timber in Kuwait, where the seller's mark-up naturally made it more expensive than in India. Because of this, those who had the time and means to do so – usually *nakhoda*s and existing dhow-owners – would purchase their timber direct from India.

The dhow was usually the property of a Kuwaiti merchant, who might own a fleet of them, hiring *nakhoda*s to sail them in return for a percentage of a voyage's earnings.[2] Sometimes, however, the *nakhoda* might own the dhow himself; if he did, he would get his share of the earnings as dhow-owner as well as *nakhoda* – a much more substantial sum. Should the *nakhoda* also have the money to buy the cargo himself, instead of carrying it on behalf of another merchant, then he stood to make even more. With ownership, however, came liability: were a dhow to sink and the goods be lost, then its owner and the owner of the cargo bore the loss alone, there being no insurance in view of religious prohibitions in this regard.

Specifically, a dhow-owning *nakhoda* stood to gain more than one who did not own a dhow (a *nakhoda ja'di*) in this respect: he could keep for himself the half of the profits made on the voyage that would normally go to the dhow's owner – no trifling sum. This was an important prerequisite for upward economic mobility, though things not always work out that way. By owning a dhow and keeping a greater share of the voyage's profits for himself, a *nakhoda* could eventually accumulate enough capital to finance his own voyages without having to borrow money or goods from a creditor. However, a dhow-owning *nakhoda* also bore additional liabilities in that any damage or repairs made to the dhow would be his responsibility; whereas

---

[1] Villiers in *Sons of Sindbad* has much to say about the relative merits of the *boum* and the *baghlah*: the *boum* was simpler to build and was considered more robust and seaworthy in a following sea than the square-sterned *baghlah*. See Villiers, 2006a: 98–9, 208–9; Al-Hijji, 2001: 4, 21–7.

[2] The dhow-owning merchant Thunayyan Al-Ghanim owned four dhows that brought him a gross profit of Rs 38,353 in 1943–44. After deducting the expenses incurred in dhow maintenance, he was left with a net profit of Rs 31,221. Interview with Khalid Thunayyan Al-Ghanim in 1995–96.

a dhow-owning *nakhoda* transporting goods on behalf of a merchant bore no liability for the loss or damage of the goods. The custom in Kuwait was that, while a *nakhoda* would do everything in his power to safeguard the cargo whether it was his own or a merchant's, if things went wrong and the cargo was lost, nobody would be held responsible; as was universally accepted, it was God's will.

As for the sale of the dhow, it is interesting to note that, unlike a car today, its market value did not plummet immediately after being put into commission. On the contrary, if the vessel developed a reputation as fast and seaworthy, its value could actually rise over the course of the first few years. Indeed, it was only fifteen years after its maiden voyage that the average dhow began to show signs of wear and tear, and it often had at least another fifteen years' sailing left in it. Thirty years of plying the Indian Ocean was the usual span of a cargo dhow's useful life, at which point it would be sold off by its owner to a used-dhow merchant, fetching around one-third of its original price. It would then be dismantled and its planks sold on to boatyards for building fishing and water-carrying craft, or to homes for firewood.

The expenses of a voyage, of course, went far beyond mere dhow ownership and maintenance, to cover the cost of goods, services and other transactions. Such costs would vary according to the destination and the nature of goods purchased. We now move on, therefore, to a case-by-case description of the various costs incurred during the various types of voyage.

Cost and profit on cargoes to and from India

In 1939 there were approximately 75 dhows shipping dates to India, on average carrying 3,000 *mann* (225 tons) each. The price of a *mann* (two *gallahs*) of dates at source in the Shatt al-'Arab during this season was anywhere between Rs 2 and 3, for the shipping of which a *nakhoda* would be able to negotiate a freightage of between Rs 1.5 and 2. In the markets of India, a *mann* could fetch between Rs 5 and 7 depending on its quality and market conditions. This meant a profit per *mann* of Rs 1.5 to 2 for the seller. These prices would fluctuate, of course. Following the end of the Second World War, for example, a *mann* was being sold for Rs 15 in the Shatt al-'Arab and Rs 20 to 23 in India, and a *nakhoda* could charge a rate of anywhere between Rs 6 and 8 per *mann* for transport.[3] Naturally a number of variables affected the price of dates at either end, the most immediate of which was supply; if several dhows arrived at their market at the same time they might create a glut and so drive prices down. In such a case, a merchant would be forced to sell his dates at a very small profit, recovering the value of his time only if he also happened to be the owner of the vessel transporting the dates.

Dhows going on to Calicut purchased timber there by the *kandi*, a local unit of measurement equal to 13 cubic feet, with each cubic foot called a *kweek*. An average dhow could carry approximately 225 tons of timber, usually teak, which in the mid-1930s would be purchased by a timber merchant's agent for between Rs 20,000 and 30,000. For a freightage of between Rs 3,000 and 5,000 – and, by the early 1950s, Rs 10,000 – a *nakhoda* would transport the timber on the merchant's behalf to Kuwait, where it would be sold for a total profit of 10 to 20 percent. A *nakhoda* able while in Calicut to secure a cargo to ship to another Indian port stood to make even more money on the side, adding to the freightage earned from the transport of dates and timber over the course of one or two return trips. From this, however, would have to be subtracted the cost of provisions for the voyage, taxes on goods, and brokers' and customs fees, a process that will be detailed below.

Cost and profit on cargoes on the India–East Africa run

As described in the last chapter, some dhows – usually about a quarter of those on the India run – sailed to Mangalore to load tiles for shipment to East Africa, particularly Mombasa. In Mangalore, a *nakhoda* could expect to pay between Rs 80 and 120 per 1,000 tiles, his dhow being able to carry roughly 90 times this much.[4] For each 1,000 tiles, a freightage of anywhere between Rs 95 and 145 could be expected, depending on market conditions.[5] Upon reaching East Africa, if he was trading on his own behalf,

---

[3] Interview with *nakhoda* 'Isa Bishara, 1999.

[4] In 1953, for example, 1,000 tiles cost Rs 111 (information gleaned from the files of the *nakhoda* 'Isa Al-'Uthman).

[5] In the 1930s, for example, a *nakhoda* could expect to receive between Rs 60 and 65 freightage per 1,000 tiles. In the 1940s, this rose to about Rs 145, and then to Rs 160 in the 1950s (information gleaned from interviews with various *nakhoda*s).

he could expect to sell every 1,000 tiles for roughly Rs 250, a profit of nearly 200 percent.

From there he would purchase a quantity of mangrove poles to sell in the ports of the Gulf, but he would usually have arrived too late to sail to the Rufiji to obtain them from the source. Instead, he would buy his poles from Zanzibar or Lamu at a higher rate, of around Rs 4 for a *kurijah* (or score, a bundle of 20) of Lamu poles, and Rs 8 for Rufiji poles, with an average-sized (i.e. 3,000-*mann* or 225-ton) dhow being able to carry 400 *kurijah*s. Because he was buying on his own account, using funds already amassed, as described in the last chapter, he would receive no freightage for the transport of the poles to the Gulf, hoping instead to sell them at a good profit. All the mariners would be entitled to their shares of these profits, which would be between Rs 12 and 18 per *kurijah* of poles, depending on the quality and season. Again, this was subject to fluctuation: in 1948, for example, a *kurijah* of poles could fetch between Rs 48 and 60 in the markets of Bahrain and Kuwait, even though the price of the poles in East Africa at the time was, at roughly Rs 51, comparatively high.

Cost and profit on cargoes to and from Yemen

Only a few dhows sailed to Yemen without extending the voyage to East Africa, and these were usually the smaller ones – on average, about 1,800 *mann* or just under 150 tons. The *nakhoda*s of these vessels would buy dates from the Shatt al-'Arab for the same price as would the larger dhows, and in the 1930s received freightage of around Rs 4 per *mann* for shipping them to Yemen, where they would fetch a price of about Rs 7 per *mann*.[6] From the Yemeni ports, usually Aden, they would purchase used tin cans at the rate of 1 rupee for a box of two, buying on average 2,000 boxes. They would then fill the cans with fish oil from the Mahra coastal settlements at the rate of Rs 1.25 (or two Mahri riyals) for two cans' worth. The *nakhoda*s would ship the fish oil back to Kuwait, where it would be sold by the merchant, who might be the *nakhoda* himself, for roughly Rs 3.5 per box. If the *nakhoda* was not the owner of the cargo, he would charge a freightage of roughly 12 annas (i.e. Rs 0.75) per box of two cans.

---

[6] In the 1940s, freightage for a *mann* of dates rose to between Rs 7 and 8 (information from interviews with various *nakhoda*s).

Cost and profit on cargoes on the East Africa run

*Nakhoda*s planning to sail on to East Africa from Yemen made sure to stop in Aden to unload whatever dates they were still carrying, and to purchase goods to trade along the East African coast, including salt, ghee (clarified butter), rice and other commodities. Once again, it must be emphasized that this was a trading venture that the *nakhoda* and his crew undertook on their own account, receiving no freightage other than fares from passengers. In the 1930s, a mid-sized dhow of 3,000 *mann*/225 tons could purchase enough salt and other goods to carry for around Rs 450, on the sale of which in East Africa they could expect to receive about Rs 800. To these receipts a *nakhoda* could add the fares collected from passengers making the journey from Yemen to East Africa. A one-way fare was around Rs 8 per head in the early 1940s, and mid-sized dhows could carry around 130 passengers in addition to crew and cargo.

From the income received from the trading venture and from freightage of dates to Yemen and passengers to East Africa, a *nakhoda* would buy a cargo of mangrove poles from the Rufiji Delta. In the 1930s, the cargo cost about Rs 5.3 per *kurijah* after deducting all the associated taxes and expenses, but it could be sold in Kuwait and Bahrain for almost three times that much (Rs 15). When added to the other income from the voyage – and even after subtracting such costs as provisions – the amount was not insignificant; in the year 1950, for example, *nakhoda* 'Isa Al-'Uthman netted around Rs 11,500 for his voyage to East Africa.[7] Of course, not all of the profits went to the *nakhoda*, for they had to be shared with his crew and the ship-owner according to the complex arrangement detailed below.

Calculating and sharing the profits of long-distance trade

While profit-sharing in the long-distance trade sector bore an overall resemblance to that in pearling, there were significant differences in the detail. It must first be borne in mind that the only proceeds to be split between ship-owner and mariners comprised freightage (*noul*) and any profit from the sale of mangrove poles or other goods bought by the *nakhoda* on the crew's own account out of freightage already amassed during the

---

[7] From the files of *nakhoda* 'Isa Al-'Uthman.

voyage. Before such proceeds were divided, however, the expenses of the voyage were deducted from the gross amount, including any money spent on provisions and customs duties. In addition to this, a *nakhoda* was given between Rs 300 and 400 as a bonus if his skills included navigation, thereby eliminating the need for a navigator on board. This amount, known as the *ta'lum*, was likewise deducted from the voyage's gross profit. Following these deductions, the net profit was divided into two halves, one of which went to the dhow-owner and the other to the crew including the *nakhoda*.

Then, just as in the pearling sector, the crew's half of the profits would be distributed as shares, with each individual receiving the number of shares appropriate to the status and importance of his job. However, unlike profit-sharing in pearling dhows, some individuals received one portion of their shares from the crew's half and the other from the dhow-owner's half. Shares were calculated as they would be on a pearling dhow, with the value of a share being determined by dividing the sum of money by the total number of shares to be distributed from that half. The total number of shares by which the amount was divided, however, excluded the shares to be paid from the dhow-owner's half. The unit value of each share from the dhow-owner's half was then determined as equal in value to each share from the crew's half. The number of shares allotted to each mariner is set out in the table below.

Division of profits from the voyage by shares

Name	Shares from crew's half	Shares from dhow-owner's half
Captain (*nakhoda*)	1	3
Deputy captain (*nakhoda shira'*) if on board	1	1
Navigator (*mu'allim*) if on board	1	1
Helmsman (*sukkuni*), of which there were usually three	1.5	0.5 to the third helmsman only
Shipwright (*qallaf*)	1	0.5
First mate (*mujaddimi al-kabir*)	1	1
Assistant to the first mate (*mujaddimi al-saghir*)	1.3–1.5	–

Cook (*tabbakh*)	1.25	–
Main singer (*nahham al-kabir*)	1.5	–
Assistant singer (*nahham al-saghir*)	1.25	–
Musician (*mutrib*)	1.5	–
Sailor (*bahhar*), of which there were usually 18 or so	1	–
Owner of the longboat, who was also the dhow-owner	1	–

The process of determining the value of a share can best be illustrated by a hypothetical scenario. If a trip grossed Rs 30,000 in freightage and other proceeds, and the total cost of the provisions and customs fees was Rs 2,000, the remainder would be Rs 28,000. Let us assume that the *nakhoda* of this voyage doubled as navigator, meaning that the latter was unnecessary, and that no assistant *nakhoda* was needed on board. The deduction of the *nakhoda*'s bonus – let us say Rs 300 – would leave the ship with Rs 27,700, from which we can deduct another Rs 100 to be given as bonuses to exceptional sailors, leaving Rs 27,600. This amount would then be divided into two, with one half equalling Rs 13,800. Assuming there were 28 sailors, the crew's half (Rs 13,800) would be divided by 42.5, which is the total number of crew's shares, calculated according to the table above, if we exclude the navigator and *nakhoda*'s assistant, leaving us with a value of Rs 324.7 per share.[8]

While the dhow-owner in this example would appear to have to pay 5 shares in total to selected crewmen, in actuality he only paid 4 shares as he was owed one share from the crew's half as rent for the longboat. Although this might at first seem as if he was being paid doubly – gaining one share from the mariners' half and saving another from what he owed to them – this was not the case. The dhow-owner's share for the longboat was included in the crew's half for the purpose of calculating the value of a share; he was never actually paid the share, but was able to discount it from the amount

[8] Naturally the value of a share fluctuated from season to season. In 1939, for example, the highest share paid out was only Rs 130. During the World Wars, this value rose dramatically, and in 1946 a share was worth Rs 500. In the early 1950s, however, it dropped to roughly Rs 400. These were values for voyages to India; profits made on voyages to Africa varied depending on the price that dates commanded and the number of passengers transported.

he was expected to pay. What remained from the crew's half after the money had been distributed – i.e. the one share that the dhow-owner never took – was then given to whoever was to be paid by him but who was still waiting for one share. Thus, in the hypothetical scenario laid out here, the dhow-owner would receive the difference between his half of the net profit from the voyage (13,800 Rs) and the equivalent of 4 shares (Rs 1,298.8), being a net amount of Rs 12,501.2.

The actual sums paid out to the parties involved in this transaction were never equal to the amount to which their shares entitled them because, as with pearling, there were debts to be repaid at all levels of the hierarchy. The crewmen owed the *nakhoda* whatever amount he loaned them before and during the voyage, and a *nakhoda* who had not financed his own voyage owed money in turn to his creditor, whoever he might be (usually a merchant or dhow-owner), to advance loans to his crew – all of which was to be deducted from the dividends of the trip. Even the dhow-owner was not without his debts; he had to reimburse the *nakhoda* for whatever had been spent on repairs during the course of the voyage, a cost that he alone was expected to bear.

So, it was only after these debts had been taken into account, and balanced against the dividends, that the net amount due (the *fadilah*) was paid out to each party to this rather complex set of transactions.

Exports from Kuwait

We have already dealt, in Chapter 3, with pearls, Kuwait's highest-value export during the period of the dhow trade; and the various goods imported by Kuwaiti dhows from the Indian Ocean into the Gulf, and shipped by them between those ports, have also been discussed in varying degrees of detail in the preceding sections. What follows is an in-depth look at the goods in this system exported from Kuwait itself, at the beginning of the annual trading cycle, to give a clearer idea of what goods were traded, where they came from and what their qualities were.

The dates of the Shatt al-'Arab

Of all of the goods transported on Kuwaiti dhows out of the Gulf during the late 19th to mid-20th centuries, the dates of the Shatt al-'Arab were perhaps the most important. Indeed, in the areas that produced them, dates were perhaps the most important export before the discovery of oil, and while there were other areas that exported dates in the region, those of the Shatt were the most plentiful, accessible and varied. A Kuwaiti dhow sailing into the Shatt was flanked by dense groves of date palms extending inland for between 0.5 to 2 miles and containing more than 15 million palms – not to mention the 1.3 million or so palms lying between the nearby cities of Hilla, Karbala and Najaf. There were more than a hundred different varieties of dates available in the Shatt, most of them falling into four general categories: *hallawi*, *khadrawi*, *zahdi* and *sayir* – especially the latter two, with the *sayir* type alone comprising more than forty different varieties.[9] Not all date varieties were for export, the *khadrawi* dates, for example, being grown only for local consumption. Nor did all dates come from Basra and the Shatt al-'Arab, although the vast majority did; some came from Najaf, while others from Baghdad made their way to London via the British merchants there. Finally, not all the dates of the Shatt were shipped by dhow to India and Yemen, for large quantities were also exported by steamship from the Basra port of Margil to the markets of Europe and the United States.

Of all Shatt dates, those of the *sayir* group were the cheapest and most abundant, and were preferred by buyers in Aden; whereas in India, it was the *zahdi* variety – rarely bought by consumers in the Gulf – that found the readiest market, although far more so in Bombay than in Karachi.[10] Steamers to Europe, however, carried chiefly the *hallawi* variety, which was renowned for its superior taste and sweetness. The Shatt dates formed an important part of western Indian Ocean diets, making their way into various local dishes and desserts, and early on establishing themselves as a regular accompaniment to meals and coffee in Yemen, the Levant, North Africa and Turkey. That said, the dates were not always consumed as food, but were sometimes processed: in India, and even as far away as Marseilles, France, they were often used to make alcoholic beverages.

An abundant date harvest depended in part on climatic factors beyond the farmers' control. The weather had to be right for the dates to ripen in the first place, and other factors too had to be taken into consideration.

[9] Lorimer, 1908–15/1986, vol. 5 (Historical): 2298.
[10] Interview with the *nakhoda* 'Isa Bishara, 1999.

The flooding of the Shatt waterway, for example, and the consequent over-saturation of the palms had an impact on the produce, as did the persistence of hot or humid winds. Weather even affected the date packing process: the dry *shamal* winds were preferred during this time, as any moisture could cause the dates to rot during long voyages to faraway ports. In addition, *nakhoda*s had to be aware of the ripening times of the different varieties so as to know the right time to call for them. Najaf *zahdi* dates, for example, ripened at the very end of the season, with the consequence that a *nakhoda* late in setting out from Kuwait would most probably be able to sell his cargo only in the markets of Bombay.

Once harvested, dates were packed into disc-shaped packages called *gallah*s, woven from the leaves of palm fronds, with every two *gallah*s making up a *mann*. Local peasants toiled non-stop weaving these packages and filling them with dates to load onto the boats, of which there were two types, *balam*s and *muhailah*s. These local river craft would then transport the dates to the dhows, which anchored for weeks off-shore amassing their cargoes of between 4,000 and 6,000 packages. Before this process began – usually in September – the date merchants and exporters of Basra and nearby areas would get together in Faw, or somewhere else near the Shatt, to determine the prices of the different types of date and the average freightage rate to be offered to the *nakhoda*s coming to them.

Kuwaiti *nakhoda*s often dreamed of owning a palm grove on the Shatt, but while some Kuwaiti merchants established themselves as date exporters, only a handful of them actually owned any land near the river. Notable among these was Hamad Al-Saqr, dubbed the "King of Dates" for his success, and the brothers Muhammad and Thunayyan Al-Ghanim, both of whom also owned a small fleet of dhows. When the trade in dates proved to be highly profitable before and during the two world wars, the number of Kuwaiti merchants and members of the ruling Al-Sabah buying plantations in the Shatt, particularly on its western bank, increased.[11] This was especially the case when the decline in the pearl market was being felt:

[11] Mubarak Al-Sabah, for example, owned a large estate in Faw. See also Hopper, 2006: 101–3. Hopper bases his data on date exports to the United States, largely ignoring the more important Indian Ocean markets. Though his estimates are slightly skewed by his disregard of regional date markets, they are still are useful in understanding overall fluctuations in the date trade. He notes, for example, that the date trade of Basra plummeted around 1925.

the pearl merchant Hilal Al-Mutairi and those of the Al-Ibrahim family, in particular Yusuf Al-Ibrahim, all owned date plantations in various parts of the Shatt, as did the sons of 'Abd al-Latif Al-Hamad, the merchant Falah 'Abd al-Muhsin Al-Khurafi, and members of the Al-Ghanim, Al-Humaidi, Al-Sayir, Al-Anbaghi and Al-Khalid families, all of whom saw opportunities in the date trade.[12] While many of these merchant families employed agents in the area, some of them went personally to the Shatt each year to visit their plantations and to oversee the date packaging and loading process.

Some Types of Dates Available in the Shatt al-'Arab

Name	Comments
zahdi	Mostly sold in the Indian ports of Bombay and Kathiawar. Transported by dhow and steamship alike.
sayir	Favoured in Karachi and the ports of southern Yemen.
diri and *chasb*	Favoured in Karachi.
barhi and *khadrawi*	Not grown in large quantities and intended only for local consumption and as gifts.
dosan	The first to ripen and to be exported.
hallawi	Packed in the factories of Gardalan and Yusufan, for export to Europe. Any left over were shipped by dhow to India and Yemen.

Arabian horses

The Arabian horse, renowned for its beauty, stamina and physique, was an important, high-value export during the 19th century, when there was a brisk demand for them in India both from locals and from the British Indian cavalry regiments, for their military campaigns in the north. These horses were raised not on the Gulf coast but in the desert interior, particularly in the Jabal Shammar region around Ha'il in northern Najd, and were shipped east by steamship and dhow from Basra and Kuwait. To facilitate their transportation, the dhow-builders of Kuwait built a special kind of vessel: a *baghlah* with an upper and a lower deck able comfortably to carry and

---

[12] The Al-Saqrs, for example, bought land in Dawasir, while the Al-Ibrahims did so in Dawra and the Al-Hamads in Mu'ammar, Zayadiyyah and 'Ashar. The Al-Khurafis bought land in Qasbah, on the east bank of the Shatt.

accommodate an equine cargo.[13] Some Kuwaiti merchant families specialized in this trade, including the Al-'Abd al-Jalil and the Al-Badr. Yusuf Al-
Badr played host to Colonel Lewis Pelly during his visit to Kuwait in 1865,
and maintained a farm and fort in Jahra where he collected the horses that
he bought from the Bedouin of the interior, and where he got them into
condition before sending them off to India.[14] Other families involved in
the trade included the Al-Mudairis, the Al-Barghash, the Al-Adwani and
the Al-'Amir.

As early as 1816, the value of a horse in Kuwait was around Rs 300 and,
after spending Rs 200 on fodder and shipment to Bombay, a merchant could
expect to sell it there for around Rs 800, thus being assured of a minimum
profit of Rs 100.[15] An average dhow could carry between 80 and 100 horses
per voyage and would take three to four weeks to reach Bombay, with stops
en route at Bandar 'Abbas and Hormuz to pick up horses from there too.
Horse transport by dhow, however, faded rapidly in the face of competition
from steamships, though there were always merchants who chose to
persevere with dhows, attracted by the low cost or because they themselves
owned the vessels. This was especially the case during the two World Wars,
when the scarcity of steamships conferred an advantage on dhows and
brought the *nakhoda*s a freightage of Rs 150 per horse, the total number of
horses not exceeding twenty per dhow.[16] After this temporary boost, however,
the trade quickly died out. Demand finally tailed off with the introduction
of mechanized warfare and, before long, the only buyers left were equestrian
enthusiasts, who hardly generated sufficient demand to fuel an entire sector.

Gold

With the outbreak of the Second World War in 1939, the price of the British

---

[13] In a 1997 interview, the *nakhoda* Sa'ud Fahad Al-Sumait recalled how he had seen
such dhows in the western part of Kuwait town as late as 1920, and that they
belonged to the Al-'Abd al-Jalil and Al-Kulaib families.

[14] Pelly, 1978 (1866): 8–9, 89.

[15] Buckingham 1829: 385.

[16] The main deck of a standard cargo dhow was unable to accommodate more than
twenty horses on a voyage. However, in the 1800s the *baghlah*s with double decks
referred to above, specially built for the 'Abd al-Jalil family, were capable of taking up
to thirty horses.

gold pound skyrocketed in the Gulf, to the extent that, by 1940, it could be exchanged for Rs 60 in Kuwait while fetching only just Rs 28 in India. Such a large price differential inevitably caught the eye of Kuwaiti merchants, many of whom sent whatever money they had to India to buy gold pounds to resell in Kuwait. The trade in gold was quickly restricted by the British India government, which outlawed the export of gold from the Reserve Bank of India in Muscat and the sale of Indian gold abroad. These restrictions on the trade in gold induced a number of Arab merchants in India to co-operate with their fellows in Kuwait and other Gulf ports to smuggle specie by dhow, for which *nakhoda*s commanded a freightage of Rs 1.5 to 2 per gold pound. The British government even went so far as to appeal to the ruler, Shaikh Ahmad al-Jabir Al-Sabah, prompting him to issue a warning that anyone caught smuggling gold would incur the severest of penalties. This warning, however, was largely ignored by Kuwaitis, who carried on smuggling in the face of inspections by British officials and the impounding of Kuwaiti dhows. The rationale behind their persistence was simple: the money to be made from gold was good and, because of the nature of the trade, was not subject to duties or taxes.[17]

Kuwaiti dhows continued to carry gold out of India until the end of the Second World War, at which point the price of gold there rose sharply and the government decided to discontinue the 1,000-rupee note. Kuwaiti merchants in India and their Indian counterparts reacted to these developments by asking their fellow merchants in Kuwait to buy gold for them with their 1,000-rupee notes and bring it back to India. This trade was just as lucrative as the export of gold from India had been; a *tola* (see Appendix D) of gold in Kuwait would cost the merchants Rs 50 but would fetch between Rs 100 and 120 in India. Kuwait's merchants were able to purchase gold from the markets of Beirut, which were well stocked with gold from Europe and Latin America, and send it by dhow to India.

It should be stressed, however, that the trade in gold lasted no more than a decade or so and played but a minor role in Kuwait's involvement in the Indian Ocean trade system. Facing ever tighter restrictions, it grew

[17] In an interview with the *nakhoda* 'Isa Al-'Uthman, he observed that even in the late 1940s gold could be bought in India for around Rs 11 per gold pound and sold in Kuwait for Rs 18.

[18] One local historian records the names of Rashid Al-Baddah and his sons Ahmad and 'Abd al-Muhsin. Al-Rashaid 1926, vol. 1: 65.

increasingly costly to undertake until, by the start of the 1950s, it had all but
ceased. However alluring a topic the trade in gold may seem, it should not
be over-emphasized. While vast numbers of British official archives concern
themselves with the minutiae of the issue, this was only because it was of
importance to the British government itself. For Kuwaitis, the gold trade
was just a business opportunity, no different from the commerce in dates or
horses, except in terms of the profits to be made.

Ghee, hides and currencies

Occupying a much smaller yet equally important part of Kuwait's exports
was the trade in animal ghee (used in cooking, particularly as a flavouring
and a nourishing addition to rice), dried leather and hides, and currencies.
Individually, these trades did not bring in as much as those in pearls, dates
or timber, but in combination with other smaller commodities they made
a significant contribution to Kuwait's relatively weak export sector. Both
animal ghee and hides were traded into Kuwait by the Bedouin of the
interior, who would bring whatever surplus animal products of their pastoral
nomadic life the merchants of Kuwait would accept, in return for necessities
of life brought in from the ports of the Gulf and the Indian Ocean. Ghee
was especially in demand in those pearling ports of the Gulf, such as Bahrain,
with no direct access to a desert interior like Kuwait.

The Bedouin traded a variety of hides, including cow, lamb and sheep
hides, many of them still with their wool attached. These were used to make
coats and hats for sale in colder climes, especially Persia, from where they
would be sold on, either as hides or finished products, to the markets of
Central Asia. In a few instances, Kuwaiti merchants themselves journeyed to
the Caucasus regions bordering the Caspian Sea, where they sold their
goods at considerable profit.[18] Most hides, however, were transported by
steamship to India, from where they would eventually make their way to
Europe.

6

Al-Qita'ah: Short-distance Trade

HOWEVER VITAL long-distance trade might have been as the engine of the Kuwaiti maritime economy, by bringing in goods from India and East Africa, it was, like large-container traffic today, reliant on the short-distance trade sector (*al-qita'ah*) for the onward distribution of goods within the Gulf from the hub of Kuwait. Gulf ports great and small were served by these short-distance traders, who would pick up the goods shipped by dhow and steamship alike to Kuwait, and carry them on to smaller ports for sale. Indeed, Kuwaiti seamen had been undertaking this kind of short-distance commerce well before the evolution of their long-distance trading, and as a prelude to it. For, prior to developing the maritime technology and experience necessary to reach India and East Africa, and before political conditions in the Gulf moved in their favour, it had been the Kuwaiti practice to purchase goods from Muscat – then the dominant Gulf participant in the trade of the Indian Ocean – and take them on for sale in local ports.

Their small size conferred an advantage on short-distance trading dhows over their ocean-going, long-distance counterparts: it meant that they drew less water, so being able to put in at ports and roadsteads too shallow for larger dhows. They were of course able to call in at the larger ports, such as Bahrain, Bushehr and Muscat, but they could also use those on the Hasa

coast (Jubail, al-Qatif, Darin, Dammam, al-'Uqair), and those on the coast
of Qatar (Zubara, Doha, Wakra), as well as Abu Dhabi, Dubai, Sharjah,
'Ajman, Umm al-Qaiwain and Ras al-Khaimah. By the 1930s and after,
however, Kuwaiti dhows rarely visited ports on the Iranian side, because
Iranian short-distance *nakhoda*s had increasingly taken over the shipping of
goods to and from Kuwait.

The chief waterway visited by the short-distance craft was the Shatt al-
'Arab. While its shallow entrance prevented most of the large dhows from
sailing into it to take on cargo, smaller ones were able to sail right up to
Basra. Such vessels proved especially crucial in carrying goods from the Shatt
port of Muhammarah, which had been brought there by steamship, to
Kuwait and other ports of the upper Gulf – the steamer service to Kuwait
of the British India Steam Navigation Company was started as a regular
service only in 1903 during the reign of Shaikh Mubarak.[1] By the early
20th century, a special type of dhow was being developed for short-distance
traders to take the place of the *baqqarah*s and *battil*s of former times. The
boum qita', built on the lines of a deep-sea *boum* but smaller, proved easier
to build and far more seaworthy than its predecessors, and quickly replaced
them as the favoured craft in this sector.

As well as being able to use the shallower Gulf ports, short-distance
traders had a comparative cost advantage, as entry into this business required
far less capital than did deep-sea trade or even pearling. Not only were the
dhows less expensive to build, but fewer sailors and, consequently, less
money in loans, were necessary to enable a successful voyage to be made.
Also an advantage were the much shorter voyages, which lasted on average
no more than a month, thus affording both dhow-owner and *nakhoda* –
often one and the same man – great flexibility in terms of time.

None of this should be taken to imply that this type of business was easy.
An intimate knowledge of the Gulf ports and the shoals and reefs littering
their entrances was absolutely essential, as a careless *nakhoda* could expose
his vessel to risk and severe damage. A *nakhoda* had also to be competent to
deal with the ever-changing weather conditions of the Gulf, as squalls and
storms could suddenly blow up, with the risk of capsizing and shipwreck,
though this was less commonplace than in the Indian Ocean.

---

[1] Lorimer, 1908–15/1986, vol. 8 (Geographical): 1058.

The economics of short-distance trade

A typical short-distance trader – whether *boum qita'* or otherwise – had a carrying capacity of between 40 and 75 tons and required a crew of 6 to 12 sailors. The low outgoings associated with this sector and the small distances involved meant that the freightage charged by the *nakhoda* could be little enough to attract plenty of business, and even to compete with steamships for cargo. And because the *nakhoda* himself was often the dhow owner and sometimes even the merchant too, he stood to make a substantial profit from a successful trading voyage – though of course he also stood to incur a heavy loss should his dhow or cargo be damaged.

The value of the trade in this sector was far from insignificant. In his report of 1863, Col. Lewis Pelly noted that Kuwaiti dhows imported Rs 16,300 worth of tobacco, dyes, seeds and rugs from Bushehr alone, to which they exported roughly Rs 32,250 worth of coffee from India, cotton, pepper and other foodstuffs.[2] By 1927/28, exports to Iran had risen to Rs 785,730, while imports too had risen sharply, to a total of Rs 937,755. This sector was an important source of revenue for the Kuwaiti government, which imposed customs duties ranging from 4 to 6 percent during the early 20th century; in 1919/20, for example, duties alone totalled Rs 651,055.[3]

Because a short-distance trading voyage lasted just one month, or two at the most, *nakhodas* could make as many as eight trips in a single year as, unlike the deep-sea dhows, they did not have to stop during the summer months because of the south-west monsoon season or for their crewmen to go pearl diving. The number of trips a *nakhoda* could make depended on the availability of cargo; if there were none in Kuwait, he might sail north to the Shatt al-'Arab in search of dates or building materials to transport locally. If he had the means, he would purchase the goods himself, so standing to gain the profits of sale instead of having to charge freightage. On the usual kind of trading voyage, however, a *nakhoda* could expect to earn a freightage of no more than Rs 500. Earnings on this meagre scale were scant remuneration for the efforts of the *nakhoda* and his crew, some of whom have unpleasant memories of their time on these dhows.[4] This attitude is

[2] Pelly, 1863: 109.
[3] This figure includes receipts from the long-distance trade sector. *Records of Kuwait, 1899–1961*, 1989, vol. 4: 663.
[4] Interview with the *nakhoda* Muhammad Jasim Al-Shmais in 1999.

reflected in the number of dhows participating in this sector; while they might have been high during the 19th century, by 1904 there were only 50 short-distance trading dhows, a number that dropped still further, to 30, in the 1930s.[5]

Profit-sharing in short-distance trade

The profit-sharing arrangements in this sector closely resembled those in pearling and long-distance trade but involved different proportions. *Nakhodas* rarely borrowed money to cover the vessel's expenses, for as dhow-owners this responsibility was theirs alone. This money, however, was paid back to them once the voyage was over and the freightage had been collected. The remainder (i.e. the net profit) was divided into two halves: one half went to the dhow-owner (usually the *nakhoda* himself), while the other was divided among the crew, some of whom were additionally entitled to money from the dhow-owner's half. The arrangement was as follows:

Position	*Shares from sailors' half*	*Shares from dhow-owner's half*
Nakhoda	1	1
First mate	1	0.5
Helmsman (usually two)	1	0.5
Cook	1	0.25
Sailor (usually 5)	1	–
Longboat owner	1	–

On the basis of this table, if an average voyage were to gross Rs 500 and average expenses amount to Rs 70, leaving a net sum of Rs 430, the sailors' half (i.e. Rs 215) would be divided by 11, resulting in a value of Rs 19.5 per share – a figure that varied from voyage to voyage depending on market conditions. During the two World Wars, for example, there was a great deal needing to be transported within the Gulf (see discussion in Chapter 4, pp. 74–5) and freightage increased as a result.

[5] Lorimer, 1908–15/1986, vol. 8 (Geographical): 1053. 30 short-distance dhows in the 1930s: author's estimation.

As was the case in all other profit-sharing arrangements in Kuwait's maritime economy, the crewmen never received the full value of their share of the profit, as the loans that had been advanced to them before and during the trip had to be deducted first.

Goods carried by short-distance traders

As pointed out above, before the development of Kuwaiti long-distance trading to India, a wide range of goods such as timber, weapons, coffee, sugar, rice, textiles and the like were carried by Kuwaiti short-distance trading dhows from Muscat to the various Gulf ports on the Arabian side. Once Kuwaiti dhows began trading directly with India, however, the short-distance traders were able to find plenty of cargoes in their homeport of Kuwait for shipment, so reducing the amount of time necessary for a voyage. While dhows from other ports such as Bahrain and Dubai also took part in short-distance trade, the prominence of Kuwaiti dhows in the long-distance trade gave the short-distance traders in their own homeport a comparative advantage.

As well as distributing goods from their homeport, Kuwaiti short-distance traders continued to carry goods from other ports. From the Shatt al-'Arab, for example, they shipped various types of dates as well as hides and fleeces, dried palm fronds (for fuel), and the fruits and vegetables in constant demand in Kuwait. From the southern ports of Persia, until they were squeezed out by Persian vessels later on, they carried grains, flour and tobacco, and sold sugar, tea, rice, hides, ghee and sometimes weapons there.

The end of short-distance trade

Their versatility and comparative advantages enabled Kuwait's short-distance traders to survive economic shocks far better than their long-distance counterparts. While long-distance trading dhows were able to continue and even expand their role after the introduction of steamships into the region in the 1860s, they had to modify the scope and nature of their activities as merchants began using steamships to transport goods. This was not the case with the short-distance fraternity, whose dhows were able to enter smaller ports and roadsteads, while low prices for freight kept their services in high demand even during the steamship era.

It was really the introduction of oil into the Kuwaiti economy that dealt the death-blow to short-distance trade. As the oil industry developed and the demand for labour in the oilfields accelerated, Kuwaiti mariners grew more inclined to stay in Kuwait and earn a wage working for the oil companies than to sail with their *nakhoda*s and earn an uncertain share of a voyage's profits. This left the *nakhoda*s, who were never eager to abandon life at sea for one on shore, with no seamen to staff a crew. This is perhaps best ilustrated a popular question posed among seamen at the time: "*Ish lak bi-l-bahr wa-ahwalah, wa rizq Allah 'ala-l-sif?*" ("What do you want with the sea and its woes, when God's bounty is on the shore?"). As more and more *nakhoda*s were forced out of the short-distance trading sector and into the wage-earning oil industry and government employment, the owners found themselves with no *nakhoda*s to sail their dhows. With no prospect of earning money from their vessels, they were forced to sell their dhows at low prices, often to Persians.

In this respect, short-distance trade was affected in the same way as its long-distance counterpart: in both cases, manpower was lured away by better and easier prospects. This is not to say that short-distance trading died out completely in the Gulf as a whole. The numerous motorized dhows still lining Dubai Creek and other Gulf harbours are testament to the persistence of this line of business and its powers of renewal. It is an activity, however, increasingly dominated by southern Iranians, who have enjoyed fewer economic opportunities than the people of the Arabian side of the Gulf, in part because of the sheer size of their country's population. In the case of Kuwait, by contrast, short-distance trade had breathed its last by the end of the 1960s.

7

Al-Naql: Lighterage and Rock-carrying

EQUALLY IMPORTANT to the efficient functioning of long-distance trade was lighterage (*al-naql al-sahili*, coastal transport), the business of transferring cargo from ship to shore. Dhows returning heavy-laden from India and East Africa were unable to sail close inshore on reaching port, as they drew too much water. Their practice was to anchor offshore at Shuwaikh and await the arrival of lighters, small craft specialized in handling cargo and taking it ashore to the warehouses. These lighters (locally, *tashalah*s) could deal with light and heavy cargo alike, whether rocks (used in the construction of houses and breakwaters along the shore), timber, foodstuffs, manufactures, mangrove poles or even passengers.

Lighterage

As the tonnage calling in at the port of Kuwait mounted, so too did business for lighters. Steamships also contributed: the large size of many meant that they had to anchor right out in Kuwait Bay, making lighters even more indispensable for the transfer of goods and passengers to shore. To co-ordinate this burgeoning activity, the Kuwaiti government in December 1935 established the Hammal Bashi Company (also called *Sharikat al-Naql wa-'l-Tanzil*, or the Transport and Discharge Company), specializing in the transfer of cargo from steamships to the harbour near the Sif Palace.[1]

In the 1930s, this company also transported sand and gravel to the Anglo-Persian Oil Company (APOC), which had begun its operations in Abadan in 1913 and was in need of building materials for the construction of a huge refinery there. The latter activity came about as the result of an agreement between APOC and the local merchant Yusuf Ahmad Al-Ghanim, who undertook to supply the company with these materials by means of his fleet of Kuwaiti-manned *tashalah*s, each of which would carry sand and gravel from Shuwaikh to Abadan, where they would be sold by the lighter load. On the profits, the government levied duties of 4 percent – at the beginning, Rs 7 – on each lighter loading sand and gravel from Kuwait's shores.[2] From Abadan, these boats transported cans of benzene, for which they were paid a freightage of Rs 15 per 100 containers.

As demand for lighters rose, the local *ostad* Ahmad bin Salman began to build lighters called *hammal bashi*s, like the *tashalah*s on the lines of the *boum* but larger, and with an open hold allowing them to carry more cargo.[3] While it is difficult to ascertain the number of lighters and *hammal bashi*s owned by the Hammal Pashi Company, the fleet must have been sufficiently large to accommodate the ten steamers calling in each month in addition to the long-distance trading dhows arriving at the end of the season. Lighterage from dhows, however, took up only two months of the year, in summer; the rest of the year's business came from the steamships, which regularly imported large quantities of commodities from India and Europe for local consumption and re-export. During the 1920s, lighters would charge steamships roughly Rs 23 to transfer 100 sacks of rice, Rs 29 for 100 sacks of sugar, and Rs 28 for 100 4-gallon cans of benzene.[4]

---

[1] The name, derived from Turkish title Pasha to reflect the company's dominance in this sector, was changed in 1938 to *Maslahat al-Naql wa-'l-Tanzil* (The Transport and Discharge Interest) by the Legislative Council, which then changed its name back to *Sharikat al-Naql wa-'l-Tanzil* in 1939.

[2] Shaikh Ahmad Al-Jabir increased this amount to 4 Rs per *itgar* (a lighter could carry roughly seven *itgar*s) in view of the amount that was being sent out. After APOC renewed its contract with Al-Ghanim, duties were set at 5.5 Rs per sodrum of sand and 6.5 Rs per sodrum of gravel. Records of Kuwait, 1989, vol. 4 p. 648; *Persian Gulf Administration Reports* for Kuwait, 1940.

[3] For the hull forms of *tashalah*s and *hammal bashi*s, see Al-Hijji, 2001: 25 and 27.

[4] *Records of Kuwait, 1899–1961,* vol. 4 (Economic): 652.

Rock-carrying

While lighters were used chiefly to transport goods from ship to shore, another important function undertaken by them was the carriage of coral rock from the tidal area to the port, for use in the construction of houses and the breakwaters protecting the boatyards from waves. Teams of four or five seamen under a *nakhoda* would work together, going to the rock beds at low tide. There they would pound at the beds with iron crowbars (*haybs*) roughly two metres in length and, as the tide rose, would sail out with a *tashalah* and load it with the rocks they had hewn. Although the seamen would never venture out too far into the sea to do the work, the whole process would usually take a full twenty-four hours.

Rock-breaking was an arduous task that took its toll on the men, for wielding a crowbar and driving it into the rock beds could cause intense muscle pain. When undertaken during the winter, as it often was, the work exposed them to cold weather and water and endangered their extremities. Also, the job required skill, especially when rocks of particular shapes and sizes had to be cut to meet special demands from builders. As a final ordeal, the men would have to row their *tashalah* back to the shore if there was not enough wind to sail back, a task that only added to the accumulated exertions and discomforts of the day.

On their return with the rocks, the men would unload them in the dhow basins along the shore. Here they were sold by the pile or, if the rocks were of a particular size and shape, by the rock. Buyers would hire a mule to carry the rocks to the construction site, this not being a service provided by the mariners themselves. On sale, one-quarter or one-fifth of the profit went to the dhow owner, who was often a local *nakhoda*. The cost of provisions for the trip were then deducted and the remaining net profit was divided among the men, each of whom would get one share, while the *nakhoda* was entitled to two shares in view of his liability for any damage to the boat.[5]

The profits generated never amounted to much. In the 1930s, an average load would be sold for Rs 5 to 10, though by the 1950s this had risen to around Rs 50. Although business was steady, it was only during times of brisk demand for construction materials – for houses or breakwaters, or even for a dam in the Shatt al-'Arab – that one could expect to earn a

[5] Interview with the *nakhoda* Jasim Al-Khalil Al-Najm, 2000.

decent amount of money. Thus, there were only 30 to 40 rock-carrying dhows in lean times of the 1930s, and mariners in this sector often participated in other activities that were more lucrative, such as lighterage, pearl diving or work on the trading dhows.

The end of lighterage and rock-carrying

High demand for their specialized services ensured business for lighters in Kuwait until well after the introduction of oil into the economy. Indeed, lighterage of the traditional kind did not cease until 1960, when Kuwait's ports were developed and deepened to allow larger ships to dock directly at quaysides and unload. Rock-carrying too became obsolete as new building materials such as cement blocks and reinforced concrete made their way into construction. In addition to which, the unappealing nature of rock-hewing and rock-carrying as a form of employment, and the growing availability of more comfortable salaried positions, were strong disincentives to continue with the old ways. As a result, construction of lighters and specialized dhows ground to a halt, and the few surviving vessels were sold off to nearby ports.

8

Naql al-Ma': Water Transport

THE QUESTION of fresh-water supply has been a continuous preoccupation of Kuwait's people throughout their history, and indeed remains an important issue today. While Kuwait's inhabitants collected rainwater and had access to wells tapping into underground aquifers, the amount of fresh water – or at least water with a low salt content – provided by these wells was never reliably adequate for all the townspeople's drinking and cooking needs. Years of minimal rainfall meant that there was simply not enough potable water to go round. As early as 1820, it was observed by one British officer that Kuwaitis frequently went over to Failaka Island to collect water in view of the relative abundance of fresh water there.[1]

As the need for fresh water increased with the size of the population – between 40,000 and 50,000 in 1911 during the reign of Shaikh Mubarak – even that proved to be inadequate.[2] One local historian records that it was only in 1909, after a winter season in which hardly any rain fell, that a Kuwaiti dhow-owner came up with the idea of making a profit by fitting his *tashalah* with a wooden tank that he could then fill with fresh water from the Shatt al-'Arab.[3] Of course long-distance dhows must have

---

[1] Report by Major Colebrook, 1820, in *Persian Gulf Précis*, vol. 5: 1.
[2] Population figure in 1911 given by Mylrea, 1951.
[3] Al-Hatem 1980: 156.

sometimes filled their wooden water tanks in a similar way before setting out on their voyages, so an old idea was being adapted to a new purpose. Whatever the case may be, it is clear that by 1910 Kuwait had 40 to 50 large ships, each with a capacity of 3,000 to 5,000 gallons, carrying water from the Shatt to supply the needs of its people.[4]

The transport of water did not solve the problem. Unfavourable weather conditions could prevent the dhows from reaching the Shatt for three consecutive days and thus spark a water crisis in the town. Also, a busy pearling season could divert mariners to the pearl banks, thus leaving the water-carrying dhows under-manned, as was the case in 1911. The growth of the Kuwaiti population during the 1910s, with the influx of immigrants from Persia, put such pressure on the water supply that in 1912 Shaikh Mubarak purchased a 300-ton motorized barge to be used strictly for the transport of water, and in 1913 he asked the British to send a steamer laden with water containers every three or four days to help alleviate the hardship.[5] During that time, he also wrote to the Gulf Resident inquiring about the possibility of finding new sources of water, including the digging of new wells or the establishment of a desalination plant in the area similar to the one the local agent had told him existed in Aden.[6] The Resident responded by asking the Government of India to send someone to survey the area and study the possibility of digging wells. In 1913 the geologist E. H. Pascoe arrived and began his work, sinking wells in Shuwaikh, on Kubbar Island and in various other areas.[7]

When even the new wells proved to be inadequate to the needs of the people, the ruler was left with no option but to set up a desalination plant. After lengthy negotiations, the Government of India and Mubarak agreed that a plant would be built by the Anglo-Persian Oil Company (APOC) and funded by the ruler, who would recover the Company's loan to him or to the state of Rs 187,500 through receipts from water sales. Local merchants

[4] Letter from Captain W. H. I. Shakespear to the Gulf Resident, November 13, 1912; *Arab Gulf Cities*, vol. 4: 80.
[5] The barge or motorized cargo vessel, whose name was *Isa'id*, was imported from England via India.
[6] Letter from Shaikh Mubarak to Percy Cox, 9 November 1912; *Arab Gulf Cities*, vol. 4: 82.
[7] *Persian Gulf Administration Reports, 1873–1957*, Kuwait reports for 1915, 1916 and 1919.

also undertook to help the government with the project, offering a total of Rs 109,000 in return for commensurate shares in the plant.[8] Although the outbreak of the First World War delayed the project considerably, by 17 March 1919 the plant was able to produce 4,800 gallons of fresh water.

However, the plant suffered from a number of technical difficulties and proved unable to satisfy the needs of the population. Though desalinized, the water was not nearly as fresh as that of the Shatt al-'Arab. It was also more expensive than Shatt water, and so had to be sold at a price beyond most Kuwaitis' means. This led to tensions between the operators of the plant and the then Shaikh, Salim Al-Sabah (r. 1917–21), who gave orders for between 400 and 500 tons of fresh water to be produced per day.[9] Despite being upgraded by a firm operating from Muhammarah, near APOC's base at Abadan, the plant was still unable to produce water that was fresh enough. As a result it was forced to pay Rs 250,000 in compensation to the ruler (by that time Shaikh Ahmad Al-Jabir Al-Sabah, who had acceded in 1921) and its shareholders, and to suspend operations.[10] Further setbacks occurred in 1927, when the ruler signed an agreement with Eastern and General Syndicate Ltd to drill water wells in the area; the costly operations, which drilled wells of nearly 500 feet, proved fruitless.[11]

As government efforts to secure a local source of fresh water waxed and waned, the dhows continued to ply back and forth carrying water from the Shatt al-'Arab to meet local needs. To cap profiteering from this water, Shaikh Ahmad set a price ceiling and, in partnership with a group of local merchants led by Khalid al-Zaid Al-Khalid, established the Kuwait Water Company in 1940. With capital of around Rs 100,000, the company was able to purchase a number of water-carrying dhows and quickly corner the trade in fresh water.[12] A critical water shortage in the summer of 1941, however, led the company to impose restrictions, including prohibiting the sale of water to those with a water cistern in their home. It was also forced

[8] This is confirmed by a 1914 list of shareholders in the desert plant that was kept by Abdullah bin 'Abd al-Ilah Al-Qina'i and published in the newspaper *Al-Qabas*, 21 September 2001.

[9] *Persian Gulf Administration Reports, 1873–1957*, vol. 7: 70, Kuwait report for 1919.

[10] Ibid., vol. 8, Kuwait reports for 1922 and 1923.

[11] Ibid. for 1927.

[12] "Kuwait Intelligence Summary" in *Political Diaries of the Arab World: Persian Gulf 1904–1965*, vol. 14, 1–15 February 1940.

to hire steam launches to tow the water-carrying dhows when the wind was not up to the job, and to construct five new dhows to augment the fleet. Despite these costs, however, the company was able to declare profits for that year totalling Rs 11,946.[13] As demand for water kept on rising, the company was compelled in 1942 to raise the price of a 4-gallon can to 9 Annas, or just over a half a Rupee.

Efforts by the Kuwait Oil Company that year to find an underground source of fresh water met with the same result as previous efforts. This served further to concentrate the water trade in the hands of the Kuwait Water Company, which had developed a new administrative body, increased its capital by Rs 200,000 (Rs 130,000 of which came from the merchant investors) and purchased no less than ten new dhows.[14] Even these developments, however, could not stem the rising price of water, which in 1943 grew by 8 Annas and now stood at more than 1 Rupee per 4-gallon can. A jump in demand in 1944 to more than 800,000 gallons placed the company under great pressure, and it had to request the British government to allow it to import the necessary timber from India (a temporary ban had been imposed during the Second World War), so that it could build enough dhows to meet the demand.[15] As pressure mounted, the company gave consideration to the purchase of a steamship to carry water at an estimated rate of 1,652,000 gallons per day.[16]

In 1948, when the water supply position was reaching an all-time low, an Iraqi named Hanna Al-Shaikh made an offer to the government to supply Kuwait with fresh water at the rate of 1 Anna per gallon, although nothing came of the proposal. Meanwhile, the price of water that summer hit 1 Rupee per gallon – a hefty price at the time – despite efforts by the Kuwait Water Company to build water storage facilities and continue providing its services.[17] That same year, a British offer to build a new desalination plant at a cost of between $6 and $8 million was rejected by Shaikh Ahmad Al-Jabir on the grounds of its high cost.[18] The idea of building a water pipeline

---

[13] *Political Diaries of the Persian Gulf*, vol. 15, p. 8.
[14] Ibid. p. 358.
[15] *Kuwait Political Agency: Arabic Documents*, vol. 8: 588.
[16] *Records of Kuwait*, vol. 6: 41.
[17] *Persian Gulf Administration Reports*, vol. 11: 40, Kuwait report for 1948.
[18] *Records of Kuwait*, vol. 6: 561.

from the Shatt al-'Arab to Kuwait had occurred to a number of merchants, who were willing to pay up to £1 million sterling to fund the project, but the lack of security guarantees from the Iraqi government effectively scuttled the project.[19]

Following the death of Shaikh Ahmad Al-Jabir in 1950 and the subsequent accession of Shaikh Abdullah Al-Salim, the Kuwait Oil Company developed desalination facilities capable of supplying 120,000 gallons of fresh water per day to Kuwait's inhabitants from its headquarters in Ahmadi. The ruler then decided to build a similar plant in the city, which by 1953 was being supplied with no less than 1 million gallons of water every day. This, however, came very late in the day for Kuwait. We shall now return to the proper subject of this chapter – the business of supplying Kuwait with water before the advent of the oil industry and desalination processes.

Early sources of fresh water

As we have seen, prior to the development of the water transport sector, Kuwaitis met their fresh water needs with supplies from Failaka Island and from the numerous wells in or near the town of Kuwait itself, including those in such areas as Shamiya, Dasma, 'Adailiyya, Kaifan and Nugra. These wells depended on rainfall for their replenishment and were thus dry for most of the year, and what little water was extracted from them was used mainly for cooking. Other wells tapping into underground aquifers produced drinkable water, such as those discovered in Sha'b and Hawali in 1907. Wells were also to be found in Jahra, al-Qurain, al-Subaihiya, al-Wafra and other places that were inhabited but too far from the town of Kuwait itself to reach on foot, though they were visited by caravans on their way out of Kuwait. The people of the town and the desert around it dug wells locally to collect fresh water after rain, which they would then carry back to their homes.[20] Those able to do so brought donkeys to these wells and filled large water sacks, which they then sold in the water market right by

[19] *Water Resources of the Arabian Peninsula*, vol. 2: 86. The idea came up again in 1955, although by then the successful desalination by the Kuwait Oil Company had rendered the scheme obsolete.
[20] Al-Rashaid 1926, vol. 1, p. 34.

the residence of Shaikh Mubarak.[21] Mubarak himself had no need to worry about his water supply, for he owned private wells near his palace in Surra and elsewhere.[22]

Another less common source of water was the *sabil*, or well donated by a prominent individual, who had taken it upon himself to ensure that it was always full of water available free of charge to the townsfolk. A famous *sabil* was that of 'Abd al-'Aziz Ahmad Al-Du'aij, who purchased a camel to bring water from the dhows or other wells to a large tank in the centre of one of the markets (later known as the Bin Du'aij Market, or Suq Bin Du'aij) for free consumption. Other merchants too, many of them involved in the water trade, contributed similar *sabils*, and also allowed the mariners working for them to take water home gratis or chose not to take their half of the profits from a voyage. Some even went so far as to finance an entire voyage to the Shatt for the honour of providing free water to the townspeople, many of whom were their kinsfolk, friends and neighbours. Another example of such charity was Ahmad Al-Khurafi, who supplied the American Mission Hospital with a large tank and undertook to keep it filled with fresh water every day free of charge.

Bringing water from the Shatt al-'Arab

Before leaving for the Shatt, a water dhow's wooden storage tanks were always unshipped and inspected onshore for cracks, which were then stuffed with cotton by the *qallaf* to make the tanks waterproof.[23] Each tank was then floated to the dhow at high tide, while the vessel was gradually flooded until the tank could be floated above its position in the hold. With the tanks in position, the crew would cause them to descend slowly into the hold by bailing out the dhow. The men would then hoist sail and set out northwards for the Shatt, sailing past Ras al-Subiyya, Mischan and Bubiyan Islands and

[21] By order of the Kuwait Municipality in 1930, those who brought donkeys to the market were forbidden to rest their water sacks on the donkey's back all day, this being considered cruelty to animals. They were required instead to rest the sacks on the ground until a buyer came, at which point they could hoist them back up onto the donkey to take them to the buyer's home. See Al-Jasim 1980: 144.
[22] Lorimer, 1908–15/1986, vol. 8: 1052.
[23] See Al-Hijji 1998: 55 and 2001: 27 for a plan of a typical water dhow holding ten tanks.

taking advantage of the water dhow's shallow draft to hug the shore.

On reaching the mouth of the Shatt, the sailors would begin loading the storage tanks with fresh water. This they did by standing on wooden platforms secured to the side of the dhow and filling the tanks by hand using buckets. Sometimes they would have to sail right into the Shatt itself to obtain their cargo but, during the summer months, the northerly winds pushed the fresh water towards the mouth of the Shatt, allowing the dhows simply to anchor near its mouth to fill their tanks. When filling the tanks, the men were always sure to fill both sides of the dhow at once so as to maintain its balance and prevent listing. During the winter, when they were forced to sail into the Shatt, they were obliged to stop at the customs post in Faw to pay duties.[24] Winter was made even more irksome by the prevailing winds that drove against the vessels, often forcing them to seek refuge near the banks of the waterway. Taking on water during this season was no easy task, as the winds that rocked the boats made the task of filling their tanks while trying to maintain balance a very tricky one. In favourable weather, by contrast, the filling of the tanks might take little more than an hour. Most dhows had storage capacities of around 13,000 gallons.

Aside from water, crews liked to take on fruit and vegetables from the Shatt gardens to sell in the markets of Kuwait. Also, they would aim to carry as many passengers as possible between Kuwait and Basra, a service in particular demand in the autumn among crewmen of long-distance trading dhows who were late and had to catch up with their fellow sailors on the Shatt. Ordinary passengers were charged a fare, but etiquette in the Kuwaiti seafaring community exempted mariners trying to get to their dhows from payment.

Water-carrying voyages to the Shatt and back were short – a typical round trip took two to four days, allowing about eight trips per month – but they were never easy. Dhows and their crews were often subjected to harassment by the authorities at Faw and were sometimes even raided by local boats. While these raids resulted mostly in property loss or damage, in a few cases Kuwaiti crews were physically beaten or even killed, resulting in complaints being filed with the local authorities in the area.[25] A safe return,

---

[24] In the 1930s these amounted to roughly Rs 3 per load, but were later doubled.
[25] References to these complaints are to be found in *Kuwait Political Agency: Arabic Documents, 1899–1949*, vol. 8: 560.

however brief the absence, occasioned much excitement. The sighting of water dhows would bring people flocking to the dhow basins, bringing donkeys and buckets and other containers to be filled with the sweet, fresh water of the Shatt. To instil order into its distribution to the populace, every dhow had a bookkeeper of sorts (*karrani*) whose job was to record all transactions and ensure that due payment was collected. At times of weak supply and strong demand, water distribution could be a very trying process for the crew, who would be subjected to the pleas and remonstrations of thirsty Kuwaitis, most of whom were clamouring for nothing more than a few gallons of water for drinking and cooking. Such moving sights were a source of inspiration to local poets and artists, many of whom strove to convey the pity and emotion of the scene in verse and painting.[26]

Profit-sharing in water transport

The total amount of water brought back from the Shatt varied according to the season. During the winter months, for example, Kuwaitis consumed much less water than during the summer, and hence fewer dhows went out. This freed captains to use their vessels for short-distance trade instead. Prices were also seasonal, with water being far cheaper in winter than in summer due to the drop in demand.

From the profits of the voyage, the *nakhoda* had first to deduct the expenses, which included the customs duties at Faw as well as the cost of provisions. Following these deductions, the net profit was divided in two, and, just as in other sectors, one half went to the dhow-owner and the other to the crew. From the crew's half, each sailor was entitled to one share and the *nakhoda* to two, the value of each share depending on the price the water commanded on the Kuwait market.

It is noteworthy that with the establishment of the Kuwait Water Company came the introduction of wage labour into this sector. The company paid *nakhoda*s and their crews set wages – anywhere between Rs 5 and 10 per trip in the 1940s – as opposed to shares in the profits, and

[26] See for example the poems of Khalid Al-Faraj and Fahad Bu Risli, and the art of Ayyub Husain; also, Al-Rashaid 1926, vol. 1: 35.
[27] Interview with the *nakhoda* 'Isa Bishara, 2000.
[28] Interview with the *nakhoda* Khalid Muhammad Al-Shahin, 2000.

covered the cost of provisions. This competition from the company combined with the fixed wages paid to its employees forced a number of dhow-owners in the water trade either to sell their dhows to it or to switch to short-distance trade, as they were unable to compete with the company's prices, capital and guarantees.[27]

Selling to the pearling dhows

Not all dhows brought their water to the town of Kuwait for sale. During the pearling season, some *nakhodas* found a readier profit in taking their supply to the pearl banks, where demand for water was brisk because of the precious time it would otherwise take the pearlers to sail to the mainland to replenish supplies. Water dhows making the trip to the banks sold not only water but also provisions such as fruit, vegetables, rice, dates, coffee, firewood for cooking (mainly dried palm fronds) and the like, and the convenience factor fetched them much higher prices than mainland markets. These dhows only sailed out to the banks a month or so after the pearling season had begun, as it was around then that the pearling dhows would begin to run out of provisions. Having sold their stock, they would return to the Shatt al-'Arab to refill their holds and repeat the exercise.[28]

This, however, was not the only supply of fresh water available at sea to the pearling dhows. Dhows from Bahrain, or those from Kuwait which sailed southwards, for example, had access to fresh water in an area called 'Ain Ighmasa, 7 miles off the Saudi fishing village of Jubail, where freshwater springs were to be found welling up in the sea at depths of roughly 1.5 fathoms. Here it was a simple matter for divers to swim down to the upwelling currents to fill water sacks, which were then stowed on board for later consumption. Smaller pearling dhows that were unable to reach the area, however, either bought their supplies from the water dhows or else had to sail to the coast to draw from whatever well or spring they could find.

9

Sayd al-Samak: Fishing

O F ALL GULF MARITIME activities, perhaps the most visible and enduring has been fishing, which traces its origins back to time immemorial and continues up to the present day. Evidence of Neolithic fishing has been found at Subiyya, for example, dating back at least 7,000 years.[1] This is no surprise considering Kuwait's prime geographical situation, the alluvial deposits of the Shatt al-'Arab and its warm, shallow waters making Kuwait Bay and its surrounding inlets and islands an attractive breeding and nursery environment for fish. Various travellers in more recent times commented on the abundance of fish in the area, particularly in Kuwait Bay itself.[2]

It is important to note at the outset that bulk fishing was not a year-round activity, but was restricted to the spring and summer months, when fishermen went after the famous *zubaidi* (the Silver Pomfret or Butterfish, *Pampus argenteus*, prized for its taste and fleshiness). Those from Failaka Island sought it off the islands of 'Awha and Mischan, while those from Kuwait Town went to the waters off Ras al-Qaid on Bubiyan Island. Other species of fish congregated in Kuwait Bay during March and April, and of these the *nagrour* (Silver Grunt, *Pomadasys argenteus*), the *shi'm* (Yellowfin Black

---

[1] Carter and Crawford, 2002: 1–13.
[2] See for example Felix Jones, writing in 1839 (Jones, 1839/1985: 52): "The harbour [of Grane/Koweit] abounds in fish."

Seabream, *Acanthopagrus latus*), and the popular *hamour* (Brown-spotted Grouper, *Epinephelus coioides/tauvina*) were particularly sought-after by fishermen. Only in the middle of winter, when the sea off Kuwait becomes too cold for some species of fish to remain, did fishing dwindle.

During the off-season, many fisherfolk would turn their hand to the collection of firewood in the interior for sale as fuel in town. Despite its seasonal nature, however, fishing was one of Kuwait's chief activities. While no firm evidence exists for the nature and extent of fishing in earlier times, we do know that, at least after the arrival of the 'Utub in the 18th century, it became central to the livelihood and diet of the people, providing a vital part of the staple diet of the maritime community. Fishermen carried on their work not only off mainland Kuwait but also on Bubiyan and Failaka Islands, where a range of techniques was used to catch an even wider variety of fish species.

Fishing methods in Kuwait

Each community in Kuwait and the surrounding islands developed its own methods of catching the species of fish particular to its area, although some exploited other zones too. The people of Failaka Island, as we have seen, fished for the *zubaidi* (Silver Pomfret) off their island and off nearby 'Awha and Mischan during the summer, but would also move to the eastern shore of Bubiyan during April and May. To catch these fish they would use a long, floating net called an *'iddah*, of local manufacture, which was usually cast at night so that the schools of fish did not try to avoid it. Whatever they caught that was surplus to local needs would be taken to market in Kuwait town, where it would be sold fresh, or else it would be salted and sold to outgoing dhows. Any left over would be salted and kept for consumption during the winter months, during which fish stocks were less abundant.[3]

Fishermen from Kuwait town too would sail to Bubiyan Island, to Ras al-Qaid on its eastern tip, to catch the *zubaidis* that came there to breed. They would fish in small groups out of small boats, and sell their catch to passing dhows en route to or from the Shatt al-'Arab, salting whatever they were unable to sell straight away to preserve it during the homeward voyage. At other times they would fish inside Kuwait Bay, using hooks, lines and

---

[3] See Al-Bakr, 2001.

sinkers but not rods (a method known as *hadag al-khait*), and fashioning whatever ropes and lines they needed from local materials such as palm fronds and palm fibre.[4] The boats would hoist sail when they could, but on days of little or no wind the men would have to row their boats out and back.

By contrast, fishermen in the villages near Kuwait town and on the smaller islands – notably the 'Azmi tribespeople – used the distinctive fish-trap method known as *hadrah*, whereby a fence was constructed onshore below the high tide mark and into the sea, so that the ebb tide would funnel fish into a small enclosure at the apex.[5] While the benefits of such a method, which was commonly used by all coastal communities on the Arabian shore of the Gulf, are obvious, such as the elimination of the need to go to sea, the drawbacks lay in the investment of money and time that building and maintaining the *hadrah*s required. One fisherman, for example, recalled that building a single *hadrah* had cost him Rs 40, with more money required for its maintenance.[6] These *hadrah*s were fashioned from bamboo, reeds or palm fronds lashed together with cord and increasing in height as the shore shelved downwards, the offshore section measuring as much as 12 feet or almost 4 metres in diameter. During high tide, the fish trap would be submerged and, as the tide ebbed, fish in its vicinity would find themselves enclosed by it. All the fisherman then had to do was walk into his *hadrah* and collect the fish trapped inside. Particular weather conditions favoured this activity: as Richard Bowen observed in his article, certain currents and winds allowed for greater numbers of fish to be trapped within the *hadrah*.[7] This technique, however, was only effective for catching shallow-water fish; others, like the *zubaidi*, had to be caught in deeper waters.

Fishing was also sometimes carried out from a *huwairiyyah* or *warjiyyah*, a small, one-man boat, more like a raft, made of palm fronds lashed together. These tiny craft were a very ancient type dating back to the Neolithic period, and were only useful for fishing close to shore.[8]

[4] This process is recorded by Dr Mylrea (1951) in his memoir "Kuwait before Oil".
[5] These were also set up near 'Azmi habitations on Bubiyan Island: Al-Rashaid, 1926, vol. 1: 29.
[6] Interview with Mubarak bin Da'san in *Al-Watan* newspaper, 11 July 1997.
[7] Bowen, 1951: 8.
[8] See Carter and Crawford, 2002, for evidence of a small bitumen-coated reed boat at the Neolithic site of Subiyya.

Another and more popular method of catching fish was by means of the *gargoor*, a dome-shaped mesh cage with a small opening, like a lobster pot, that fish could easily swim into but find it difficult to swim out of again. Still in use today, the *gargoor* is tied to a floating marker and dropped into the water, where it is left for days before being pulled up by its owners, catch and all. Each person knew exactly where his own *gargoor* was; it was simply not done to draw up someone else's *gargoor* and take his catch. It was only regarded as acceptable, in Kuwaiti maritime custom, for mariners desperate for food on a deep-sea voyage to draw up someone else's *gargoor*, then they were expected to leave the value of what they had taken in coins for its owner.

Main varieties of fish in Kuwait

It is beyond the scope of this book to describe all the various species of commercially important fish in Kuwait. Instead we shall briefly identify the most sought-after species.[9]

The *zubaidi* (Silver Pomfret), already referred to, was so popular that from at least the early 20th century it has been the most sought-after fish in the market, being caught in quantities three times larger than any other fish.[10] The most prolific areas for *zubaidi* lay between Failaka and 'Awha, as well as in the Khor Abdullah surrounding the north of Bubiyan, at depths of between 2 and 12 fathoms. The largest quantities were found between December and April though, as we saw above, fishermen from Failaka would go to these areas in April and May too. While *zubaidi* were caught in large quantities and fetched high prices in the fish markets, stocks always had time to regenerate so that a catch was ensured for the following season. This was not done on purpose. It was merely because the relatively simple fishing methods, coupled with the relatively small market for them (the fish were caught only for local consumption and not for export), meant that there was no danger of overfishing.

In addition to the *nagrour* (Silver Grunt), *hamour* (Brown-spotted Grouper) and the *shi'm* (Yellowfin Black Seabream) mentioned above, other important species were the *nuwaibi* (Silver Croaker, *Bairdiella chrysoura*), and

---

[9] For more on these species of fish, see Al-Bakr, 2001; Al-Mattar *et al.*, 2006.
[10] Lorimer, 1908–15/1986, vol. 3: 1053.

the small but popular *maid* (Largescale Mullet, *Liza macrolepis*) caught close to the shore in December and January, along with shrimp (chiefly Green Tiger Prawn, *Penaeus semisulcatus*). All of these were caught in varying quantities from season to season. The *nagrour*, caught during March and April, was the most popular of them, making up roughly a quarter of all of the fish caught, for example, in the 1904 season.[11]

Profits from fishing and their distribution

Lack of hard data about the quantities of fish caught in the pre-oil era makes it difficult to determine what profits might be made from a traditional fishing venture. What one can say with some certainty is that in the 1930s, in the town of Kuwait itself, there were approximately 40 fishing boats of various medium-sized types, such as the *jalbut*, fishing *lanch* and *shu'i*, and about 50 smaller boats such as the *balam fudiri*.[12] Such numbers, however, cannot account for fish caught on shore and outside the town itself, nor can they throw any light on variations in the size of the catch from season to season and from place to place. Interviews with fishermen reveal that the price of fish in the markets of Kuwait was never high, and that in earlier times fish left unsold after the evening prayer either had to be left in the market to be taken free of charge because of the lack of refrigeration, or else were salted and dried for sale the next day.[13]

After a crew of fishermen had returned and the catch of the day had been sold, the expenses of the trip – namely provisions – had first to be deducted from the gross profit. From the remainder, one-tenth went to the boat-owner, and the remaining nine-tenths was divided into two halves, one of which was distributed among the fishermen in equal shares, and the other among the owners of the nets (usually the fishermen themselves, but not always). If no nets were used – that is, if the fishermen only used hooks, lines and sinkers – one-fifth of the profits went to the boat-owner and the

---

[11] Ibid.

[12] For these fishing boat types, see Al-Hijji, 2001: 8–10, 15, 17.

[13] Interviews with various fishermen, 2001. In the 1930s, *zubaidi* was sold in Failaka Island for roughly Rs 3 per 100 fish during the appropriate season. Interview with the *nakhoda* Ali Faraj, 2001.

[14] Lorimer 1908–15/1986, vol. 7: 513.

[15] Interview with fisherman Salih bin Jabal, 2001.

rest was divided among the fishermen. On Failaka Island, however, the boat-owner received only the equivalent of one share, with another going to the headman of the community there.[14] The value of a share could fluctuate widely from season to season: while it was usually between Rs 1 and 3 per trip in the pre-oil era, during the 1940s and 1950s it shot up to almost Rs 50.[15]

Fishing today

As noted at the start of this chapter, fishing, unlike other maritime activities, did not come to an end with the gradual penetration of oil into the Kuwaiti economy. If anything, the sector expanded during this period, but in a modernized form. Boats were fitted with motors and fishing gear became much more sophisticated, to enable larger catches to be made to feed a growing population. Increasing water pollution, however – especially following the 1990–91 invasion and occupation of Kuwait – has had a negative impact on local fish stocks. While fish is still readily available in the Kuwait fish markets, the quantities have decreased, leading the government to impose regulations on the timing and intensity of fishing operations. Furthermore, fishing is no longer practised by Kuwaitis as a means of livelihood, being largely now the domain of foreign business, Arab and otherwise. Overfishing by the private companies of Kuwait poses the danger of destroying local breeding grounds and there have been calls for further regulation of fishing. This is especially true of shrimp, the high demand for which has already led to regulations specifying months during which individuals and companies alike can trawl for shrimp.

That said, many Kuwaitis continue to fish for sport, some on a regular basis and others only from time to time. Thus, if there is one activity that continues to bind Kuwaitis to the sea and preserves their knowledge of it – even if only minimally – it is fishing.

10

Al-Nahmah: Songs of the Sea

No ACCOUNT OF KUWAITI maritime traditions can be complete without a brief, general description of the songs and instruments that accompanied the dhows' departure, voyages and return, and which had a profound influence on the development of music not only in Kuwait but elsewhere in the Gulf too.

Performed as an accompaniment to both work and leisure, *al-nahma*, or *al-fann al-bahri* (the "art of the sea") as it is still called, had a dual purpose on board ship. Its primary function was practical, to co-ordinate the crew's efforts, lift their morale and lighten their fatigue during arduous teamwork such as lifting a sail or rowing a longboat; these work songs were the equivalent of the rhythmic sea shanties common to other maritime cultures. The second function was as pure entertainment at times of rest and recreation or celebration. For both reasons a *nakhoda* always took trouble to hire the best singer, or *nahham*, available. The importance attached to music is shown by the fact that an exceptionally skilled *nahham* could earn bonuses in addition to his share of the profits of the voyage, and almost always commanded the respect of *nakhoda* and crew alike, often dining with the former on the poop deck of the dhow. *Nahham*s were hired only for voyages on pearling or long-distance trading dhows, and never for short-distance traders and fishing boats.

Sea songs and shanties

The lyrics of sea songs and shanties derive their essential characteristics from a type of folk poem called the *mawwal*, which is a blend of the *zuhairi* and *muwaili* types of poetry of the Gulf and Arabian Peninsula. *Zuhairi* poems consist of seven verses broadly falling into two stanzas: the first stanza comprising the first three verses, which share rhythm, alliteration and rhyme; with verses four, five and six, forming the second stanza, also sharing their own similar characteristics. The seventh and final verse, called the *rabbat* or *guful*, reverts to the features of the first stanza.[1] Thus, a poem would run somewhat as follows: AAA, BBB, A, with each group (A or B) sharing the same rhythm, alliteration and rhyme. A *muwaili* poem resembles a *zuhairi* one in its conventions – that is, adherence to similarities in rhythm, alliteration and rhyme – but differs in containing fewer verses and in being more obvious in meaning than its *zuhairi* counterpart. A *muwaili* shanty tended to be sung when a sail was being lifted. Other shanties, called *shailah*s and *handah*s, were made up of shorter rhyming verses repeated over and over again during other tasks. While there were conventions to these, they were usually simple in structure and their function was solely to lend rhythm to the work.

With these conventions in mind, songs of the sea can be split into three broad categories: *yamal*s, *khatfah*s, and *haddadi*s. The *yamal*, developed on *zuhairi* conventions, was a shanty sung by the *nahham* in the company of the *nakhoda* and his crew as they rowed out to the dhow to begin their voyage. Sitting in the back of the longboat by the *nakhoda*, the *nahham* would sing to encourage and harmonize the oarsmen's efforts. His tone was usually cheerful, but occasionally could be sad, conveying the sorrow of the men as they left their families and homes to earn a living. The *nahham* always sang the *yamal* a cappella, with no music or percussion other than the rhythm of the oars as they splashed and pulled through the water in unison. If the singing – and thus the rhythm of the oars – was slow, it was called a *yamal rakid*; a faster pace was known as a *yamal muharriqi*. As soon as one song was over, the *nahham* would begin another, without letting up until the dhow was reached. A typical *yamal* would go:

[1] Al-Rifa'i, 1985: 187.

> I bid you farewell, O light of my eye
> For I sleep not when leaving you.
> I waited long to meet you, my sight weakened by my longing,
> And I remain, O Master of mine, a body bereft of a soul,
> Without a mind, a discarded carcass.
> All the Arabs have rested, but for my grief-stricken soul,
> O light of my eye, care for me as I care for you.

On embarkation, the crew would hoist the sails to the chanting of the *khatfah*, which was sung in the *muwaili* style to the beat of an *iqa'* – one of a broad category of drums characteristic of vernacular music. During this operation, the *nahham* typically chanted a particular song, the *istihlal*, replete with references to the sailors' dependence on the grace of God for a safe journey. As the mainsail inched upwards, the sailors would occupy the short breaks they took during the labour by joining in the music with rhythmic hand-clapping. This on-and-off working and singing continued until the sails were fully raised and billowed by the breezes as the vessel began to move off. A *khatfah* went somewhat as follows:

> O my benign Prophet,
> O Most Gracious, Most Merciful,
> We are hastening, dependent on Allah.

After which the first *nahham* sings:

> O Allah! O Allah! O Allah!
> We have lifted, [and are] dependent on Allah.
> My Lord, in You we trust,
> For You are Gracious, and You know of our plight.

To which the second *nahham* replies:

> I am patient, O He Who wields sovereignty,
> [He] Who taught you the blackness of night.
> I seek refuge with you, O Muhammad,
> [On the] day of resurrection, O supporter of mine,
> My treasure and utmost desire.

The first *nahham* then returns:

> We are weak and wretched,
> My Master, we swallow your sight.
> You will settle the debts that burden us,
> You will settle our heavy debts,
> The first to the last,
> O Lord, pray for Muhammad.

Unlike the *yamal* and *khatfah*, which were work-related shanties, the *haddadi* was for recreation on deck, and was typified by a variety of beats, rhythms and tunes. The most famous of these melodies was known as the *sangini*, which was customarily sung after the coating of the hull to the accompaniment of the *sarnayi*, a foot-long wind instrument of African origin resembling an oboe. In the *sangini* one could also expect to hear several different percussion instruments, including *tabla*s (djembe-like drums) and *tuwaisa*s (brass drums). These were hardly ever used in songs other than the *haddadi*, to which particular conventions applied that distinguished it from other songs of the sea.

One particular song, the *'ardah bahriyyah*, was performed only on safe arrival in port following a pearling season or long-distance trading voyage. For this, the sailors would gather at the bow of the vessel and, with an ensemble of drums – including *iqa'*s, *tabla*s and the *tar* (a large, flat, circular drum with a hollow bottom) – and following the lead of the chief drummer, the *khammari*, they would drum their way into the port. The *'ardah bahriyyah* was composed not just of percussion and other instruments, but included repeated paeans of praise to the Almighty for having ordained a safe landfall. This performance was much like the *'ardah* of the desert (*'ardah barriyyah*), with the essential difference that its rhythm was slower, and while the *'ardah* of the desert was intended to stir up warriors for battle, the *'ardah* of the sea was an expression of joy and relief. So distinctive was the sound of the Kuwaiti *'arda bahriyyah* that it would prompt other Kuwaiti dhows anchored in port to raise their flags in celebration of their compatriots' arrival. While technically it could be performed to mark arrival in any port, it was customarily performed on arrival in Oman and then in Kuwait following a season's voyage.

Other types of maritime music included the *sumrah*, performed during nights at anchor in a foreign port, whether Basra, Matrah in Oman, Aden, Mombasa, Zanzibar or Bombay. Mainly celebratory and jovial in mood, the *sumrah* involved the playing of the *'ud* (lute), drumming from various percussion instruments, and the rhythmic clapping and melodic singing of the sailors, many of whom would also be inspired to dance. Such celebrations were not confined to the crew, but could draw in local onlookers and participants from whatever port the dhow happened to be at anchor in.

Still other songs were appropriate to different circumstances at sea. This *'ardah bahriyyah*, for example, composed on *zuhairi* principles, was sung while returning from a season on the pearl banks:

> Happiest is he who celebrates Eid in his land,
> And in the morning dons his finest.
> Our Eid is on the pearl banks, hauling lines.
> Our clothes are our diving shorts, the rags of the oppressed,
> Aboard the *Sultan of Dhows*, that stout *boum*,
> Which breasts the great waves that constrict its thoughts,
> With Bu Nasr, our captain, that bird of prey who roves foreign seas at his will.

The *iqa'*, or rhythms

Most songs involved different types of percussion instruments, basically drums of various materials, shapes and sizes. One was the earthenware *aihla*, which was usually used to store water but could be drummed with pleasing effect. Another, like a small *tabla*, was called the *mirwas*.[2]

The precise origin of the Kuwaiti *iqa'* or rhythms is unknown. Some maintain that they made their way into maritime music from African sailors, while others point to their resemblance to rhythms used in Indian classical music as the key to their origins. Whatever the case, it is clear that the *iqa'* instruments were played using conventions inherited from a variety of Indian Ocean cultures: for example, some rhythms were made up of a cycle of 16 beats, just as in the classical Indian style, while others, consisting of 12, 10 or 8 beats, may also have a classical Indian origin.

---

[2] For an excellent analysis of the role of the *iqa'*, see Al-Daikan, 1995.

Renowned Kuwaiti *nahhams*

While it would be futile to try to record the names of every *nahham* in Kuwait's maritime history, it is appropriate here to recall a few so as to give prospective researchers leads to follow. Perhaps the most famous *nahham* was 'Abd al-'Aziz Al-Duwaish, whose sweet voice and mastery of his art made him a celebrity in Kuwait. One might also add Farhan Buhailah, one of the older *nahhams*, who made frequent voyages with the *nakhoda* Saqr Al-Abdullah Al-Saqr in his *baghlah Al-Qundi*. Another older *nahham* was Sa'd bin Fayiz, who accompanied the great *nakhoda* 'Abd al-Latif Al-'Uthman on his *boum Taysir*. The last of the famous *nahhams* of Kuwait, Sa'd Al-'Abjal, died in 1991 during the Iraqi invasion of Kuwait.

Although these were singers of unusual distinction, others achieved equal fame. Others among a host of names that have gone down in history were Salim Al-Marta, 'Utaij bin Sharida, Sa'd bin Sharida, Sharida bin 'Utaij, Jawhar Al-Sayyid, Bu Zayid Al-'Umairi, Salih Ikhail, Ya'qub Ikhail, Muhammad Al-Khashti, Sulaiman Al-'Aziz, Sultan Al-Harbi, Faraj bin Handi, Rashid Al-Jaimaz, 'Isa Bu Ghaith, Yusuf Salman Bu Ghaith, Sulaiman Bu Risli, Fahad bin Khalaf, Ghadban Al-Ghadban, Sa'ud Al-Sarram, 'Ali Al-Mulla, Husain Al-Mulla and Muhammad bin 'Awad. All these *nahhams* alleviated life at sea for generations of Kuwaiti seafarers, assuaging their toil and bringing consolation for their troubles.

11

Al-Musabalah: The Desert Trade

NO ACCOUNT OF THE maritime trade of Kuwait, whether short- or long-distance, can be complete without considering its land-based counterpart: the desert trade, known as *al-musabalah*. It was the hinterland of northern, central and eastern Arabia that endowed Kuwait with its opportunity to carve out its niche as entrepot for goods coming in from the Indian Ocean. While other ports in the Gulf formed one primary market for Kuwaiti trade, Kuwaiti commerce with the bedouin and townspeople of the Arabian hinterland extended the market for such goods deep into central Arabia too. Here were to be found the grazing grounds of Jabal Shammar, famed for its horses, and the politically important Rashidi capital of Ha'il. To its south, in central Najd, lay the large and commercially important towns and oases of the al-Qasim region, notably Buraidah and 'Unaizah. And farther south still, in Sudair and al-Washm, lay still more populous Najdi settlements. The townspeople and bedouin of these regions in turn supplied Kuwait with goods for consumption and export. Kuwait's reputation as a free port made it a focus of far-flung caravan routes, from the head of the Gulf to Najd and the Hijaz beyond it, and to Iraq and Syria. Its reputation for security of goods and people added to its attractions for merchants from both the Gulf and the interior.

Trade with the bedouin of north-east Arabia and the caravans drawn to the town were thus a crucial factor in Kuwait's economic growth. Certainly the sheer size of such caravans must have contributed a very great deal to trade in the town: as early as 1758, one traveller recorded a train of 5,000 camels and 1,000 men leaving Kuwait for Aleppo.[1] Even after the overland trade with Aleppo had died out following that city's decline towards the end of the 18th century, Kuwait's commerce with the interior continued unabated.[2] One merchant recalled that as late as the 1930s it was accounting for roughly one-third of Kuwait's total income from trade.[3]

The number and size of caravans passing through Kuwait town fluctuated widely, making it difficult to pinpoint just how much was bought and sold in this poorly monitored sector. Lorimer notes that in 1904 around twenty-two came into Kuwait from Najd and Jabal Shammar, with the number of camels (each capable of carrying roughly three bags of various goods) ranging from 500 to 1,000 per caravan. While the general decline of the regional overland trade must have adversely affected the number of caravans passing through Kuwait, independent reports between 1915 and 1927 describe the arrival of single ones ranging from 35 to 4,900 camels in size. Generally, however, as a result of the First World War upheavals in the Hijaz and Aleppo, the Ikhwan Revolt of the 1920s and the Kuwait embargo during the 1920s and 1930s, it is safe to assume that the number of caravans dwindled sharply.[4]

Customs duties of 2 percent were collected on goods purchased by the bedouin in Kuwait and another duty of 2 percent was imposed on goods brought into Kuwait for sale by the bedouin. There was a choice of customs stations (*wadi*) that these desert traders could stop at, the most frequented being the one near the southern gate to the market within the wall. This was manned by a government appointee whose job was to collect the duty on goods carried by bedouin leaving the marketplace. Those bringing goods into the marketplace had to stop at the customs station in Safat Square, which was later moved to a new building behind the town gate at Shamiya.

---

[1] Ives, 1773: 222.

[2] For Aleppo's decline, see Abdullah, 2000: 77–81.

[3] Interview with the merchant Muhammad Thunayyan Al-Ghanim on the television programme *Safhat min tarikh al-Kuwait* ("Pages from the History of Kuwait"), Kuwait Television, 1966.

[4] Lorimer 1908–15/1986, vol. 8 (Geographical): 1057. Before the embargo of 1922, it is estimated by the author that the desert trade was bringing in about Rs 1.5 million per year.

In 1938, in combination with those levied on the maritime trade and the pearling sector, such duties amounted to almost three-quarters of government income.

The exchange and storage of goods from the interior, vital though it was to Kuwait's economy, was only part of a total package of effects wrought by this trade. There were social ramifications as kinship links grew with the desert tribes, and these in turn brought political allegiances and obligations. The security of Arabian settlements depended on reliable alliances with the desert tribes surrounding it, and close ties with the tribes of its immediate hinterland was thus vital to the defence of Kuwait. This closeness was reinforced by the participation of tribesmen in pearl diving and other maritime activities. The bedouin also acted as an information network, bringing a constant stream of news and gossip about the affairs of the interior towns and tribes, their rivalries and shifting alliances. They thus bridged the otherwise formidable barriers to communication between Kuwait and remote inner Arabia.

Credit, reputation and trust in *al-musabalah*

Trade with the interior usually took place in spring, when bedouin and merchants from the Najdi towns would come to Kuwait to purchase the commodities they needed, such as rice, coffee, cardamom and textiles, for resale at home. While the bedouin customarily brought their own desert products to market, including brushwood for fuel, ghee and hides, and sold or bartered them for some of the goods they needed, most of the goods they took back with them were purchased or taken on credit rather than for cash, which was in short supply. Such debts were to be paid back in full and without interest one or two years later. The merchants of Kuwait stood to gain a fair amount from deals of this kind, not least the extension of the market for their goods into the interior. To this end, some bedouin were employed as agents by Kuwaiti merchants to sell their goods for them, receiving a commission (in this context known as *sa'i*) for their services. When a trader from the interior (a *musabil*) had debts to pay, it was in his interest to pay them in full and on time. Anyone defaulting on the payment of debts would find his reputation tarnished and his ability to purchase goods – on credit or otherwise – severely curtailed. Under this system, recourse to courts was rare; indeed, in contrast to the pearling industry, there was no court specializing in *musabalah* cases.

A story illustrating these principles rather graphically was told by the merchant Mishari Al-Rawdan, who recalled how, during one trading season, a bedouin trader came to Kuwait town and deposited a sum of money with a merchant there for collection at a later date.[5] When the time came, the *badawi* returned to the man he remembered as the merchant, who immediately swore that he had never received any such deposit. When the *badawi* reacted by creating a scene, the merchant, to preserve his reputation, gave in and handed over the money he was demanding. As the *badawi* was making his triumphant exit from the market, however, he ran into the merchant with whom he had actually left his money. Covered in shame, the *badawi* returned the sum he had taken from the merchant he had wronged with profuse apologies. The story has undoubtedly been embellished in the telling, but it none the less powerfully illustrates the principles of reputation, probity and trust and how they operated in the marketplace. The damage to his reputation that the wrongly accused merchant could have suffered would have cost him far more than the money demanded of him. Similarly, while the *badawi* could have chosen to make off with twice the amount he had deposited, he opted instead to return the first sum to its owner so as to preserve his own reputation and keep his credit intact.

Disruptions to the desert trade

Despite forming a crucial component of Kuwait's economy, the desert trade did not always run smoothly. Early in the reign of Shaikh Ahmad Al-Jabir Al-Sabah, a disagreement with King 'Abd al-'Aziz Al Sa'ud (Ibn Sa'ud) of Najd prompted the latter to impose the embargo mentioned above on the desert trade with Kuwait. It rumbled on from 1922 and all through the following decade, and came at a particularly bad time for Kuwait's economy, which during that period was battered by the Ikhwan Revolt in Najd, the decline of the pearl trade and the worldwide depression, and was thus in a

---

[5] Interview with the pearl merchant Mishari Al-Rawdan on the television series *Safhat min tarikh al-Kuwait* ("Pages from the History of Kuwait"), Kuwait Television, 1966. The year in which he witnessed the event was not recorded during the interview.

very fragile state. The cause of the conflict was Ibn Sa'ud's insistence on receiving duties of up to 7 percent on goods purchased in Kuwait by bedouin from his extensive domain – a measure that was regarded by Shaikh Ahmad and Kuwait's merchant community as unreasonable, an infringement of Kuwait sovereignty (since Ibn Sa'ud proposed to appoint an agent in Kuwait to collect the tax on his behalf), and unfavourable to the growth of trade.[6] While 7 percent might not now seem a significant amount, when one adds it to the 2 percent levied by Kuwait's rulers on goods bought by bedouin, and compares it with the 4 percent on goods brought in from the interior that were re-exported abroad, and the 4 percent on imports from abroad, the amount demanded by Ibn Sa'ud represented a substantial increase. So profound was the impact of the embargo that many in Kuwait were left facing starvation, forcing the merchants to pool resources to help alleviate hunger.[7]

This disruption in trade relations continued throughout the 1930s until, in 1942, an agreement to lift the embargo was reached by both sides. It was no coincidence that during the 1930s oil concession agreements had been signed in both Saudi Arabia and Kuwait and exploration had confirmed the existence of commercially exploitable resources, bringing the promise of new money pouring into the coffers of the ruling families. As oil income trickled down to the merchants and other Kuwaitis, an expanding range of business and job opportunities began to emerge, eclipsing the significance of the desert trade to Kuwait's economy, and so rendering the embargo futile.

Prices and receipts in the desert trade

Among the commodities purchased by the bedouin of the interior were

---

[6] *Persian Gulf Administration Reports, 1873–1957*, vol. 8: 75.

[7] The merchants were able to raise roughly Rs 8,000 in just two days. *Records of Kuwait, 1899–1961*, vol. 7 (Foreign Affairs): 235.

[8] There were various kinds of rice on the market. At first, Japanese rice was preferred, with Rangoon rice eventually taking its place. Karachi rice too (*balm Karachi*) was purchased in large quantities. Among the more expensive varieties were Zeira rice, Rishti rice, 'Anbar rice, Dawood Khan rice, and American (*Amrekani*) rice.

[9] *Political Diaries of the Arab World: Persian Gulf, 1904–1965*, vol. 6: 520.

[10] "Report for Kuwait, 1942" in *Persian Gulf Administration Reports, 1973–1957*, vol. 10: 12.

23. *Above* Having reached Zanzibar, some Kuwaiti dhows would head south for the treacherous Rufiji Delta, to cut and load up with mangrove poles to carry back to the Gulf. Mangrove trunks, seen here in 2000, were in heavy demand for use in house-building. The Rufiji was notorious for malaria, crocodiles, hippopotami and snakes. Dhows would have to spend up to a month there, an ordeal for the sailors.

24. *Below* A cash receipt to the Kuwaiti *nakhoda* Miflih Salih Al-Falah, for his purchase of mangrove poles (*boriti*) in April 1949. It was issued by the company responsible for the sale of poles, which was based at Dima, on the edge of the Rufiji Delta.

M. GHAUI
RUFIJI DELTA.

Station. *Dima*

No. *132/49.* **CASH MEMO.** Date. *1 - 4 -* .... 194*9*.

Sold to *Maflah Salch*. *D. Maimuna.*

Date	Quantity supld.			Description	Rate @	Amount	
	Scrs.	Pls.	C. Ft.			Shs.	Cts.
	6	05	–	*Boriti No 1*	25/-	156	25
	41	18	–	„ No 2	22/-	921	80
	58	07	–	„ No 3	20/-	1167	00
	38	02	–	„ No 4	18/-	685	80
	144	12					

TOTAL. *2930 = 85*

Received With Thanks.

for M. GHAUI.

25. *Above* Lamu, on the Kenya coast, was an alternative source of mangrove poles, and dhows that had not made the voyage to the Rufiji could call in here for them. Here mangrove poles are seen stacked on the beach at Lamu in 2000.

26. *Below* Mangrove poles lie stacked on Kuwait's waterfront in the 1940s.

27. This small *boum* in the Shatt al-ʻArab, *ca.* 1960, has taken on a cargo for distribution within the Gulf.

28. A Gulf trade dhow of the *balam* type under sail, *ca.* 1960.

29. Small cargo dhows used in the short-distance Gulf trade lie moored along the waterfront of old Kuwait in the 1950s.

FRESH WATER

30. Kuwait's first desalination plant was installed towards the end of the reign of Shaikh Mubarak (1896–1915) to ease the permanent water shortage in the town. This photograph of it was taken *ca.* 1916.

31. A water carrier fills his waterskins at the town's main reservoir in the 1950s. This was after a new desalination plant had been installed in 1953 by the Amir, Shaikh Abdullah Al-Salim, which put an end to the reliance on water brought by dhow and steamer from the Shatt al-'Arab.

32. By the 1950s, water was being hawked through the streets of Kuwait in handcarts as well as by the traditional porters carrying oil cans yoked over their shoulders.

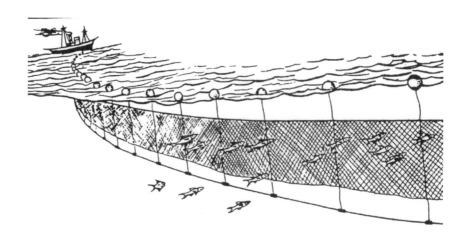

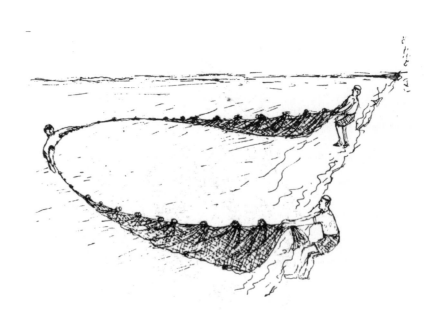

33. *Opposite, top* Long floating nets, or gillnets, such as this, with floats at the top and weighted at the bottom, were used offshore to catch pomfrets (*zubaidi*) and other species.

34. *Opposite, below* Seine nets, similar to gillnets, were operated from the beach. One end was secured to the shore while the other was taken out and round to enclose whatever fish might be close inshore.

35. *Below* A *hadhra*, or semi-permanent tidal fish trap, was a commonly used method of catching inshore fish, which would be swept into the enclosure by the ebb tide. They were made of reeds, palm fronds or bamboo canes.

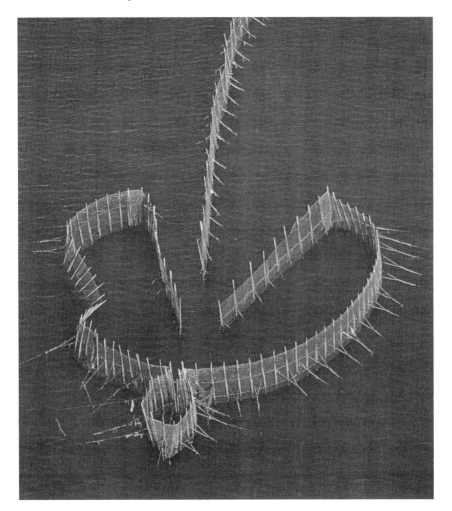

36. *Above* Cast-nets, made of fine mesh, were bell-shaped with weights round the edge. The fisherman would wade into shallow water and skilfully cast it onto the surface so that its full circumference was deployed. The net would then sink round the fish.

37. *Opposite* The *gargoor*, a dome-shaped cage with a small opening like a lobster pot, was a popular method of catching fish: the fish found entry easy through the funnel opening, but exit almost impossible.

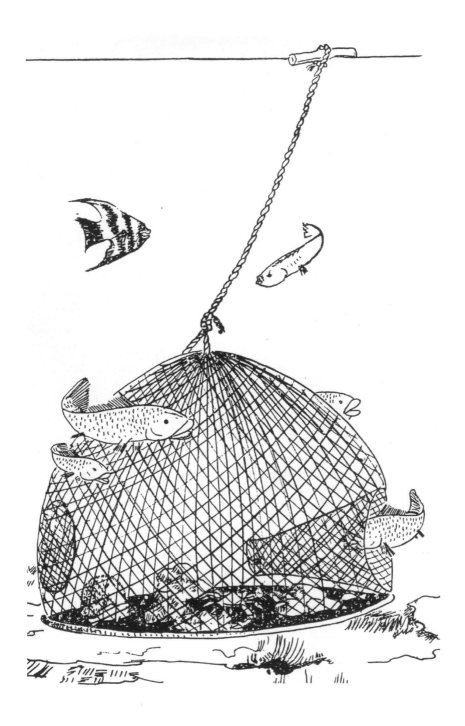

38. In the past made of palm basketry, in recent times *gargoor*s have been made of steel wire. Here they are seen loaded on a Kuwait fishing vessel, a *balam fudiri*, in the 1960s or 1970s.

39. *Above* Kuwaiti sailors sing and drum near a newly completed *boum* on Kuwait's waterfront, 1997.

40. *Below* Kuwaiti sailors performing on earthenware *aihla*s, water jars, in the 1970s.

41. *Above* Safat square, the large, protected open space inside the wall of the old town, was the site of Kuwait's trade with the desert hinterland, and was frequently bustling with Bedouin doing business. Here it is seen in the 1950s.

42. *Below* A bedouin tribesman and his camel transport brushwood (*arfaj*) from the desert to Kuwait town for firewood, *ca.* 1900.

43. Bedouin and camels in Safat square, Kuwait, 1950s.

rice, flour, dates, coffee, sugar, barley, tea, tobacco, cardamom and other spices, as well as a variety of textiles, weapons and ammunition, and household items.[8] While there were standard weights for each commodity, costs naturally varied from year to year: in 1920, for example, rice and flour cost about Rs 35 per bag, barley about Rs 8.5 per bag, sugar about Rs 77 per 1-*mann* bag, and coffee Rs 60 per 80-*ratl* bag.[9] In 1939, however, prices dropped sharply: rice to Rs 7 per bag, flour to Rs 5 per bag, dates to Rs 1.5 per *mann*, and sugar to Rs 8 per bag. Rising wages caused these prices to skyrocket again just three years later, to Rs 29.25 per bag of rice, Rs 29.5 per bag of flour, Rs 18 per *mann* of dates, and Rs 60 for a bag of sugar.[10]

12

Oil and its Impact on Kuwait's Maritime Economy

THE DISCOVERY OF OIL and its impact on Kuwait's various maritime pursuits has formed a thread running through this book, particularly as an explanation of why, by the new economic opportunities and income that oil brought, the ties that bound Kuwait to the sea were severed. So, although much of what will be said here has already been stated in one form or another, the purpose of this concluding chapter is to provide a synthesis presenting a clear picture of this seismic economic and social shift.

Though oil was discovered in commercial quantities in Kuwait in 1938, the outbreak of the Second World War prevented any from being exported until 1946, when the fighting stopped and tankers to transport it could once again be made available. The income and employment opportunities that followed quickly unravelled the traditional maritime economy of Kuwait, sector by sector, until, by the 1960s, its people had become so utterly reoriented away from their maritime livelihoods to the desert oil rigs and government jobs, that the sea had been rendered little more than a body of water to swim and fish in.

However, one sector had fallen apart even before the introduction of oil, in the face of an inimical force that few had foreseen. The pearling industry first showed its vulnerability in the early 1920s, when the less expensive

Japanese cultured pearl began to infiltrate the markets of India. By the mid-1920s, the effects of this competition were being felt by the Kuwaiti pearl merchants who, by 1929, were experiencing difficulties in selling off their season's catch. The impact of the Japanese cultured pearl was merely compounded by the worldwide economic depression that came with the 1930s and undermined the market for pearls in Europe and the United States. This is vividly illustrated by the experiences of pearl merchants (*tawwashes*) such as Husain bin 'Ali Al-Saif, his sons 'Ali and Yusuf, and his nephew Muhammad bin Shamlan Al-Saif, who made visits to Paris during 1930–32 to sell pearls that they had failed to find buyers for in Bahrain and Bombay. They failed in Paris too, and a letter survives from Muhammad to his father in Kuwait begging forgiveness for having burdened the family's resources with a journey that bore no fruit.[1]

By 1934 the pearl merchants of Kuwait had given up all hope of an upturn in the market for their pearls, and the next year far fewer pearling dhows set out than ever before. Many merchants found themselves in a financial bind, with most of their money tied up in pearls that were unsellable. Only a handful survived the crash, and the years up to 1945 saw scores declaring themselves bankrupt. One early survivor was Hilal Fajhan Al-Mutairi, who was able to weather the storm with the help of his date plantations on the Shatt al-'Arab and his property in Bombay and Bahrain, which had been acquired before the market disintegrated. He had even been able to sell Rs 3 million worth of pearls to the French pearl merchant, Albert Habib, just before the decline was being sharply felt in both Kuwait and Europe. He had had foresight, having heard early on that pearls were being cultured in Japan, and had tried in vain to warn his peers, many of whom refused to believe that pearls could be cultivated rather than just harvested from the sea. By taking precautionary measures he was able to survive the initial downturn in the market, and his death in 1937 shielded him from seeing the worst of its effects.

It should be borne in mind, nonetheless, that the market for natural pearls did not disintegrate all at once, but fell apart gradually. Some demand persisted among the Indian princely and upper classes, many of whose members continued to purchase pearls for ceremonial attire until well into the 1950s. In 1955, for example, a group of pearling *nakhodas* was able to sell

---

[1] Al-Shamlan 1975, vol. 2: 296; Al-Shamlan 2000: 167–75.

a season's catch for almost Rs 191,000, although this was the last sale of such magnitude.[2]

Hard on the heels of the downfall of the pearl market came the discovery of oil and the concomitant demise of all the other maritime trades. As oil revenue enriched both government and citizenry, new employment opportunities emerged that paid the lower levels of the labour hierarchy far more in guaranteed wages and offered a far easier life than did the uncertain profits and prolonged absences that had plagued the pearling industry and the dhow trade. *Nakhoda*s trying to plan voyages to India and East Africa soon found themselves without crewmen, as mariners opted for secure employment with the oil companies and elsewhere.[3] Because of the considerable profits still to be made from long-distance trading, many *nakhoda*s sought sailors from elsewhere in the Gulf, but soon gave in to the pull of the oil current.[4] In 1957, the last practising *nakhoda*, 'Isa Ya'qub Bishara, abandoned the business for good and joined the scores of his fellows taking up jobs in government. They sold their dhows to traders in other parts of the Gulf to be adapted for engines and put to whatever uses their new owners saw fit.

The demise of the dhow trade also sounded the death knell for maritime music, by making redundant its vital role in life at sea. However it did leave an indelible mark on later musical forms, and even today one can hear recordings by new groups whose music has been profoundly influenced by that of their fathers and grandfathers.

Lighterage and rock-carrying proved a little more tenacious than the long-distance dhow trade, but were ultimately destined for the same fate. Both activities endured until the port facilities in Kuwait were developed to accommodate the larger cargo ships. By 1959, upgrading of the port of Shuwaikh had progressed sufficiently to allow modern vessels to tie up at the docks to discharge their cargo, most of which by this point included cement and steel, modern building materials which were keenly adopted by Kuwaitis at large and rapidly supplanted the rocks, mud bricks and mangrove poles that had characterized Kuwaiti construction up till then. The development of port facilities also eliminated the need for lighters to

---

[2] Al-Shamlan 1975, vol. 2: 296.
[3] Shuhaiber 2003: 105–8.
[4] Among these one can include the Al-'Amiri group and that of Hamad bin Husain.

transport goods from ship to shore, so sealing the fate of the Hammal Bashi Company (the Transport and Discharge Company).

It was inevitable that the waning of the long-distance dhow trade should also drag down its complement, short-distance trading, which by the mid-1960s had all but fallen out of Kuwaiti control and into the hands of those who could still man and afford to run it. While the last Kuwaiti short-distance trading *nakhoda*, Yusuf Al-Hashil, embarked on his final voyage in 1965, there are still today numerous motorized dhows from the ports of Iran and Pakistan lining the creeks of Dubai and Sharjah, for example. None of these, however, are owned and operated by Kuwaitis, all of whom had disengaged from this sector by the mid-1960s.

As Kuwait's dhow trade dwindled, so too did its renowned dhow-building industry, once its chief glory. The drop in demand for dhows was just one of several factors conspiring to strangle this sector. Successive restrictions and then the ban imposed by the Government of India on the export of teak, for instance, rendered the procurement of building timber difficult, though not impossible. Then there was the gradual introduction of fibreglass and other new materials, which many traditional dhow builders simply lacked the expertise to use. While some shipwrights were still able to find work modifying existing dhows for engines for the fishing sector, this made up but a fraction of their previous workload. As demand for wooden vessels inexorably shrank, the sons of the *ostad*s and *qallaf*s opted for different career paths, preferring education and modern technical skills to the pursuit of what was coming to seem an archaic and outdated craft tradition. With the death of the last generation of dhow builders, then, came the disappearance of their historic industry.

Finally, the advent of oil to Arabia brought about the eclipse of the desert trade, as the flood of oil revenues into Saudi Arabia and the Gulf States, and the consequent development of ports, road systems, air transport and even, in the early 1950s, a railway from Dammam to Riyadh, rendered this sector obsolete. As early as the 1940s, many bedouin in eastern Saudi Arabia, while clinging to a lifestyle ostensibly resembling that of the past, were losing their dependence on the markets of Kuwait, and were turning instead to the economic opportunities, welfare benefits and markets developing in their own country.

In conclusion, one can clearly see how the introduction of oil wealth choked to death all of the maritime pursuits, with the exception of pearling, that had sustained the people of Kuwait for hundreds of years prior to the mid-20th century. The sole such activity to survive intact, if heavily modernized, has been fishing, and even that has long since passed into the hands of foreign businesses based in Kuwait. Kuwaitis themselves fish today not as a livelihood but as a pastime. All in all, life for most Kuwaitis has been transformed by oil from one of dire hardship and exploitation into one of material ease and comfort. In many ways an undeniable blessing, this has also been, in the eyes of many, a double-edged sword. Oil wealth, consumerist affluence and material security, with all their benefits, can at the same time exact a price in terms of social cohesion, political security, and the environment. More specifically, they have rendered obsolete, with obvious and irresistible force, an entire traditional system of manual skills, maritime knowledge, commercial practices and cultural forms built up over centuries. In doing so they have also consigned to the past, at a more subtle and profound level, the distinctive sense of human worth and dignity that formed such an essential part of Kuwait's unique maritime society and economy.

APPENDICES

Appendix A

The Pearling Law of May 1940

PRIOR TO THE CREATION of Kuwait's Legislative Council in 1938–39, the Emirate's pearling industry did not enjoy formal, written laws. Rather, it was structured by a complex set of unwritten customary rules and arrangements, all of which were recognized and adhered to by participants in the industry. It was only after the establishment of the Shura Council (which succeeded the short-lived Legislative Council) that legislators, inspired by legal reforms in the Bahraini pearling industry, formulated a set of laws which spelled out in very clear terms the rights and obligations of mariners, *nakhoda*s and merchants. The legislation was in large part a response to changes taking place within the industry: by the late 1920s, the competition brought on by the Japanese cultured pearl dealt the industry a blow that only worsened with the onset of the worldwide economic depression in the 1930s (see Chapter 3). Furthermore, when the laws were being formulated many divers were in the process of leaving pearling for wage-based work in the oil industry, a phenomenon that is reflected in the text itself.

In drafting the laws, the council members sought the assistance of experienced pearling *nakhoda*s and merchants alike. While legislators kept the interests of these two parties in mind, the resulting legislation also included a number of protections for mariners. These included *inter alia* protections against *nakhoda*s who forced the children of deceased divers to dive for them, the introduction of account books to clarify how much the diver owed or was owed, and the establishment of public institutions (e.g. the Department of Pearling Accounts) to oversee the industry. Some *nakhoda*s cancelled their divers' debts on their own initiative. This, however, was uncommon; many *nakhoda*s (for example those of the Abu Gammaz family) have preserved account books which still show outstanding debts by divers who have long since passed away.

One matter deserves further clarification: the one-third earnings *barwa* mentioned several times in the Pearling Law. As the author has related in Chapter 3, the *barwa* was a document that *nakhoda*s issued to mariners upon releasing them to the employ of another *nakhoda*. A *nakhoda* who could not afford to keep his divers or was unable to sail out during the pearling season would issue *barwa*s to his divers, asking whoever wanted to hire them to repay him the entire loan or, if he was planning on returning the following season or wanted to lower the hiring costs involved, some proportion of the debt. In some cases, the new *nakhoda* was asked to pay the entire amount to the old one; in others, he was instead asked to reserve one-third, one-quarter, one-fifth or one-tenth of the mariner's earnings towards the repayment of the debt. Other *barwa*s stated that the mariner was free of debt and could be hired by any *nakhoda* at no cost. Over time, an agreement emerged among *nakhoda*s whereby no *nakhoda* could hire another's divers without first seeing their *barwa*s and repaying the former *nakhoda* according to the terms dictated by him. This complex but largely informal system of overlapping rights and obligations was formalized under the laws presented here.

Understanding the pearling laws is no easy task for the uninitiated reader. The language of the legislation is full of idiomatic expressions as well as references to customary arrangements intelligible only to participants in the industry themselves and, to a much lesser degree, historians of the pearling industry. While an attempt has been made here to clarify ambiguities in the law, the industry's complexities, coupled with the fact that few of its participants are alive today, make the job of rendering the legislation comprehensible to the lay reader difficult at best. In translating the text of the laws, we have tried to remain as faithful as possible to the spirit of the wording, but have taken some editorial liberties to make the text as clear to the reader as possible. Those who wish to make use of the laws as a primary source are thus advised to refer to the original Arabic text rather than this translation.

Yacoub Yusuf Al-Hijji and Fahad Ahmad Bishara

The Pearling Law

Under the authority of Ahmad al-Jabir Al-Sabah, Ruler of Kuwait.

Further to the proposals submitted to us by the head of the Shura Council, and building on our desire to implement reform for the benefit of our country and people, we issue the following edict:

Article 1
This law shall be entitled the Pearling Law and comprises 51 articles.

Every mariner on a pearling dhow must present himself to his *nakhoda* half a month before the start of the season to help prepare the vessel. This applies to all mariners, whether at home or abroad; those with no legitimate excuse will be punished.

Article 2
Every mariner must follow the orders of his *nakhoda* during the pearling season, whether on land or at sea, and has no right to disobey him or to object to his instructions under any circumstances. In the event of insubordination or infringement of rules during pearl diving, the *nakhoda* is to bear witness against the offender – whether crew member or otherwise – and the case is to be brought before the ruler.

Article 3
If a diver receives a loan from a *nakhoda* and, without legitimate cause, fails to participate in the dive in question, he must repay the loan in addition to a settlement determined by the government at the end of the diving season.

Article 4

If a diver embarks with a *nakhoda* on a diving voyage and absconds from the vessel while at anchor at another port, his case will be brought before the ruler.

Article 5

If a mariner postpones or is late in joining his vessel by one month or more without legitimate excuse, the *nakhoda* may decide either to accept a payment in settlement, to be determined, or to loan him half the sum set for the season and despatch him to his vessel. If half the diving season or more has elapsed, then the diver must pay whatever settlement is determined.

Article 6

If the entire season elapses without the diver reporting for duty, then he must pay whatever settlement is determined.

Article 7

If a mariner deserts his vessel twice or more and is apprehended, he will not be released without bail being paid by a person responsible for him.

Article 8

If a mariner disobeys the orders of his *nakhoda* on land or sea, the *nakhoda* may choose either to pay him half the requisite loan for the season, or to take from him half what he has already loaned him, or to discharge him with a paper[1] stating that he must hand over to the *nakhoda* one-third of his earnings until his loan is repaid.

Article 9

Should a mariner fall ill at sea, the *nakhoda* is to take care of him and take him to a nearby place on shore. If the man is too sick to rejoin his vessel, the *nakhoda* is to ensure that he returns home. Upon returning home, the mariner is to see a doctor immediately and, on his recovery, is to return to his *nakhoda*.

---

[1] This paper will hereafter be referred to as the one-third earnings *barwa*, although the original text refers to it only as a *waraqah*, or document.

Article 10

If on his return home a mariner is found to be feigning his illness, he is to be punished forthwith and returned to his *nakhoda*.

Article 11

No amount demanded by the *nakhoda* in settlement shall exceed the amount set by the government as the standard loan to pearlers for that season.

Article 12

If a *nakhoda* hires a mariner whose *barwa* shows an obligation to pay a settlement to a another *nakhoda*, and the new *nakhoda* is unable to pay it, then the diver is to work off his debt to the first *nakhoda* during the following season. The second *nakhoda* has no right to ask the mariner to repay any debt owed to him until the first *nakhoda* is completely repaid.

Article 13

If the second *nakhoda* [referred to in Article 12] is unable to sail for the season and is unable to pay the amount owed to the first *nakhoda*, then the first *nakhoda* is to issue the mariner with a *barwa* allowing him to continue to work under the second *nakhoda* provided that the latter places no claim on the mariner's earnings, which are earmarked for the first *nakhoda*.[2]

Article 14

If a mariner borrows money from his *nakhoda* during the off-season, then he is compelled to take the loan advanced at the beginning of the season and go on the dive with that same *nakhoda*. He may not ask for a *barwa* in that year.

Article 15

All mariners working on the pearling dhow are under obligation to cover

---

[2] In this case, the mariner's "earnings" refer to the one-third earnings he would normally receive after payments are made to meet the terms of his discharge from the first *nakhoda*. The terms of discharge (i.e. repayment of the amount owed to the first *nakhoda* using one-third, one-quarter or one-fifth of the mariner's earnings) are clearly stated on the *barwa*s themselves.

for one another, the alive for the dead and the present for the absent, the only stipulation being that every mariner must be above the age of consent [i.e. an adult]. All participants must attend with signed and witnessed documents stating their eligibility, and no participant can ask to be released until everyone has completed their assigned task.

Article 16
No *nakhoda* can loan money to any individual crewman unless all crewmembers are present, or, in the case of there being absentees, in the presence of their legitimate representative(s). If such a loan is made without the consent of all crewmembers, then it is to be considered a private transaction.

Article 17
If a mariner dies during the dive and leaves assets other than his house, such assets are to be distributed among his creditors, including his *nakhoda*, in proportions commensurate to his debts to them. The house is to be dealt with according to the rules set out in Articles 18 and 19.

Article 18
If a mariner dies without an heir and leaves a house, then that house, if it was built with money borrowed from the pearling *nakhoda*, belongs to that *nakhoda* if he can provide proof to that effect. If the house was inherited or built with money from other sources, it is to be distributed among the mariner's creditors in proportions commensurate with his debts to them.

Article 19
If a mariner should die while in debt to his *nakhoda* and owning nothing but the house he lived in and which was paid for by money borrowed from the *nakhoda*, and if that house is occupied by his sons, then the sons may choose either to pay off their father's debt to the *nakhoda* or, when they reach the age of maturity, to dive for that *nakhoda* under the obligation to pay back their father's debt. If the house was built with money borrowed from elsewhere, the sons may choose either to pay off their father's debt immediately, or to wait until they are of age and then be held responsible for settlement of his debts.

Article 20

A pearling *nakhoda* may not advance a mariner, who is under an obligation to pay one-third of his earnings towards settling a debt, more than the amount set by the government each year; and the *nakhoda* must pay the one-third of the mariner's earnings to the issuer of the *barwa* at the end of the diving season without delay.

Article 21

If a *nakhoda* issues a mariner with a new paper stating that the latter owes him one-third of his earnings until his debt is repaid, and the mariner then joins a new *nakhoda*, the first *nakhoda* may not demand the return of the mariner until the second *nakhoda* is repaid whatever he advanced the diver, unless the first has valid pretext for doing so.

Article 22

If a *nakhoda* is unable to take part in a pearling voyage having bound a mariner carrying a one-third earnings *barwa*, then the *nakhoda* who issued the *barwa* is to send him to sail with whomever he pleases or issue a new *barwa* reflecting the changed situation. The *nakhoda* who was unable to participate thus relinquishes all rights over the mariner until the latter has repaid his debt to the previous *nakhoda*, who in the meantime is to pay one-third of the mariner's earnings to the *nakhoda* who was unable to participate.

Article 23

If the mariner referred to in Article 22 holds a one-third earnings *barwa* and has profits left over after his net earnings have been determined and after he pays one-third of his earnings to his previous (i.e. first in Article 22) *nakhoda*, then he is to give one-quarter of the remainder to the non-participating (i.e. second in Article 22) *nakhoda* or pay off Rs 5 of the debt he incurred from that *nakhoda*.

Article 24

If a financially hard-pressed *nakhoda* who has paid his mariners between Rs 10 and 15 is unable to recover the amount at the end of the season, then during the next season the mariners shall not be entitled to ask him for the official loan amount set by the government, but are to be advanced the amount set during the previous season or to pay off the amount loaned to them.

Article 25

If a mariner is unable to sail on a larger boat but finds a place on a smaller vessel or a [independent] *khammas* boat and is in debt to a *nakhoda* via the one-third system, then one-third of his earnings are to go to his *nakhoda* creditors, be they one or more.

Article 26

If a mariner possesses a one-third earnings *barwa* and fails to attend the dive (either with the *barwa*-issuing *nakhoda* or any other), then he is to pay the settlement appropriate to his case. Any dispute in this regard is to be brought before the ruler.

Article 27

If an independent diver sails with a vessel and receives an advance, however small, from the *nakhoda*, he has to then pay the *nakhoda* one-fifth of his net profits, unless the *nakhoda* agrees to a lesser sum or proportion. If the independent diver receives no advance from the *nakhoda*, then he is obliged to pay him one-tenth of his net profits. If, however, he owes a different *nakhoda* money, then the diver is only allowed to keep one-tenth of his profits, the remainder being used to pay off his debts.

Article 28

If a *nakhoda* rents a vessel from its owner at a rate of one-tenth of the season's net profits [i.e. instead of the usual one-fifth] and takes on an independent diver, then the diver is to pay the *nakhoda* one-twentieth of his net profits, unless he and the *nakhoda* previously agreed that he would pay the usual one-tenth.

Article 29

If an assistant [*tabbab*] dives headfirst [i.e. without the help of a hauler or weight] and God blesses him with good fortune, then his *nakhoda* has a right to one-tenth of the price of his catch when it is sold, as well as whatever expenses the assistant incurred over the course of the voyage. If he dives with the aid of a weight, then the *nakhoda* is to receive one-tenth of the catch's value, expenses incurred by the assistant, and an apprentice's [*radif*'s] share. If he dives with the assistance of a hauler, then the *nakhoda* has a right to the one-tenth, expenses incurred and a hauler's share.

Article 30
If a *nakhoda* hires a pearling dhow [at the standard rate of one-fifth of the net profit of a diving season, paid to the dhow's owner] and spends money on whatever repairs and maintenance may be necessary, and he then finds that these expenses exceed the dhow-owner's share, then the latter owes the difference to the *nakhoda* and is to subtract it from the amount to be collected the following season. If the dhow-owner decides to sell his vessel, then he is to pay the *nakhoda* the amount he owes. If the boat sinks, then the debt to the *nakhoda* is cancelled. However, if the damage to the vessel is repairable, the debt remains.

Article 31
If a *nakhoda* hires a boat for a fixed sum, all expenses incurred in repairs and maintenance of the boat are to be subtracted from the sum owed to the ship-owner. The *nakhoda*, however, must be able to show an itemized invoice detailing the amount spent on the vessel.

Article 32
Every mariner employed by the government or the oil company must pay the pearling commissioner 15 percent of his monthly wage.[3]

Article 33
A *nakhoda* whose mariner is employed by anyone other than the government or oil company has the choice either of accepting money in settlement of the mariner's debt, or of forcing the mariner to dive for the pearling season.

Article 34
If a merchant loans a *nakhoda* money to be repaid from the earnings of the

---

[3] This amount was to be allotted to cover debts the mariners had previously incurred to their *nakhoda*s.

season's catch and the *nakhoda* is unable to repay the loan, the merchant is not entitled to repayment from the *nakhoda*'s property in compensation. In such a case, he may take the *nakhoda*'s mariners and his vessel. If that is insufficient to cover the amount of the loan, then the merchant may make up the shortfall from the *nakhoda*'s property with the exception of his residence.

Article 35
If a *nakhoda* mortgages his house or any other property to a creditor through an official mortgage deed [*sanad*] and is unable to repay the amount, he must sell the property specified in the deed and is not entitled to offer his mariners or vessel in settlement instead.

Article 36
Whoever advances money to a pearling *nakhoda* must take care of the affairs of the dive, including loaning whatever money is necessary, purchasing provisions [for consumption] on land or at sea, the mariners' shares [after making the standard deductions] and the amounts due to *nakhoda*s of mariners working on a one-third earnings *barwa*, but is not entitled to any surplus. For his part, the *nakhoda* must give his creditor all of the proceeds from the pearls' sale [both during and after the voyage] and is not to keep anything from him. If he does keep anything from him, he has no right to ask him for whatever was left over from the crew's share of the proceeds or from the one-third earnings *barwa* mariners, and will be punished [by the ruler].

Article 37
Any mariner wishing to settle his account with a *nakhoda* must do so within one month following the end of the pearling season [i.e. the *guffal*]. Should he fail to do so within this period, he is not entitled to make the request again until the following year. If, during this period, a person [i.e. another merchant or *nakhoda*] legally claims the vessel and its crew [in settlement of a debt], then all of the mariners' debts (and other debts) are settled, and the claimant has no right to hold the *nakhoda* responsible for any debts in any way.

Article 38

During the sale [of the catch], the *nakhoda* is not entitled to stipulate to the pearl merchant [*tawwash*] that any portion of the money be set aside from the proceeds of the sale for himself, his son or any of his relatives. If he is found to have done so, then the money must be returned and added to the overall value of the catch. Furthermore, the *nakhoda* may not claim any of the pearls themselves as part of his share of the profits.

Article 39

A *nakhoda* must inform his mariners of the value of the catch immediately on sale.

Article 40

A *nakhoda* who gives his mariners money for the spring or the return dive [*al-khanjiyyah* and *al-raddah*] following the publication of this law, may not claim repayment of such money if the return dive proves unprofitable for the mariners.

Article 41

If a *nakhoda* is owed by his mariners any money advanced to them for the return dive prior to the publication of this law, then the amount will be settled by the ruler. However, if a mariner sails with a *nakhoda* to whom he is in debt and the amount of the advance is earned during the trip, then the *nakhoda* may take that sum to cover the mariner's debt.

Article 42

If a mariner possessing a one-third earnings *barwa* is hired by another *nakhoda* – for pearling, short-distance trade or otherwise – then whoever hires him must settle the full amount of the debt. If a *nakhoda* hires a mariner without asking for his paper then he will be admonished and must settle the amount. If he repeats this action then he will incur a fine in addition to the amount to be settled.

Article 43

If a [long-distance trading] *nakhoda* taking a mariner to Zanzibar or Malabar is 15 days late in returning him for the beginning of the pearling season, then he must pay that mariner's pearling *nakhoda* the required sum of money [i.e. the *fasil*[4]]. In this case the pearling *nakhoda* may choose to either accept the sum or take the mariner on for the season. If the mariner is late for the second voyage of the pearling season, then the same rule applies.

Article 44

If a long-distance trading *nakhoda* wants a mariner to join his crew, the mariner's paper from his pearling *nakhoda* must give him permission to go on such a voyage. If the *nakhoda* does not ask to see the mariner's papers and the latter does not arrive in time to sail with his pearling *nakhoda*, then the long-distance *nakhoda* must pay the pearling *nakhoda* one-and-a-half times whatever settlement is determined by the government and shall be disciplined by the ruler. If the pearling *nakhoda* does not sail that season, then the long-distance *nakhoda* must pay the settlement applying to a mariner who fails to sail with his pearling *nakhoda*.

Article 45

If a mariner arrives from a long-distance trading journey in time for the pearling season, his [long-distance] *nakhoda* is not entitled to ask him to stay on board to go to Basra to unload cargo.

Article 46

If the [pearling] *nakhoda* of a mariner who is 15 or more days late for the pearling voyage because of a long-distance trading voyage, chooses not to sail [to the pearl banks], then he has the right to choose either to take on the mariner, or to take half the loan [that would have been paid to mariner], to be paid by the long-distance trading *nakhoda*.

Article 47

No person owed a debt has the right to raise a complaint against a mariner after the latter has taken a loan from his *nakhoda*, but must raise the issue with the ruler beforehand.

---

[4] The *fasil* is a sum equal to that set by the government as the standard amount *nakhoda*s can loan to mariners.

Article 48

If a mariner is made 15 or more days late for the dive by his long-distance trading duties and is a crew member among the mariners who are to sail out later than the rest, then his [pearling] *nakhoda* can choose either to take him on or to accept in settlement a sum equal to the average loan for that season, which is to be paid by the long-distance trading *nakhoda*.

Article 49

If a mariner holds a one-third earnings *barwa* and then hires a boat [to go diving], then one-third, one-fifth, or a half of his share's value shall be deducted from his earnings, whether he is a mariner or a *nakhoda*.

Article 50

No *nakhoda* may hire a mariner already attached to another *nakhoda* if the mariner is not in possession of his account book from the pearling accounts manager, recording his credits and debts. Both *nakhoda*s must go before the accounts manager to settle the amount.

Article 51

The Shura Council must execute our order here promulgated on 22 of al-Rabi' al-Thani 1359 AH, corresponding to 29 May 1940.

President of the Shura Council,
Abdullah al-Salim Al-Sabah

Ruler of Kuwait,
Ahmad al-Jabir Al-Sabah

Appendix B

Addendum to the Pearling Law of 1940

ONLY DAYS AFTER the Shura Council's promulgation of the Pearling Law of 1940, Kuwaiti *nakhoda*s and merchants with experience in the pearling industry reviewed the legislation and highlighted the need for further clarification on a number of points. To satisfy these experts, the Shura Council added two more articles and issued them as an addendum to the 1940 legislation.

It has been decided that two new articles are to be added
to the Pearling Law:

Article 1
Should a mariner die after setting out on a pearling voyage – even if after only a short period – then he is entitled to one full share, just as if he had survived until the end of the season.

Article 2
If a [pearling] *nakhoda* is late in setting out and one of his mariners wants to sail with an earlier crew, then the *nakhoda* can either advance the mariner the loan and have him sail with him, or advance him the loan and let him sail on the earlier vessel. In the event of the *nakhoda* being incapable of

sailing that season, he must issue his mariners with a one-third earnings *barwa*.

(Decided in the Shura Council session of Tuesday, 6 Jumada Al-Awwal, 1359 AH)

Clarification

The crewmen on board a pearling dhow are called the mariners, and they can be divided into three categories:
The diver (*ghais*), who collects the oysters from the sea bed.
The hauler (*saib*), who is responsible for pulling up the diver.
The apprentice (*radif*), the boy responsible for performing all kinds of services to *nakhoda* and crew.

As for the profits of the catch, they are to be distributed as follows:
One-fifth is deducted and goes to the owner of the dhow.
The cost of provisions is then deducted.
The remainder is then divided as follows:
    3 shares to the *nakhoda*
    3 shares to each diver
    2 shares to each hauler
    1 share to each apprentice

On the vessel there should be a young boy (*tabbab*) to perform such light tasks as handing out provisions and water and the like. He has no share in the profits of the voyage, but shall go through the flesh of the oysters after the mariners have done so and can keep what pearls he finds.

Should there be an independent diver on board who has not taken a loan, he is to pay half one-fifth of the value of his catch to the *nakhoda* and the share of his puller. If he does take a loan, then he is to pay one-fifth of the value of his catch to the *nakhoda* and the share of his puller, and that is after he has paid his share of the cost of the dhow's provisions.

Appendix C

The Long-distance Trade Law of 1940

THE CORNERSTONE of Kuwait's maritime economy, the long-distance trade sector was less complex both financially and contractually than the pearling industry. The primary difference between the two, in terms of both finance and contractual rights and obligations, was that mariners employed on long-distance trading dhows rarely incurred any steady debts, as they were paid out of the freightage that the *nakhoda* received. Also, because of the less seasonal nature of the sector, long-distance trading *nakhoda*s faced less pressure to repay whatever debts they incurred from merchants – and not all of them had to, as many were in good enough financial standing to finance their own voyages. While *barwa*s were employed in the long-distance trading sector, only mariners who also worked on pearling dhows ever encountered them. Those who worked exclusively on long-distance trading dhows were paid the difference between their share of the freightage and the expenses they incurred during the voyage, and needed a *barwa* only to confirm their debt-free status when changing vessel or *nakhoda*.

The Long-Distance Trading Law of 1940 was promulgated under circumstances similar to those of its pearling counterpart. While this sector of the maritime economy had not experienced a decline similar to that of the pearling industry, the economic depression of the 1930s and the emerging oil industry all placed strains on long-distance trading. Moreover, the transport boom that Kuwaiti dhows experienced during the Second World War necessitated the establishment of a formal legal framework to structure the sector and minimize the number of disputes that could arise. With the help of *nakhoda*s who had long experience in long-distance trade – one of the most famous of whom was the *nakhoda* 'Abd al-Latif Al-'Uthman – legislators issued the long-distance trade law only days after issuing the pearling law.

Yacoub Yusuf Al-Hijji and Fahad Ahmad Bishara

The Long-distance Trade Law

I, the ruler of Kuwait, Ahmad Al-Jabir Al-Sabah, having given consideration to proposals submitted to us by the head of the Shura Council, and building on our desire to implement reform for the benefit of our country and people, issue the following edict:

Article 1
This law shall be entitled the Long-Distance Trade Law and comprises 62 articles.

Article 2
The *nakhoda* must be alert at all times and aware of the conduct of his sailors, and must himself be of sound character and good behaviour.

Article 3
The dhow owner must appoint an experienced mariner to assist the *nakhoda* and take his place when necessary. The dhow owner is not exempt from this requirement unless it is impossible to find an appropriate deputy.

Article 4
If the dhow runs into trouble or encounters unexpected danger, the *nakhoda* must do everything in his power to save the vessel. The mariners must attend to their duties and follow the *nakhoda*'s orders, whether he orders the rescue of their own vessel or of any other. Anyone failing to do so faces punishment at the hands of the government.

Article 5

Neither the first mate (*muqaddimi*) nor any other mariner may oppose the destination agreed for the voyage between the *nakhoda* and the owner of the capital or merchandise.

Article 6

The first mate may not leave the dhow at any time except with the permission of the *nakhoda* if he is present. If he chooses to disembark in the absence of the *nakhoda*, he shall be deemed to have committed a violation. If he amasses a number of violations or disobeys the *nakhoda*, the *nakhoda* may choose to demote him to the rank of sailor, and compel him to forgo his additional shares.

Article 7

Should a mariner fail to obey the orders of the first mate or carry out his duties, the *nakhoda* has the right to subtract whatever he deems the appropriate sum for such a violation from the mariner's share of the profits, and to distribute it among his fellow crewmen. The opposite shall also apply: if a mariner carries out more than his share of work and distinguishes himself in his job, the *nakhoda* may award him a bonus to be taken from the gross freightage collected on the journey.

Article 8

The helmsman (*sukkuni*) must be endowed with good eyesight, a sound understanding of maritime matters, a familiarity with the area, an ability to manage the rudder and adjust the vessel's course, and alertness to unexpected changes in wind speed and direction. When the vessel is at anchor, he is to carry out his duties when they are requested of him and when he is responsible for them. When the vessel is at sea and someone else is at the helm, he is to join his peers in whatever work is required of him. Should he fail to do so, he shall be deemed derelict in his duties and shall be liable to punishment according to Article 6.

Article 9

Once the gross profits of the voyage are known, the cost of provisions and other port expenses as well as the navigation bonus for the *nakhoda* (the *ta'lum*) are to be subtracted. The remainder is to be divided into two halves, one for the vessel and the other for the mariners, the latter being divided between them. Whatever extra shares are to be awarded are to be derived from both the vessel's half and the mariners' half according to the following rules:

1. Extra shares for two of the helmsmen, the *nakhoda*, the navigator, the *nakhoda*'s deputy, the first mate and other sailors shall all be deducted from the vessel's half.

2. Extra shares for the longboat's owner, the singer (*nahham*) and the cook shall be deducted from the mariners' half.

Article 10
If the vessel sails to Basra and some of the crew are absent for most or all of the loading process, those present and bearing the burden of taking on the cargo are to be awarded bonuses, the nature of which is to be determined and guaranteed by the *nakhoda*.

Article 11
Should a mariner fall ill en route to Basra, the *nakhoda* must take him to the nearest doctor and see that he is cared for right away. If the doctor prescribes an extended convalescence for the man, the *nakhoda* must return him to Kuwait and give him a share of the profits of the trip commensurate with the amount of time and labour expended by him.

Article 12
Should a mariner break a bone in the course of his maritime duties, he is to be given a full share of the profits irrespective of the amount of time he has spent on board. Furthermore, the *nakhoda* is to exert every effort to render him aid, taking him to a hospital if one exists not too far off the vessel's course, and to afford him all he needs in terms of medical, transportation and food expenses provided this amount does not exceed Rs 200. On his recovery, the man is to make his way back to his vessel by means of any dhow available, Kuwaiti or otherwise. If he is unable to do so, he is to find a passage home by dhow or steamship.

Article 13

If the vessel is at Basra and a crewman requests permission to disembark to procure items on his own account, the *nakhoda* is to determine the duration of his leave. If the sailor fails to return on expiry of his leave, so that the vessel has to leave port without him, then he shall forfeit his share of the profits and shall be deemed to be in debt. However, if the sailor is sent ashore by the *nakhoda* and the vessel departs before his scheduled return to it, the sailor is to use his best endeavours to catch up with it in any way possible, and, should he manage to do so, then his rights are secured. If he is sent ashore by the *nakhoda* and overstays his scheduled return, then the *nakhoda* is to use his discretion in estimating the man's pay at the end of the voyage.

Article 14

If a mariner on board a long-distance trading dhow dies at Basra, he is to be awarded a whole share of the proceeds of the outward-bound leg of the voyage. If he dies on the return voyage, he is to be awarded a whole share of the entire trip's proceeds.

Article 15

If a mariner goes missing without good reason in one of the ports of India, Yemen or East Africa, he forfeits any right to the profits of the voyage and shall remain indebted to the *nakhoda* to the sum of the amount he borrowed for the voyage. If he goes absent on the return voyage from Muscat to any one of the Gulf ports, then he shall be entitled to one share of the profits, minus a sum calculated on the basis of the average amount he would have earned per day according to his full share, multiplied by the total number of his days absent. Should the *nakhoda* have to hire another crewman to take his place, the latter's hire is to be paid by the absent mariner, who shall also face punishment by the government. This applies to vessels at sea; in the case of absenteeism in Kuwait, the workman's pay is to be equal to the average wage paid to workmen on the dhows.

Article 16

If a vessel anchors in port temporarily for an indeterminate period, the crew must stay on board for the entire time that the *nakhoda* is ashore and must be present upon his return. If one of the crew goes absent and the *nakhoda*, upon returning, is compelled to leave port, then he is entitled to leave the man behind, and shall not be liable for any of his expenditures aside from those incurred in trying to return to his vessel. If the man fails to return, he shall be deemed to have deserted and so forfeited his share of the profits of the voyage. He shall owe the *nakhoda* the amount of his advance and may be liable to punishment by the government.

Article 17

If, having left port, a laden vessel runs into difficulties compelling the *nakhoda* to unload the cargo, he is entitled to do so without consulting the owners of the cargo, though he must inform them of his decision immediately, whether via their agents, by mail or by telegraph. If it is difficult for him to do so, he has the right to act for the benefit of both parties. Whatever expenses are incurred in loading and unloading is borne by the cargo owner; the dhow's owner is only to pay for what was spent on his dhow.

Article 18

The *nakhoda* must see to it that maintenance and repairs are carried out to his vessel after the discharge of every full cargo. If maintenance and repairs take more than twenty days, the merchant to whom he is under contract shall be entitled to consign his goods to another vessel. In the case of Article 17, the merchant must pay freightage to the dhow owner for the unloading of the goods at the place of discharge. If the merchant wishes to delay receipt of his goods until the arrival of the vessel then its owner must comply with this request, for which he will receive full freightage. Goods damaged beyond recall by water can be discounted from the freightage; those only partially damaged are to be inspected and assessed accordingly. Freightage for goods such as wood and coir is to be paid in full; anything missing is to be paid for from the freightage receipts of the *nakhoda*.

Article 19

If a merchant and dhow owner agree on the transport of dates or any other kind of merchandise from Basra, then the merchant has 30 days to send the cargo from the time the vessel clears the customs house at Faw if the vessel is loaded, or from the time it unloads its cargo and is ready to load the new cargo. If the 30 days elapse, the merchant is to pay 4 Annas [in demurrage] to each mariner for every day spent loading the ship.

Article 20
If a merchant and dhow owner agree on the transport of cargo to a particular port and the merchant changes his mind after the dhow owner has already begun preparations, the merchant must pay a cancellation fee equal to half of the agreed freightage. If the merchant has begun to load the vessel with cargo but fails to complete the process within the agreed timescale (as specified in Article 19), he must pay the freightage in full. If the dhow owner fails in this regard without good reason, he must repay half the freightage to the merchant.

Article 21
No dhow owner is entitled to take on additional cargo without first consulting the merchant whose cargo he is carrying.

Article 22
If a merchant contracts a vessel to transport cargo from one foreign port to another, he must ensure that it is loaded according to the duration specified in Article 19. If it is not, then he must pay half the freightage and the dhow owner is free to do as he pleases with his vessel.

Article 23
If a merchant contracts a vessel to ship cargo from Basra to Aden or any other port in that direction and, when the vessel reaches Muscat, he decides to change its course to India, he must pay the full Aden (or other port) freightage. If it was agreed [in the *satami*, or manifest] that the merchant has the right to choose which course to take, then he is to pay the freightage to India only. If, once the vessel reaches India, the merchant again decides to send it to Aden, then he must pay the difference between freightage to India and freightage to Aden and the *nakhoda* can choose whether or not to accept it.

Article 24
If a merchant contracts a vessel to ship his cargo to the ports of India, and

there was no agreement [between the merchant and the *nakhoda*] as to where in India or how much freightage the *nakhoda* was entitled to, then the value of the freightage paid will be equal to that paid to the majority of the *nakhoda*s [that season]. If the vessel discharges the cargo in the port of Kutch or Bhavnagar, then the *nakhoda* is to receive 12.5 percent more than the average freightage paid that season.[1]

Article 25

If a *nakhoda* is forced to jettison cargo to save the vessel and the lives of those on board, either in port or at sea, he must use his best judgment in such a crisis. What remains of the cargo after jettisoning is to be charged for freightage, with the proceeds being distributed evenly amongst the transporters; no freightage is chargeable on cargo lost. No cost is to be incurred by the dhow owner or the crew, and what applies to Kuwaiti merchants in this respect applies equally to foreign merchants.

Article 26

If several sailors fall ill or die and the *nakhoda* is forced to hire replacements from another vessel, each hired hand is entitled to a full share of his previous vessel's profits and one-quarter of a share of the profits of his new vessel. The remaining three-quarter share on his new vessel is to go to the vessel he has left, the value of the share to be determined by the latter vessel's *nakhoda* according to the distance the man has sailed on it.

Article 27

The crewmen have no right to ask the *nakhoda* to pay their shares until they reach Kuwait, at which point their accounts will be settled. Anyone jumping ship without permission shall be deemed absent without leave and shall be dealt with according to Article 6. Even if a sailor wishes to pay off his debt to the *nakhoda* and to leave the vessel at a particular port, he has no right to do so and must stay with the vessel until it reaches Kuwait. The *kharijiyyah* [loans advanced to mariners while at other ports] of mariners in India and other ports, however, is recognized as done according to local custom.

---

[1] Transporting cargo to Kutch and Bhavnagar earned more in freightage because these ports were more difficult to sail to and unload cargo at.

Article 28

If a *nakhoda* hires a foreign sailor without a letter of attestation of his debt status[2] and on the man's promise that he is free of debt and, when in port, the man's previous *nakhoda* spots him and wants his loan repaid, the *nakhoda* hiring the man has no right to him unless he agrees to cover his debt for him. If the man stays with the new *nakhoda*, the latter must take into account the money owed to the previous *nakhoda* and subtract it from the hired hand's net share from the voyage. If the man is hired and his previous *nakhoda* fails to approach him before the settling up of accounts at the end of the voyage, then any request for repayment shall be null and void. The same applies equally to Kuwaiti mariners serving on foreign vessels.

Article 29

If a mariner has sailed on board a vessel and has taken money from the *nakhoda*, and subsequently finds that a claim is laid against him, the claimant has no right to delay or impede him from carrying out his sailing duties.

Article 30

If a mariner agrees to take ship with one *nakhoda* and accepts money from him, and then does the same with another *nakhoda* with the intention of playing them off one against the other, he will be subject to punishment later and only the first *nakhoda* shall have a legitimate claim to him.

Article 31

If a mariner sails to India and, upon returning to Kuwait, wishes to receive his share of the voyage proceeds and not sail the second leg of the voyage, he has the right to do so. If he is found to have made a profit during that voyage, it must be handed over to him; if, however, he is found to still owe money [because he borrowed more than the value of his share], he can choose either to pay off the debt or to serve on the vessel again.

Article 32

If a vessel destined for Basra puts in at Kuwait and a crewman wishes to disembark there, he has no right to do so. All mariners must stay with their

---

[2] "Letter of attestation of his debt status": a *barwa*; see preamble to the Pearling Law of 1940 in Appendix 1 for an explanation of this.

vessel until it reaches its destination and its cargo is fully discharged. Permission to disembark may be given at Basra if the vessel is committed to another outward voyage, and those wishing to do so can then be taken back to Kuwait.

Article 33

A *nakhoda* has no right to hire a sailor without a letter of attestation as to his debt status [a *barwa*; see note 2 above] from his previous *nakhoda*. If the letter attests that the man owes money, the *nakhoda* must pay the debt and then come to an agreement with him over repayment, with no variation in the amount. If the mariner's letter certifies him to be free of debt, and then having been hired he receives a demand for repayment of an old debt, such a demand is null and void as from the enactment of this law.

Article 34

If a mariner is requested for an early (*harfi*) voyage because of what he owes to a *nakhoda* and is too late in his return from a pearling voyage to join the vessel, then the pearling *nakhoda* must pay the *nakhoda harfi* an agreed sum in compensation.

Article 35

If a trading *nakhoda* relieves a mariner of his pearling debt by paying the amount stated in the mariner's letter of attestation [a *barwa*; see note 2 above], and the mariner then wishes to sail with the pearling fleet, the mariner may not do so without a letter of attestation from his trading *nakhoda*. If a pearling *nakhoda* hires the mariner without such a letter of attestation, he shall be liable for payment of the sum paid on behalf of that mariner by the trading *nakhoda*.

Article 36

A *nakhoda* must settle all his mariners' accounts once work on the vessel has been completed, and must pay any overdue share of the freightage, to whomever is owed one, at the same time as payment of shares of the profit for that voyage.

Article 37

If a mariner leaves a *nakhoda*'s crew with a letter of attestation [a *barwa*; see note 2 above] declaring a debt to be payable and then, having taken ship with another *nakhoda*, gets into debt with the latter and wants to leave his crew too, then he is liable for his debts to both *nakhoda*s. If he returns to his first *nakhoda*, then he must settle his debt with his last *nakhoda*.

Article 38

If a mariner with debts to settle with two or more *nakhoda*s asks permission from one of them to let him stay in Kuwait rather than sail and the *nakhoda* agrees without notifying the others, then he is held responsible to the others for that mariner's debts to them.

Article 39

If a mariner has a debt remaining from a trading voyage and then sails with a short-distance trader or on a "return" (*raddah*) pearling trip, whoever takes him on must pay a sum in settlement of the debt commensurate to the amount of the loan determined for that season.

Article 40

In the event of collision or shipwreck, whether in harbour or at sea, leaving crewmen marooned in a foreign port, all Kuwaiti vessels at hand are to distribute the men amongst themselves according to their capacities and assist them in returning to their home port.

Article 41

In the event of a vessel having the good fortune to happen upon jetsam with a trade value, such as ambergris or other commodities, one-fifth of its value is to be given to the dhow owner and the rest is to be distributed amongst the crew in proportion to their entitlement to shares.

Article 42

In the event of a vessel having the good fortune to come across useful flotsam such as timber, anchors and other gear, whether afloat or submerged, their value is to be added to the freightage. If their owner subsequently identifies himself, half of their value is to be given to him if they were found a great distance away. Such items found close to Kuwait are to be distributed among the mariners in proportion to their efforts in recovering them.

Article 43

If a mariner comes into conflict with his fellow crewmen or his *nakhoda*, all men on board must assist the *nakhoda* in disciplining him. Should his decision go against keeping the man on board, the *nakhoda* is entitled to disembark him at any port of his choosing, and if there is a Kuwaiti vessel there it is to take him. The offender's share of the profits shall then be determined according to the length of his service on the vessel before the clash.

Article 44

If a mariner takes money [a *kharjiyyah* loan; see Article 27 above] from his *nakhoda* and fails to attend to his duties, then the *nakhoda* has the right to discharge him and take from him what he is owed if the mariner owed no previous debts to other *nakhoda*s. If the mariner owed debts to other *nakhoda*s by way of a *barwa*, then he [the mariner] is responsible for them.

Article 45

If a mariner deserts a trading vessel when it is at sea away from Kuwait and he owes money to a pearling *nakhoda*, the latter has no right to hold the trading *nakhoda* responsible for the debt because the mariner is absent without leave from the both of them. If someone claims a mariner as a debtor or a slave, then the *nakhoda* is to expend his efforts in defending the mariner. However, if the mariner is forcibly taken away from him, then the *nakhoda* cannot be held responsible by anyone.

Article 46

If a mariner deserts his vessel or commits a crime meriting redress or imprisonment – either on the vessel or in a foreign port – and the government of that foreign port orders him to pay a fine, then he alone is to pay it. If he is imprisoned and his vessel leaves him behind, he is to receive a share of the freightage proportional to the amount of time he has spent on board.

Article 47
If a mariner is fined or jailed in consequence of actions in defence of his vessel, the fine and whatever other costs he incurs are to be added to the vessel's expenses. In the event of his incarceration delaying his return to his vessel, his share of the profits shall not be affected thereby.

Article 48
In the event of a *nakhoda* hiring a pilot to guide him into port, the pilot's wage shall be added to the vessel's expenses unless the *nakhoda* has previously agreed with the merchant that such an expense be covered by the latter.

Article 49
If the vessel suffers an accident at sea and as a result needs repairs or provisions, the *nakhoda* has the right to take action without having to consult anyone.

Article 50
If a mariner stays behind or goes missing in a foreign port and wishes to make his voyage home on board one of the vessels there, he is not entitled to request any share of profits from that voyage, though the *nakhoda* may decide to give him a tip.

Article 51
If a vessel sustains impact damage to its hull or gear, whether out at sea or near the coast or a port, and it needs to be towed by a sailing vessel or steamship, then the cost incurred in so doing is to be deducted from the freightage collected.

Article 52
If a laden vessel heading for Basra is towed into port by a tugboat in order to hasten the process and neither the *nakhoda* nor the dhow owner gave instructions for this to be done, the cost incurred is to be covered by the merchant. If either the *nakhoda* or dhow owner hired the tug, then the cost is to be deducted from the gross freightage of the voyage, as is done with provisions.

Article 53

If a dhow owner settles his mariners' accounts and gives them all *barwas* certifying them to be clear of debt, and then later realizes that there was a surplus or deficit in the accounts, the matter is to be settled between both parties even if a full year has passed [since the discovery of the deficit or surplus].

Article 54

If a merchant contracts a *nakhoda* to carry money for him and it later comes to light that there is money missing, the *nakhoda* is to be held responsible. Furthermore, if the *nakhoda* carries money for a merchant on the latter's word that the amount was handed over in full and he later discovers this not to have been the case, the *nakhoda* shall be held liable for the difference.

Article 55

If a mariner and his sons, brothers or paternal cousins sail together as a party, pooling their efforts, and they find themselves in debt at the end of the voyage, then they are all held responsible for it. If one of them is incapacitated or dies, another is to take his place. If a dispute breaks out amongst them, whatever money they have earned is to be distributed among them proportionally to their share of profits and their status on board (such as helmsman or first mate), the only stipulation being that they all agree to such a division.

Article 56

When a vessel is in a foreign port, no more than half the crew may leave it at any one time, the other half having to stay on watch. No mariner apart from the *nakhoda* is permitted to spend the night ashore.

Article 57

A *nakhoda* not in possession of his own vessel must comply with the requests of the dhow's owner in its management, provided such requests do not infringe the law as set out herein and do no harm to the crew. Furthermore, the *nakhoda* shall not spend more money than is necessary to cover the mariners' loans and the vessel's expenses, and any money left over is to be handed over to the dhow owner or his agent.

Article 58

The *nakhoda* must declare in the manifest [*satami*] that he and his fellow cargo-carriers are subject to the laws of Kuwait.

Article 59

In the event of fire on board the vessel, goods that are fire-damaged or destroyed shall be treated in the same way as jettisoned goods.

Article 60

In the event of their vessel being sold due to a rise in its value or by decision of its owner, then the crewmen are each to be given one share commensurate in value to that of an average season's round trip profits. The owner must also see to it that the crewmen are given their passage home either by sail or, if no such option exists, by steam.

Article 61

If the vessel is forcibly sold or otherwise disposed of because it is no longer fit to sail, the *nakhoda* must see to it that his mariners are returned to their home ports. If it is sold after the season is over, the *nakhoda* must settle the mariners' accounts and may deduct the cost of their passage home.

Article 62

The head of the Shura Council is enjoined to execute the orders herein.

Promulgated on 28 Rabi' al-Thani 1359 AH, corresponding to 4 June 1940 AD.

Head of the Shura Council
Abdullah al-Salim Al-Sabah

Ruler of Kuwait
Ahmad al-Jabir Al-Sabah

Appendix D

Common Weights, Measures and Exchange Rates

Weights

1 ton: 1,016 kilograms

1 *mann* of dates: 75 kilograms: 168 *ratl*s, or pounds (UK)

1 *mann* (in customs houses): 125 pounds

1 *mann* of flour, barley or rice: 139 pounds

1 *mann* of fabric: 55 pounds

1 *mann* of fats, oils and plaster: 11 pounds

1 *mann* of sugar only: 222 pounds

1 *kara*: 1·5 tons/40 *mann*s

1 *mithqal* (used in weighing pearls): 5 grams

1 Indian *tola* (used in weighing gold): 2·25 *mithqal*s

1 *itgar* (usually of sand): 2,800 pounds

1 *haqqah*: 1·25 kilograms

1 *fraselah* (used in Somaliland): 20 pounds (UK) or 35 pounds (Berbera)

1 *kontal* (used in Somaliland; Eng. Quintal; Ar. *qintar*): 100 kilograms

1 *yaluq* (used in Oman to signify a package of dates): 50 kilograms

1 *gallah* (of dates): 0·5 *mann*s: 37·5 kilograms (also called a *nisfiyyah*)

Distances

1 *jireeb* (a unit to denote an area of land in Basra containing roughly 100 date

palms): approx. 3, 680 square metres

1 *zam* (used in calculating distances travelled by ships): 12 miles

1 *darr* (used in calculating distances in terms of time): 10 days

Lengths

1 *dhra'*: 19 inches, or roughly 1·5 feet

1 *ba'*: a fathom/ 6 feet

1 *waar*: 1 yard/ 3 feet

1 *tasu*: 1 inch

Sizes

1 imperial gallon: 4 litres

1 *zila* (tin can used in trading waters, or oils, fats and molasses): 4 imperial gallons

1 *mdawwar*: unit used in measuring quantities of grass

1 *kurijah*: 20 pieces

1 *gandi*: 10 cubic feet plus 29 cubic inches

1 *sodrum* (of sand): 100 cubic feet

Average exchange rates (during the 1920s and 1930s)

1 Indian Rupee (R): 16 Annas

1 Anna: 4 Bezas

1 French Franc: Rs 1–2

1 British Pound (Sterling): Rs 15–18

1 British Pound (Gold): Rs 70

1 Swahili Shilling: 18–10 Annas

1 Maria Theresa Thaler: Rs 1·25; 5 Persian Krans

1 Persian Kran: 7 Annas

1 Irani tuman: Rs 3

1 Iraqi Dinar: Rs 12

1 Ottoman Lira: Rs 6·5–8

1 Mujaidi: Rs 2·5

1 Turkish Pound: 0·9–1 British Pound (Sterling); 13 Rs

1 Turkish Lira: 1–1·1 British Pounds (Sterling): 100 Piastres

1 German Crown: Rs 2

1 United States Dollar: Rs 2

1 Mexican Peso: Rs 5

GLOSSARY

Glossary

NOTE: A fuller list of Kuwaiti seafaring terminology can be found in the glossary of Al-Hijji, 2001: 146–55, and many pearling terms appear in the glossary of Al-Shamlan, 2000: 178–83. This glossary follows the system of transliteration used in Al-Hijji, 2001.

'abrah An open-sea crossing.

'Adān The coast south of Kuwait City.

aḥaimir A squall in the Gulf and Arabian Sea.

aihla Earthenware drum.

'alqah A short rope used to make a loop on the *zaibal* above the diver's lead or stone weight, in which he put one foot, to make his descent to the seabed. The *'alqah* was fastened at its top to the *zaibal* by the *qalṭah*, allowing it to be adjusted to the size of the diver's foot.

'Akkāz A small island in Kuwait bay surrounded by a coral reef.

amīr al-ghawṣ Admiral of the pearling fleet.

al-'arḍah al-baḥriyyah Literally, "sea performance"; the drumming and singing of Kuwaiti sailors celebrating their arrival home.

al-'arḍah al-barriyyah Literally, "land performance"; the Arabian tribal war dance.

azyab The north-east wind prevailing in the Arabian Sea near the Gulf of Aden, from September to April.

'azzāl A pearl diver not required to share his catch with others on board the same boat, but instead paying for his food and for a place on deck.

bā' A fathom, the unit used to measure depth at sea.

baghlah An old long-distance cargo dhow with an ornate transom stern, later largely replaced by the *boum*.

baḥḥār Mariner, sailor, seaman.

balam A type of small dhow used in pearling and fishing.

balam fūdirī A double-ended fishing boat, with stem- and sternpost at the same angle to the keel.

bāqah Vaka, *Albizia molveanna*, a timber used for gunwales and bulwarks.

baqqārah An old type of double-ended dhow, now extinct, with a raking bow and vertical sternpost to hold a detachable rudder. Similar in form to a *battīl*.

barrāsū Stay-behinds in India (see Chap. 4 p. 15).

barwa A letter of attestation formally recording a mariner's debts to previous *nākhodā*(s).

baṭn "Stomach" or middle-sized pearls retained by the middle pearl sieve.

battīl An old type of pearling dhow, no longer seen, with a pointed stern like a *baqqārah* and a raking, fiddle-shaped prow, later replaced by vessels such as the *sanbūk*.

bāwarah Anchor.

bild A plumb-line used in dhow building.

bīṣ Keel of a vessel.

boum A common deep-sea dhow typical of Kuwait and other Gulf ports, distinguished by its long, straight stempost, pointed stern and yoke steering.

boum qiṭā' A small *boum* built for short-distance trade in the Gulf.

boum saffār A large, deep-sea cargo *boum*.

būkah A type of pearl.

bulbus The rope tied to the sweep, for the diver to hold onto between dives.

chandal, also *kandal* Mangrove poles.

chau A unit used in measuring and evaluating pearls.

chisab A type of date grown in the Shatt al-'Arab.

dabūsah A storage room or cabin beneath the poop deck.

dairī A type of date grown in the Shatt al-'Arab.

dallāl A middleman or commercial broker.

dānah A pearl of the largest size and highest price.

dayyīn Pearl diver's oyster basket.

dhayl Pearls retained in the lowest sieve (i.e. the smallest pearls) during measurement and valuation.

dūbah Barge.

dūsān A type of date grown in the Shatt al-'Arab plantations.

faḍīlah A mariner's net profit at the end of a voyage; the value of his share of the gross profits of the voyage after loans and expenses have been deducted.

fainī Pali wood, *Palaquium ellipticum*, used in dhow building for the topmost plank of the hull.

fallāhīn Peasants, agricultural labourers.

fanaṣ Jack wood, *Artocarpus heterophyllus*, a type of timber used for making the ribs of the dhow hull.

fann Poon, *Calophyllum inophyllum*, a timber used for dhow masts.

fann baḥrī "Maritime art"; a general term used to refer to sea shanties and chants.

fāṣil A sum equal to that set by the government as the standard amount *nakhoda*s are permitted to loan to mariners.

faṭām A nose clip used by divers to prevent entry of sea water.

gallāf, qallāf Carpenter; dhow builder; shipwright.

gallah A package of dates, weighing roughly 37.5 kilograms.

gandī, also *kandī* Unit of size and weight used in India for selling timber.

gargoor A domed, cage-like fish trap, today made of wire mesh, and formerly of palm frond basketry.

gari Cart for timber, in India.

Gāz Bandar The dhow docks at Karachi.

ghaiṣ Diver.

al-ghawṣ The pearl dive; the pearl-diving season.

al-ghawṣ al-'azzāl A freelance pearl diving venture performed by a diver on his own account, bringing his own hauler and joining the crew of a conventional pearling boat on his own terms.

al-ghawṣ al-kabīr The "great dive": the main pearl diving season, from June to September.

al-ghawṣ al-khammās An independent pearl dive, carried out by divers and haulers banding together on their own account, pooling their resources and hiring their own boat.

al-ghawṣ al-khanjiyyah The unofficial spring pearl dive, usually in April, before the main pearl diving season.

al-ghawṣ al-munawwar Informal pearl diving in shallow water close to shore, with no need of a hauler. Anyone prepared to jump off a boat, or to wade out, could do it.

ghawwāṣ Pearl diver

guffāl, quffāl The close of the diving season.

guful, quful The end of a sea shanty's stanza.

ḥadāq, pronounced *ḥadāg* Fishing.

ḥaddād A blacksmith.

ḥaddadī A type of sea shanty sung by sailors in their leisure time.

ḥaḍrah A fence-like fish trap set up along the beach below the high tide mark, to catch fish on the ebb tide.

hair A pearl bank.

ḥallāwī A type of date grown in the Shatt al-'Arab plantations.

ḥalwa A sweetmeat based on date syrup and ghee; the Muscat variety is the most popular in the Gulf.

ḥammāl bāshī A large, short-distance trade dhow of the *boum* type, a larger version of the *tashālah*; a *boum*-type barge used in transporting goods from dhows and steamers to the docks in Kuwait.

ḥāmour Brown-spotted Grouper, *Epinephelus coioides/tauvina*, the most popular species of fish caught in the Gulf.

ḥandah A type of sea shanty sung by sailors while working.

ḥarfī The first deep-sea voyages to India at the beginning of the *safar* or long-distance trading season.

ḥasbā A large single pearl.

ḥaṭab Timber used in dhow building.

hayb A crowbar; a long iron pole used to pound rocks in the sea for transport to and sale on shore, for building.

hindāsah A brass quadrant with a plum-line used in dhow building.

hourī, hūrī A dugout canoe imported from India.

humbah Mango wood, *Mangifera indica*, used for making the blades of dhow sweeps.

ḥumayyir A squall in the Gulf and Arabian Sea; diminutive of *aḥaimir*.

huwairiyyah A small, raft-like rowing boat made of palm fronds lashed together with cord (also called *shāshah*, *warjiyyah*).

ʿīdah The main rope holding a pearl diver, which he holds while diving and by which he is drawn up again by his hauler.

ʿiddah A net used in fishing.

igmāsha, iqmāsha A single pearl.

igmāsh, iqmāsh The season's catch of pearls.

īqāʿ A drum used to set the basic rhythm for sea songs.

irfaʿ "Get up!"; the command to down tools and finish the day's work in the dhow-building yard.

istihlāl The beginning of a sea song.

itbābah A large collection of pearls; the season's catch of pearls.

jaddūm Adze.

jālbūt A small to medium dhow with an upright stem and transom stern used in pearl diving, and also for short-distance trade.

janqilī, jangalī Indian Laurel, *Terminalia tomentosa*, used to make dhow keels.

kabrail A type of tile made in Mangalore, India, and transported by dhow to the Swahili coast of Africa.

kandī, also *gandī* Unit of size and weight used in India for selling timber.

karrānī Vessel's bookkeeper.

khaḍrāwī A type of date grown in the Shatt al-'Arab plantations.

khaiṭ String, cord.

khammārī A type of drum, or a shroud.

khārijiyyah A loan advanced to a mariner in a foreign port.

khashab Literally, "wood"; a term used colloquially in Kuwait to refer to dhows.

khatfah The act of raising sails and setting out on a voyage; the shanty that accompanies it.

kraik A species of seabird that, when spotted, indicates that land is near.

kūrijah A score (20 pieces), usually of timber.

kweek, kwīk A unit for measuring timber, equalling approximately 1 cubic foot.

lu'lu Pearl

mafraṣ A channel between two islands or coral reefs.

maid Largescale Mullet, *Liza macrolepis*, a popular type of fish in the Gulf.

mann A unit for weighing dates, equalling two *gallas*, or roughly 75 kilograms.

maṭāf A sand bar near Bandar Daiyir, on the Iranian shore of the Gulf south of Bushire.

mawwāl A type of folk poem.

minṭāïj, mintayī Benteak, *Lagerstroemia lanceolata*, a type of timber used in dhow building.

mirwās A small hand drum used in sea songs.

mithqāl A unit of weight used in the pearl business.

muʿallim Pilot, navigator.

muhailah A type of river craft with a high curved stempost, used in Iraq and on the Shatt al-ʿArab waterway.

mujaddimī A boatswain, first mate.

Mukhā The Red Sea port (in Yemen) famous for its coffee, also known as Mocha.

musābalah The term, from the noun *musābil*, used to refer to doing business with the Arab tribespeople of the Arabian hinterland of Kuwait.

muthammin An expert in pearl valuation.

muṭrāsh A round-trip voyage from Kuwait to an Indian Ocean port during the long-distance trading season.

muṭrib Musician.

muwailī A type of Arabian poetry used in the composition of sea shanties.

nagrour, naqrūr Silver Grunt, *Pomadasys argenteus*, a popular species of fish.

nahhām A professional singer, a chanter, on board a dhow.

al-nahmah Singing.

nākhodā, or *nawkhudhā* Dhow captain.

nākhodā harfī "Start of season" *nākhodā*; one who made an early departure from the Shatt al-ʿArab with a cargo of dates.

nākhodā jaʿdī A *nākhodā* who did not own his own vessel.

al-naql Lit. "transport": lighterage from ship to shore; rock-carrying.

naql al-māʾ Water transport.

noul, nōl Freightage

nuwaibī Silver Croaker, *Bairdiella chrysoura*, a popular species of fish in the Gulf.

ostād, ustād A master shipwright; head of the dhow-building team.

'oud, 'ūd Lute.

qallāf, gallāf Carpenter; dhow builder; shipwright.

qaltah A cord used to fasten the *'alqah* to the *zaibal*, enabling the *'alqah* to be adjustable.

qarat Egyptian Thorn, *Acacia nilotica*, a hard timber used for making the sheaves of pulley blocks and the pins and shafts round which the sheaves rotate.

Al-Qawāsim The ruling tribe of Ras Al-Khaimah and Sharjah (U.A.E.), who became a maritime power in the Gulf and Oman during the late 18th and early 19th centuries, before the series of maritime truces imposed by the British on the shaikhdoms of the southern Gulf. Until that time, regarded as pirates by the British.

qilātah, or *ḥuṣṣa* A share of the profits of a pearling or long-distance trading voyage; mariners are allotted one or more of these, depending on their job.

qitā'ah Short-distance trade between the ports of the Gulf.

quffāl, guffāl The close of the diving season.

guful, quful The end of a sea shanty's stanza.

Al-Qurain "The Two Horns", the old name of Kuwait.

rabbāt The last line of a stanza in a sea shanty.

radīf An apprentice boy on a pearling boat.

rā'īs al-sālifah A member of the merchant community who, as the head of a group of others, was appointed by the ruler or selected by other merchants to arbitrate in commercial disputes.

rās "Head" or "top": the pearls retained in the upper sieve (i.e. the largest pearls) during weighing and valuation.

ratl A unit used to measure weight that can vary from port to port. In the Gulf, it is roughly equivalent to 1 lb (i.e. one UK pound).

rattī A unit of value of pearls.

rūznāmeh, rozenāmeh Captain's log book.

sabīl An act of charity; a benefaction such as a fountain free for public use.

al-safar "Voyaging": long-distance sea trade; the annual deep-sea voyages to India, South Arabia and the East African coast

saʿī A commission on sales.

saib A pearl diver's hauler on board a pearling boat.

sāj Teak, *Tectona grandis*, the main timber used in dhow building.

sakkūnī A dhow's quarter-master.

salaf Money advanced to a sailor before a voyage.

samrah A musical gathering arranged by a dhow's crew aboard their ship during their leisure time.

sanad A legal deed, e.g. a mortgage deed.

sanbūk A type of dhow with a transom stern, used in Kuwait as a pearling dhow.

sanginī Sea songs performed after coating a dhow's underside with a mixture of lime and animal fat.

ṣarnāyī A wind instrument used in sea songs.

satamī Cargo manifest.

Al-Sawāḥil "The Coasts", the term used to denote the Swahili coast of East Africa.

sāyir A type of date grown in the Shatt al-ʿArab plantations.

shailah A sea song performed while working.

shalmān A tree branch used in dhow building; a crook of timber; a rib.

shamāl The north wind that blows in the Gulf.

shamshūl Shorts worn by pearl divers to protect them from jellyfish (also called *ṣirwāl*).

shāshah A small, raft-like rowing boat made of palm fronds lashed together with cord (also called *huwairiyyah*, *warjiyyah*).

shiʿm Yellowfin Black Seabream, *Acanthopagrus latus*, a popular species of fish found in the Gulf.

shimāmīzī Swahili term for the head of a mangrove pole-cutting crew in East Africa.

shinyālī A sweet made of dates, flour and ghee, prepared in a dhow on approaching land.

shuʿī A small to medium-sized transom-sterned dhow used for fishing and pearling, with a curved bow.

shūnah A mixture of powdered lime and animal fat applied to the dhow's underside to protect it from ship worm (teredo).

siḥtīt, siḥteet The smallest and least valuable pearls.

ṣil Fish oil applied to dhows while beached to protect them from the sun.

sinyār "Follower"; unskilled learner navigator under the guidance of an experienced one.

suhailī The south-west monsoon winds.

sukkūnī Helmsman of a dhow.

tabbāb A young apprentice on a pearling dhow.

ṭabbākh A cook.

ṭabla A common type of drum used in musical performances.

tājir A merchant.

taʿlāh The return; the homeward-bound a dhow's leg of the voyage.

taʿlūm A bonus paid to the *nakhoda* if he also acts as navigator.

ṭār A type of drum used in musical performances.

ṭāsah A sieve used in sorting and assessing pearls.

tashālah A short-distance cargo dhow; a small, shallow-draught *boum*.

tawāhū Sailors staying behind in India (v. Chap. 4 p. 15)

ṭawwāsh A pearl merchant.

thulth al-makadda One-third of a mariner's net earnings.

tibrāh A generic name given to a pearl bank renowned for the quality of its pearl oysters.

ṭiraiḥ Salted or dried meat or fish.

tūlah A tola, a unit of weight used in measuring gold or perfume.

tuwaisah Brass drum.

warjiyyah A small, raft-like rowing boat made of palm fronds lashed together with cord (also called *huwairiyyah, shāshah*).

wādī The tax levied on goods exported from Kuwait to the Arabian hinterland, and collected at a customs station near the Safat market area; the customs station itself.

yāmāl A type of sea shanty.

zāhdī A type of date grown in the Shatt al-'Arab plantations.

zaibal, zībal A rope weighted with a stone, used by pearl divers to carry them down when diving.

zubaidī The Silver Pomfret or Butterfish, *Pampus argenteus*, a popular species of fish in the Gulf and especially in Kuwait.

Zubārah An old seaport, now abandoned, on the north-west coast of Qatar, which used to be pearling port and which played an important role in the establishment of the 'Utūb in the Gulf.

zuhairī A type of Arabian poetry used in the composition of sea shanties.

zuhairiyyah An oarsman's shanty.

Bibliography

ARABIC SOURCES

'Abd al-Mughni, A. (1987, 2nd ed.), *Al-iqtisād al-Kuwaitī al-qadīm* ("The Old Economy of Kuwait"), Damascus: self-published

Al-Azmah, Faisal (1945), *Fi bilād al-lu'lu'* ("In the Land of the Pearl"), Damascus: self-published

Al-Bakr, Muhammad Ya'qub (2001), *Al-ḥadāq* ("Fishing"), Kuwait: Center for Research and Studies on Kuwait

Al-Daikan, Ghannam (1995), *Al-īqā'āt al-Kuwaitiyya fi-l-ughniyya al-sha'biyya* ("The Kuwaiti *īqā'* in the Folk Song"), 2 vols. Kuwait: National Council for Culture, Arts and Letters

Al-Dhuwaihi, Abdullah (2001), *Al-Najdīyūn wa-l-baḥr* ("The Najdis and the Sea"), Riyadh: self-published

Doukhi, Yusuf Farhan (1984), *Al-aghānī al-Kuwaitiyya* ("Kuwaiti Songs"), Doha, Qatar: Markaz al-Turath al-Sha'bi li-Duwal al-Khalij al-'Arabi

Faras, 'Abd al-Hamid Salih (2007), *Quṣṣat al-mā' qadīman fi dawlat al-Kuwait* ("The Story of Water in Old Kuwait"), Kuwait: self-published

Al-Ghunaim, Abdullah Yusuf (1998), *Kitāb al-lu'lu'* ("The Book of the Pearl"), Kuwait: Dar al-Basha'ir

Al-Hatim, Abdullah Khalid (1980, 2nd ed.), *Min huna bada'at al-Kuwait* ("Kuwait Began from Here"), Kuwait: self-published

Al-Hijji, Yacoub Yusuf (1998, 2nd ed.), *Ṣināʿat al-sufun al-shirāʿiyya fī-l-Kuwait* ("Dhow-Building in Kuwait"), Kuwait: Center for Research and Studies on Kuwait

—— Al-Hijji, Yacoub Yousef, ed. (2003), *Rozenāmat al-nawkhidha ʿĪsā Yaʿqūb Bishāra* ("The Logbook of Nakhoda ʿIsa Yacoub Bishara"), Kuwait: Center for Research and Studies on Kuwait

—— (2005), *Nawākhidhat al-safar al-shirāʿī fī-l-Kuwait* ("Long-Distance Trading Nakhodas in Kuwait"), 3rd ed., Kuwait: Center for Research and Studies on Kuwait

Al-Ibrahim, Yaʿqub Yusuf (2003), *Min al-shirāʿ ilā al-bukhār* ("From Sail to Steam"), Kuwait: Al-Rubaiʿan Publishing and Distribution

Al-Isfahani (1968), *Bilād al-ʿArab* ("Land of the Arabs"), Riyadh: Dar al-Yamama

Al-Jasim, N. (1980), *Baladiyyat al-Kuwait min khamsīna ʿāmmān* ("Fifty Years of Kuwait Municipality"), Kuwait: Municipality of Kuwait

—— (2000), *Qadhāyāt fī al-tārīkh al-siyāsī wa-l-ijtimāʿī li dawlat al-Kuwait* ("Issues in the Political and Social History of Kuwait"), Kuwait: self-published

Al-Jasim, N., and Al-Khususi, B. (1982), *Tārīkh ṣināʿat al-sufun fī al-Kuwait* ("History of Dhow-building in Kuwait"), Kuwait: Kuwait Foundation for the Advancement of Science

Malik, Imam A. (2005), *Al-Muwaṭṭaʾ* (copy of the foundational Maliki work on jurisprudence, written on Failaka Island in AD 1682), Kuwait: Center for Research and Studies on Kuwait

Al-Mannaʾi, Sultan (1886), *Ḥisāb wa-awzān al-luʾluʾ* ("Pearl Weights and Calculations"), Bombay: self-published

Al-Mattar, S., *et al.* (2006), *Asmāk al-zubaidī* ("Zubaidi Fish"), Kuwait: Center for Research and Studies on Kuwait

Mylrea, C. S. G. (1997), *Al-Kuwait qabl al-naft,* Arabic translation of Mylrea's manuscript "Kuwait before Oil" (see below), Kuwait: Al-Qurtas Publishing, 1997

Al-Nabhani, Khalifa bin Hamad (1949), *Al-tuhfa al-Nabhāniyya fī tārīkh al-Jazīra al-ʿArabiyya* ("The Nabhani Masterwork on the History of the Arabian Peninsula"), 12 vols., Cairo: Al-Matbaʿa al-Mahmoudiyya al-Tijariyya

Al-Qabas, daily newspaper

Al-Qina'i, Yusuf bin 'Isa (1988), *Ṣafḥāt min tārīkh al-Kuwait* ("Pages from the History of Kuwait"), 5th ed., Kuwait: Dhat al-Salasil

Al-Qitami, 'Isa (1924), *Al-mukhtaṣar al-khāṣ li-l-musāfir wal-ṭawwāsh wa-l-ghawwāṣ* ("A Handbook for the Long-Distance Trader, the Pearl Merchant and the Pearl Diver"), Kuwait: self-published

—— (1976), *Dalīl al-mihtar fī 'ulūm al-biḥār* ("Guide for the Perplexed to the Science of the Seas"), 4th ed., Kuwait: self-published

Al-Rashaid, 'Abd al-'Aziz (1926), *Tārīkh al-Kuwait* ("The History of Kuwait"), 2 vols., Baghdad: 'Asriyyah Press

Al-Rifa'i, Hussa Zaid (1985), *Aghānī al-baḥr* ("Songs of the Sea"), Kuwait: Dhat al-Salasil

Al-Rumi, Ahmad al-Bishr (1996), *Mu'jam al-muṣṭalaḥāt al-baḥriyya fī-l-Kuwait* ("Dictionary of Maritime Terminology in Kuwait"), Kuwait: Center for Research and Studies on Kuwait

"*Ṣafḥāt min tārikh Al-Kuwait*" ("Pages from the History of Kuwait"), television series, Kuwait Television (1966)

Al-Shamlan, Saif Marzuq (1975), *Tārīkh al-ghawṣ 'ala al-lu'lu' fī-l-Kuwait wa-l-Khalīj al-'Arabī* ("The History of Pearl Diving in Kuwait and the Arabian Gulf"), 2 vols., Kuwait: self-published

Al-Siadan, H. (1993, 3rd ed.), *Mawsū'at al-Kuwait al-mukhtaṣira* ("The Concise Encyclopaedia of Kuwait"), Kuwait: self-published

Al-'Umari, Mubarak Amro (1999), *Zuhairiyyāt al-Dhuwaihī* ("The Al-Dhuwaihi Zuhairi Poems"), Kuwait: self-published

Al-Zayyani, Rashid (1998), *Al-ghawṣ wa-l-ṭawāsha* ("Pearl Diving and Selling"), Bahrain: Al-Ayyam li-l-Nashr

OFFICIAL AND ARCHIVE COMPILATIONS

Arab Gulf Cities, ed. Richard Trench, 4 vols., Farnham Common, UK: Archive Editions, 1994

Arabian Gulf Intelligence: Selections from the Records of the Bombay Government, New Series, no. XXIV, 1856, compiled and edited by R. Hughes Thomas, Bombay: Bombay Education Society Press, 1856.

Reprinted with an introduction by Robin Bidwell, Cambridge: Oleander Press, 1985

Kuwait Political Agency: Arabic Documents, 1899–1949, ed. Michael Asser, 13 vols., Slough, UK: Archive Editions, 1994

Lorimer, J. G. (1908–15; reprinted 1986), *Gazetteer of the Persian Gulf, Oman and Central Arabia*, 7 vols., Farnham Common, UK: Archive Editions

Persian Gulf Administration Reports, 1873–1957, 11 vols., Farnham Common, UK: Archive Editions, 1989

Persian Gulf Précis, 1801–1905, ed. J. A. Saldanha, 8 vols., Calcutta: Superintendent of Government Printing; reprinted Farnham Common, UK: Archive Editions, 1987

Persian Gulf Trade Reports, 1905–1940, ed. Penelope Tuson, 8 vols., Farnham Common, UK: Archive Editions, 1987

Political Diaries of the Arab World: Persian Gulf, 1904–1965, ed. Robert Jarman, 24 vols., Farnham Common, UK: Archive Editions, 1990/1998

Records of Kuwait, 1899–1961, ed. Alan de L. Rush, 8 vols., Farnham Common, UK: Archive Editions, 1989

Records of the Persian Gulf Pearl Fisheries, 1857–1962, ed. Anita Burdett, 4 vols., Farnham Common, UK: Archive Editions, 1995

Water Resources in the Arabian Peninsula, 1921–1960, ed. Anita Burdett, 2 vols., Farnham Common, UK: Archive Editions, 1998

SOURCES IN ENGLISH

Abdullah, Thabit (2000), *Merchants, Mamluks and Murder: the Political Economy of Trade in Eighteenth-century Basra*, Buffalo, NY: SUNY Press

Abu Hakima, Ahmad Mustafa (1983), *The Modern History of Kuwait, 1750–1965*, London: Luzac & Co.

—— (1988), *History of Eastern Arabia, 1750–1800: The Rise and Development of Kuwait, Bahrain and Wahhabi Saudi Arabia*, London: International Book Centre

Arabian Gulf Intelligence: Selections from the Records of the Bombay

Government, New Series, no. XXIV, 1856, compiled and edited by R. Hughes Thomas, Bombay: Bombay Education Society Press, 1856. Reprinted with an introduction by Robin Bidwell, Cambridge: Oleander Press

Bowen, Richard LeBaron (1951), "Marine Industries of Eastern Arabia", New York: *Geographical Review*, 41

Buckingham, James Silk (1829), *Travels in Assyria, Media and Persia*, London

Byford, Cecil (1935), *The Port of Basrah*, Iraq: Port of Basrah Directorate

Carter, Robert, and Crawford, Harriet (2002), "The Kuwait–British Archaeological Expedition to as-Sabiyah: Report on the Third Season's Work", *Iraq* LXIV, pp. 1–13

—— (2006, unpublished), "Maritime Interactions in the Arabian Neolithic", report submitted to the Department of Antiquities and Museums, Kuwait

Dickson, H. R. P. (1983, 3rd ed.), *The Arab of the Desert*, London: HarperCollins

Donkin, R. A. (1998), *Beyond Price: Pearls and Pearl-fishing: Origins to the Age of Discoveries*, Philadelphia: American Philosophical Society

Facey, William (1979), *Oman: A Seafaring Nation*. Muscat: Ministry of Information

—— (1992), *Riyadh: The Old City*, London: Immel Publishing

Facey, William, and Grant, Gillian (1998), *Kuwait by the First Photographers*, London: I. B. Tauris

Fattah, Hala (1997), *The Politics of Regional Trade in Iraq, Arabia and the Gulf, 1745–1900*, Albany, NY: SUNY Press

Al-Hijji, Yacoub Yusuf (2001), *The Art of Dhow-Building in Kuwait*, Kuwait: Center for Research and Studies on Kuwait, and London: London Centre of Arab Studies

Hopper, Matthew (2006), "The African Presence in Arabia: Slavery, the World Economy and the African Diaspora in Eastern Arabia, 1840–1940", Unpublished PhD dissertation, University of California, Los Angeles

Hornell, J. (1945), "The Pearling Fleets of South India and Ceylon", London: *Mariner's Mirror*, 31, pp. 214–30

Ives, Edward (1773), *A Voyage from England to India in the Year MDCCLIV* [1754], London: Edward and Charles Dilly

Jones, Felix (1839), "Extracts from a Report on the Harbour of Grane (or Koweit), and the Island of Pheleechi … November 1839", in *Arabian Gulf Intelligence: Selections from the Records of the Bombay Government*, New Series, no. XXIV, pp. 51–4

Kemball, Lt. A. B. (1845), "Memoranda on the Resources, Localities, and Relations of the Tribes Inhabiting the Arabian Shores of the Persian Gulf, submitted to Government on the 6th January 1845", in *Arabian Gulf Intelligence: Selections from the Records of the Bombay Government*, New Series, no. XXIV, pp. 91–119

Khouja, M. W., and Sadler, P. G. (1979), *The Economy of Kuwait: Development and Role in International Finance*, London: Macmillan Press

Manesty, Samuel, and Jones [Brydges], Harford (1790), "Report on the Commerce of Arabia and Persia" in *Persian Gulf Précis, 1801–1905*

Martin, E.B. and C. P. (1978), *Cargoes of the East: The Ports, Trade and Culture of the Arabian Seas and Western Indian Ocean*, London: Elm Tree Books

Mylrea, C. S. G. (1951), "Kuwait before Oil", unpublished memoir written between 1945 and 1951, held in the Middle East Centre Archive, St Antony's College, Oxford. Tr. and published in Arabic, 1997 (see above)

Niebuhr, Carsten (1792), *Travels through Arabia and Other Countries in the East*, 2 vols, Edinburgh. Reprinted 1994, Reading: Garnet Publishing

Palgrave, W. G. (1865), *Narrative of a Year's Journey through Central and Eastern Arabia*, 2 vols., London: Macmillan

Pelly, Lewis (1863–64), "Remarks on the Tribes, Trade and Resources around the Shoreline of the Persian Gulf", *Transactions of the Bombay Geographical Society* XVII, Bombay

—— (1865a), "Account of a Recent Tour around the Northern Portion of the Persian Gulf", *Transactions of the Bombay Geographical Society*, XVII, Bombay

—— (1865b), "A Visit to the Wahabee Capital, Central Arabia", London: *Journal of the Royal Geographical Society* XXXV, pp. 169–90

—— (1866), *Report on a Journey to the Wahabee Capital of Riyadh in Central Arabia*, Bombay. Reprinted 1978, Cambridge: Oleander/Falcon

Al-Shamlan, Saif Marzooq (2000), *Pearling in the Arabian Gulf: A Kuwaiti Memoir*, translated by Peter Clark, London: London Centre of Arab Studies

Sheriff, Abdul (1987), *Slaves, Spices and Ivory in Zanzibar*, London: James Currey

Shuhaiber, Suhail (2003), "Social and Political Developments in Kuwait prior to 1961", in *Kuwait: The Growth of a Historic Identity*, ed. B. J. Slot, London: Arabian Publishing

Slot, B. J. (1998), *The Origins of Kuwait*, 2nd ed., Kuwait: Center for Research and Studies on Kuwait

—— (2003), ed., *Kuwait: The Growth of a Historic Identity*, London: Arabian Publishing

—— (2005), *Mubarak Al-Sabah: Founder of Modern Kuwait, 1896–1915*, London: Arabian Publishing

Tibbetts, G. R. (1971), *Arab Navigation in the Indian Ocean before the Coming of the Portuguese, being a translation of* Kitab al-Fawa'id fi usul al-bahr wa'l-qawa'id *of Ahmad b. Majid al-Najdi*, London: Royal Asiatic Society

Toth, Anthony B. (unpublished MS), "From Maritime Amirate to Oil State: Ahmad bin Jabir Al-Sabah and the Transformation of Kuwait, 1921–1950"

Villiers, Alan (1969), *Sons of Sinbad: An Account of Sailing with the Arabs in their Dhows, in the Red Sea, round the Coasts of Arabia, and to Zanzibar and Tanganyika; Pearling in the Persian Gulf; and the Life of the Shipmasters and the Mariners of Kuwait*, New York: Charles Scribner's Sons

—— (2006a), *Sons of Sindbad: An Account of Sailing with the Arabs in their Dhows, in the Red Sea, round the Coasts of Arabia, and to Zanzibar and Tanganyika; Pearling in the Persian Gulf; and the Life of the Shipmasters and the Mariners of Kuwait.* Full reprint of the first London edition of 1940, introduced by William Facey, Grace Pundyk and Yacoub Al-Hijji, London: Arabian Publishing

—— (2006b), *Sons of Sindbad: The Photographs*. Selected and introduced by William Facey, Grace Pundyk and Yacoub Al-Hijji, London: Arabian Publishing

Index

This Index follows the system of transliteration used in the Glossary. In alphabetizing, Āl, al-, Ibn and bin (b.) are ignored. Where the family name is known, members are indexed under it, e.g. Al-Ṣabāḥ, Al-'Uthmān etc. The ambiguity in Kuwaiti usage of al- in family names (in which the definite article al-, e.g. in Al-Ghānim, has come to signify also Āl, "family of") has led the editor to capitalize the Al- in those contexts.